11.34

AN ARTIST AMONG MOUNTAINS

Gateway to tragedy: looking down into the gorge of the Vilcanota,
in the Peruvian Andes, from the last refuge of the Virgins of the Sun

AN ARTIST
AMONG MOUNTAINS

by

VICTOR COVERLEY-PRICE

(Member of the Alpine Club)

*With 33 illustrations from
drawings by the author*

LONDON

ROBERT HALE LIMITED

63 Old Brompton Road London S.W.7

First published 1957

MADE AND PRINTED IN GREAT BRITAIN BY
EBENEZER BAYLIS AND SON, LIMITED, THE
TRINITY PRESS, WORCESTER, AND LONDON

CONTENTS

LIST OF ILLUSTRATIONS

FOREWORD

In these days of restrictions and high costs, thirty-three full-page illustrations is a generous allowance for any book. But when I began to choose the subjects from among the hundreds of paintings and sketches that I have made, during the past thirty years, in many different parts of the world, I found it extremely difficult to limit my choice to thirty-three. In the case of Peru alone, I had more than one hundred and fifty pictures.

Fortunately my publisher had expressed his liking for the style of some drawings of mine that had appeared in *The Sphere* and this helped me to choose the particular treatment for my illustrations, which I have given a fairly high degree of "finish". Both slight and vigorous sketches, of a kind that might find a place in a book concerned solely with art, could therefore be eliminated. They remind me vividly of happy days among mountains, but there is not enough in them to explain their subjects to strangers. What was required was a series of *illustrations*: an extension of the text in pictorial terms. Three or four could be allotted to each chapter and I decided that, while their style should be consistent, the subjects should be widely varied. Ruthlessly, I discarded hundreds. I hope those that I have chosen will give pleasure.

I am indebted to *The Sphere* for permission to reproduce Plates Nos. V, X, XII, XIV, XV, XXVIII and XXXI.

Chapter I

AMONG THE LITTLE MOUNTAINS OF EUROPE:
MY MOUNTAIN CREED

It was six o'clock in the morning of a summer's day in 1921. I woke up suddenly, with the sun already filtering through the thin curtains, and I heard faint sounds of music mingling with the tinkle of the mountain stream just across the road.

"Are you awake?" I said, addressing my two companions impartially. We had reached this little hotel in Altenau late in the evening and we had been lucky to find a vacant room with three beds.

Milne, an Oxford graduate about five years my senior, grunted from the bed next to mine. O'Brien, his Irish friend who was a little older, was still asleep.

"It looks like another lovely day," I said. "Listen!"

The music—by now I had identified a German *Laute* and a mandoline—was coming nearer and at that moment a bird joined in the medley of sounds.

"They are coming down the road," said Milne, throwing back the bedclothes and tossing his pillow on to O'Brien's dark curly head. "Come on! We ought to be out too."

We drew the curtains aside and looked out across the forested hills of the Harz Mountains. The smell of the pines, that clothed the hills all round the little village, filled the morning air. I took deep breaths; it was good to be alive.

"There's a sketch for you!" exclaimed Milne as a party of half a dozen young Germans, wearing the typical costumes of *Wandervögel* and with rucksacks on their backs, came striding along beside the stream. One of them, a sturdy fair-haired youth with blue eyes, was strumming the melody of an old German folk song on his mandoline. Two of the others, one of them a girl wearing a brightly embroidered blouse, were accompanying him on the *Laute*. The girl had a lovely fair complexion

11

and she was singing the words of the song in a clear youthful voice. When she came to the end of the verse, just as they passed our window, the others all joined in the chorus and they marched away down the valley with the long coloured ribbons fluttering from their instruments.

That picture has remained with me until to-day, partly perhaps on account of the sounds that accompanied it. Just as the thin meanderings of the shepherd's pipe seem to belong to the Persian hills, so the mellow ripples of the guitar or the lute belong to the forest trails among the mountains, not only in Germany. Such music, that marries so well with the babbling of the streams and the soft whispering of the trees, is seldom heard now: perhaps it has been displaced by more mechanical sounds. But it is a memory of my younger days and, if only I had been able to persist in my efforts to learn to play the *Laute*, I would always take the instrument with me to the hills.

We watched them go, those Germans who were young and vigorous and happy before the days of Hitler: then we sat on a bed with a map and planned our own walk for the day. O'Brien, still half asleep, always needed goading into action at this hour of the morning; but once roused he took a lot of restraining. I had not known him long and found him rather difficult, but Milne managed him admirably.

"You missed a good picture there," said Milne. "Why don't you have your camera ready?" The question had a teasing implication.

O'Brien was out of bed in a trice, menacing with a jug of cold water. Photography, alleged to be his hobby, was a sore point with him ever since the three of us had made our first flight. That had been only a fortnight ago.

When I arrived in Hanover during the Long Vacation from Cambridge, to stay with the family of a *Hofprediger*—a former Court Preacher to the Kaiser—where I hoped to talk German all day, I found Milne and O'Brien already installed. Fortunately Milne was a good linguist, while O'Brien, a bad one, was a man of few words. We soon made friends and agreed that, whenever a German was present, we would never speak anything but German. Together we explored museums and palaces and art galleries, picking up a lot of new words from the guardians who showed us round; but occasionally we broke away from our studious routine and our walking tour in the Harz Mountains was one of these excursions. Another was our first flight.

In those days the network of airways in Europe was only just beginning to develop and, in Germany at least, most of the aircraft used were relics of the 1914 war. Milne discovered that, if we took an early train to Bremen, a couple of hours away, we could see something of that old town and then fly back to Hanover in time for lunch. The programme had the merit of being quick and cheap, including a full hour in the air for about five shillings. This compared favourably with the ten-minute "flips" that were offered at aerodromes in England for ten shillings.

We enjoyed our tour of Bremen although O'Brien, wandering in search of subjects for his camera, got lost several times. He was particularly keen on action pictures, but he always had such a rigmarole of preparation to go through that he was seldom ready to snap before the subject had disappeared. Milne teased him mercilessly about this, rousing his Irish temperament, but he never acquired the slightest qualification of a press photographer. Nearly always he was too late.

The prospect of taking photographs from the air set his ambition seething and we hoped that this time he really would be ready for action. Anything above sixty miles an hour was still a good speed for an aeroplane, but we warned O'Brien that he must have a plate ready in the camera if he wanted to get a view of Bremen as we left. There could be no question of a time exposure, so there would be no need to waste time working out problems of that nature.

We were the only three passengers at the aerodrome and, even to our inexpert eyes, the machine looked a bit ramshackle. It was a biplane with an open cockpit having just enough room for five people and it still carried its wartime camouflage paint, although this was badly weathered. The most unusual features in its construction—at least we thought they must be unusual— were sundry lengths of ordinary galvanized wire, evidently affixed quite recently, upon which the security of various parts of the fuselage appeared to depend. The pilot, a young man with a red scar across his forehead, seemed indifferent to the vulnerability of these contrivances, so we pretended to regard them with nothing but amusement and we climbed into the aircraft, leaving a seat vacant for O'Brien's photographic apparatus.

The process of taking off was exactly as I had imagined it, but it was undeniably thrilling to be airborne for the first time. When the machine lurched, rocked or dipped suddenly I found myself clutching the side of the cockpit as if that offered more security than the rest of the aeroplane. Having already climbed several mountains, I looked down without undue surprise on the ground below, but whenever we passed over a factory chimney I felt an almost irresistible desire to toss something into it.

I was so engrossed in my observation of the ground that I hardly noticed the fumblings going on beside me, where O'Brien was belatedly preparing his camera for action. But when he leant across me to take a trial sight over the side I had perforce to pay attention. Apparently satisfied that, by leaning well out, he could just manage to use the viewfinder while pointing the camera downwards, he asked me to hang on to his coat while he slipped in a plate and took his first snap. By now Bremen was far behind.

The wind was fairly strong and the first thing that happened was that a folder containing instructions about how to handle the camera was whipped out of his pocket and went whirling away in the slipstream. Half expecting him to follow, I clutched his coat more firmly. Then, with an accent that only an Irishman can command, he uttered a capacious oath as his whole box of plates disappeared over the side.

It was I think partly to console O'Brien for his loss of the plates—and of our confidence in him as a photographer—that the retired Court Preacher, his bearded and scarred face flushed with enthusiasm, embarked at lunch time on a prolonged harangue about the unsurpassed charm of the Harz Mountains. Without delay, he insisted, we must go there for a walking tour. Both O'Brien as a photographer and I as a painter would find landscape subjects at every turn. What was more, if we inadvertently dropped anything we could always pick it up again. He reverted to this subject on every possible occasion and at least one of my hour's lessons with him was devoted to the poems of Heinrich Heine's *"Harzreise"*. In self-defence, we decided to take his advice.

Those days of walking in the Harz were by no means my first experience of mountains and now, looking back with wider experience, I regard them as little more than hills. The Brocken, which is the highest point in north Germany, is less than 4,000 feet in altitude, with a railway leading to a hotel at the top. But the woods and the wild valleys, where the music of streams and waterfalls was never far away, had all the charm that the Court Preacher ascribed to them. The little towns and villages that we visited—Goslar, Schierke, Wernigerode and others—had a sleepy, old-world fascination that by now must have largely faded. In Goslar we lingered among the medieval buildings, as attractive as those in lovely Hildesheim, but it was in the Okertal and some of the other rugged valleys that I felt most impelled to sketch. (Plate I.) With rucksacks to carry food and clothing, we walked all day and every day for a week, spurning the railway and the roads and sometimes scrambling away from the footpaths. Both the people and the landscape were friendly: perhaps that is why I still remember the Harz with affection.

I stayed in Germany, for months on end, several times during the early 1920's and I got to know the country far better than I knew England. At home I had never travelled much and I might not have travelled at all if I had not decided to study foreign languages. After two visits to France and one to Spain I went to Germany for the first time in the depths of winter, a few days before Christmas.

It was an idiotic journey, undertaken at the insistence of a Swiss undergraduate at Cambridge whose elder brother proposed to drive his car to Berlin, for a brief business visit, and then to go on right across Germany to Zurich, if possible in less than three days. My Swiss friend offered me a seat in the car and I, being only too eager to see more of the world, accepted the proposal without due consideration. It snowed almost from the start. We had punctures and mechanical breakdowns. We got stuck in the snow several times, twice we skidded right off the road and once, somewhere in the neighbourhood of

Weimar, we turned completely round twice before coming to rest abruptly against a brick wall. No vital damage was done and so, without waiting to have the dents removed, we continued on our perilous way.

Travelling at night on the highway between Frankfurt and Mannheim, we struggled on relentlessly through a blizzard and emerged miraculously after about an hour without having collided with anything. Then, in the beam of the headlights, a white mound appeared at the side of the road. Several cars were coming towards us and I expected the Swiss to stop. Instead he accelerated and charged the mound at considerable speed.

I have no clear recollection of exactly what happened, but I remember getting out of the car feeling very shaken and astonished to find that it was still on the road. Several other people gathered round us and there was a lot of excited talking, but the only sign of damage was a burst front tyre. My Swiss friend had a swollen upper lip and discovered that half a tooth was missing. When the clamour had subsided and the other cars had driven away, we set about changing the wheel: no easy matter with cold hands and snow on everything. We drove on, slowly at first, until we were sure that the car was functioning as it should, then at increasing speed.

Presently, with calmer nerves, our driver explained that, as there had been no warning lantern beside the mound in the road, he had assumed that it must be a snowdrift. If he had applied the brakes we might have skidded into it and got stuck, so he had decided to go at it with sufficient momentum to carry us through. Unfortunately the mound happened to be a snow-covered heap of the neatly cut cubes of stone that are widely used for road surfacing on the continent.

My friend, who had unbounded confidence in his brother's skill as a driver, received this explanation in silence and I thought he had gone to sleep in the back seat. But suddenly he uttered an exclamation of triumph. "Wonderful! What luck!" he cried and he held up the missing fragment of his front tooth, which he had found embedded in the woodwork at the back of the front seat.

We eventually reached Zurich after midnight, three days

I. In the Okertal, Harz Mountains, Germany

II. The Kaisergebirge, Austrian Tyrol

after leaving Berlin, and I have never felt more thankful that a journey was over. My Swiss friend said that he hoped I had enjoyed it and I could only reply that it had been a great experience. When we started I had hoped to see something of the country, but we never stopped anywhere except at night. Even in Berlin there had been no time to see anything and I only remember wandering miserably round in the snow, gazing through the steamy shop windows like a moth attracted to a light.

On the following day I fled to a Swiss mountain resort, where a few days on skis seemed far less risky than that journey by car.

The house in which I stayed in Hanover was not far from that where Field-Marshal Paul von Hindenburg was living in retirement. Several times a week I had German lessons from an old German *Fräulein* near the river Leine and I usually walked there and back past Hindenburg's home. Quite often I met him walking slowly along the pavement, a fallen German god who, all the world believed, would never again appear in the limelight. Occasionally, when his mind was not too abstracted, he said *"Guten Tag"* as I passed and of course I replied to the greeting.

About three years later, early in 1925, Hindenburg became President of the German Republic in succession to Friedrich Ebert and he remained at the head of the State until his death in 1934. At the beginning of 1926 I was appointed as Third Secretary at the British Embassy in Berlin and when the Ambassador, Lord D'Abernon, retired I accompanied his successor, with the other members of his staff, at the presentation of his credentials to the President. Sir Ronald Lindsay introduced each of us in turn and Hindenburg spoke a few words to me and complimented me on my knowledge of German. But, not unexpectedly, he gave no sign of having seen me before.

After leaving Hanover I spent six weeks at Bad Oeynhausen, then a small watering-place on a tributary of the river Weser which was later to become the headquarters of the British forces in Germany after the war of 1939–1945. The German family with whom I stayed consisted of three generations, the eldest being the grandmother of ninety-four who spent many hours

2

knitting egg-cosies. I called her the *Eierwärmerfabrik*—the Egg-cosy-factory—a title that delighted her. They taught me a lot of German, including many of the folk songs that my wife and I now sing together during our tramps among the mountains. But often I went off for long walks alone among the hills along the Weser and through the forests of the Teutoburger Wald and I made many little sketches that now remind me of those days.

It was at this time that the disastrous inflation that destroyed the value of German currency began to have its most serious effects, bringing widespread ruin among all classes. But what was a calamity for Germans was a windfall for me and for other foreign students who had very little money. A pound sterling became worth millions of marks and at one time it was cheaper to write letters on the plain backs of 500-mark notes than to buy notepaper. In 1922 and 1923, when inflation reached its peak, I was able to travel all over Germany for a few shillings and I took the opportunity to see most of the finest art galleries in the country.

I spent a large part of one Long Vacation in Dresden. Some-one had told me that I would never know German really well unless I added Saxon to my vocabulary. This was true enough, but my stay there also introduced me to some more minor mountains, the Meissen Highlands extending along both banks of the Elbe. For some reason, obviously a silly one, this district was popularly known as Saxon Switzerland. It was an attractive area in its own right, but it was not in the least like any part of Switzerland that I knew. Several times I went for scrambles there with a German friend and it was perhaps fortunate that I made this early acquaintance with the often slippery limestone pinnacles that form a lofty palisade along the river. They gave me a healthy respect for rock climbing.

Occasionally, on Sunday afternoon walks, I made a few sketches among the mountains, but a lot of my time was spent in Dresden's rich museums and art galleries. I saw there and was allowed to handle portfolios of many of Dürer's finest drawings and they gave me a lasting admiration for his draughtsmanship. It was fascinating to examine the detail of so much of his original work, sometimes with a magnifying glass that enabled me to appreciate precisely how he had made each stroke. Although the designs of many of his woodcuts are very fine, I imagine that few people realize that many—perhaps most—of the prints were made from blocks cut by other hands. I must say that, having made woodcuts myself, I often wondered how one man could find the time and summon up the physical endurance to cut the large number of blocks that are attributed to Dürer.

In Dresden, when travel was so cheap for holders of foreign currency, I was bitten by the bug of travel and also by a few stray specimens of that less welcome creature, expected only east of Vienna, the bed-bug. Although I was now a multi-millionaire, in marks, I could still not afford many luxuries. Apart from a rare glass of beer, I drank nothing but water. I seldom went to a theatre and never to a cinema, but I could not resist the desire to see how other people lived and what they did with their hands. Every time I went abroad I extended my journeys farther afield and everywhere I went I tried to see as much as I could of the local arts and crafts. Somehow or other I managed to penetrate into quite a lot of factories, art schools and other places where things were being made by hand.

After visiting Meissen, to see the manufacture of what is loosely called "Dresden china", I went for a few days to Prague, the capital of the new Czechoslovakia which had acquired its independence barely four years earlier. I had not the least interest in politics and I found it most irritating, when I wanted to go and see the art galleries there, to have to obtain yet another visa in my already overcrowded passport and to be delayed at the frontier by a new set of tiresome formalities. I had had more than enough of that in Germany, where I had even been obliged to report to the police on arrival in a new town and to have my passport stamped again before departure, a procedure known as *Anmeldung* and *Abmeldung*. We have grown so accustomed to such restrictions that it is hard to believe that there was once a time when travellers could move much more freely about Europe.

On returning to Dresden I found that the currency situation had got completely out of hand. In some towns there were riots and several times, when going to my German lessons, I had to make wide detours in order to avoid demonstrators. One day I went to Leipzig, a centre of the book and fur trades, to buy sets of certain German classics to take back to Cambridge. While there I met two English ladies who wanted to buy themselves fur capes. They could speak little German and asked me to interpret for them. After going to several stores they seemed to have more or less made up their minds, but one of them thought that a fur they had seen in a shop across the road was a better bargain. So back we went to that shop; but, having examined the fur again, they agreed after all to buy the other one. Once more we crossed the road and I told the assistant that the ladies would like the fur he had shown them five minutes ago, priced at I forget how many million marks and, to them, cheap at the price. The man then explained that, while we had been absent, the latest *Kurs* had been received from the bank. As a result the price of the fur in marks was now exactly six times what it had been a few minutes earlier. The ladies were horrified, but they bought the fur nevertheless. The lesson that they learnt—that "he who hesitates is lost"— was also cheap at the price.

This was not the last of the many startling jumps in the rate of exchange and the cost of living. About a week before I was due to leave Dresden it was announced that at midnight all railway fares would be multiplied by six. As far as I was concerned this was a big jump ahead of the *Kurs* and, if I stayed on, I should have to abandon my plan to spend a few days in Switzerland, where I had promised to meet a cousin.

The family with whom I was staying—strangely enough that of another *Hofprediger*—agreed that it would be wise for me to leave at once and, while I rushed off to the police station for my *Abmeldung*, the daughter took a place for me in the long queue at the railway station. On my way back to the flat I ran into a huge crowd of demonstrators and suddenly shots were fired from two or three different directions. I had been told that it was fatal to run on such occasions: a running figure always suggested someone anxious to escape from the police, *ergo* a criminal, and it invited a shot. I certainly did not feel unperturbed, but I managed to keep sufficient restraint on my impulses to be able to walk back in the direction from which I had come. I had not gone far before I was stopped by a *Schupo*—a member of the *Schutz Polizei* whose duty it was to maintain order—and while he examined my passport I feared that I might again become involved with the demonstrators, who were surging all round us. However he let me go at last, not before there had been more shots unpleasantly close, and I made a wide detour through the town until I eventually got back to the flat.

In great haste I packed my suitcase and rucksack and, as there was no possibility of getting a car, the *Frau Hofprediger* produced an old pram and most generously insisted on accompanying me to the station. I put my luggage in the pram and together we set off through the most deserted streets that we could find. It was the only occasion on which I had ever pushed a pram. We reached the station at last and I took over the place in the queue, while my two kind friends went home with the pram.

It was now about five o'clock and I had six hours to wait before my train was due to leave. Towards nine o'clock the queue began to move slowly and I soon got sick of picking up my luggage, taking a short step and putting it down again. But an hour later I had a ticket, at the price still valid until midnight, and I squeezed on to the platform to await the train that was to carry me towards Switzerland.

By now I felt that I had had enough of Germany, for the time being. It reeked of political disturbance and financial crises—the prolonged aftermath of the Great War—and it was difficult to enjoy the beauty of the country without being affected by the fumes of discontent, regimentation and aggressive, ill-balanced argument. I longed to get away from it all, back into the refreshing atmosphere of the Swiss mountains. When at last the train arrived, already uncomfortably full, it was the pressure of the crowd rather than my own efforts that forced me into it. But I was glad to endure the night journey in such conditions, in view of what lay ahead.

My rambles about Germany, spread over a number of years, took me to every quarter of the country. Before I came down from Cambridge I knew it and the language well enough to be asked to advocate the German point of view in a debate at the

Union and to deliver a lecture in German to the German Society. But political Germany never held my real interest, which lay in the mountain regions, with their folk songs and dances, and of course in anything to do with art.

My tour of the Rhineland, where the river, the hills and the numerous old castles appeared to have arranged themselves for artists to paint, was to some extent a disappointment because the whole region was still occupied by the Allied Forces of the 1914–1918 war. Cologne, Coblenz, Mainz and other cities were overcrowded with foreign troops and visitors. The shops in the occupied zone, apparently under official instructions, charged foreigners at least double the prices charged to Germans and I generally had to show my passport before I could buy anything. This was understandable, but it created an extraordinary zoo-like feeling, though one wondered sometimes who was behind the bars.

In my student days I kept what I called my "Museum": a large box into which I put a discriminating jackdaw's collection of valueless souvenirs. This heteregeneous assembly of objects, which I still have, reminds me more vividly than photographs of many places, people and sensations. It is a kind of wordless scrapbook. There are odd coins from nearly every country in Europe, including many of the artistic local currency notes that were printed wholesale in numerous small districts of Germany during the period of inflation. There are dried flowers and grasses from the heights overlooking the Dardanelles, spent bullets picked up at Suvla Bay, bits of rock from various mountains, a fragment of rock-salt from a Tyrolese salt mine and a piece of felspar from the Libyan desert.

My more dramatic pieces include the bill for the most squalid night's lodging I had so far had, in a Turkish lodging-house in Constantinople, when two Turks fought with daggers on the landing outside my door; the soft lead bullet that was mysteriously fired by an unknown hand through my bedroom door in Trieste; the paint-box that was dented by a stone when I was pelted with stones while sketching in a suburb of Cairo and a piece of my bootlace that was cut by a falling rock fragment while I was climbing the Matterhorn.

Another fragment—a piece of striated red and white sandstone—is a bit that I broke from one of the vertical cliffs of Heligoland while trying to photograph guillemots. It reminds me of my most hideously uncomfortable sea voyage when, in a small river steamer not normally used for the trip, I clung for more than nine cold and hungry hours to a seat on the exposed deck during one of the worst storms in the North Sea. The passage from Cuxhaven to Heligoland should have taken only three hours, but there were moments when it seemed that the ship could not possibly survive the storm. When I landed in a small boat after midnight most of the population of the island were on the jetty, in spite of the wind and rain. They had been watching the ship's lights for hours, expecting them to disappear at any moment.

My companion on this trip, who lay prostrate in the bowels of the ship throughout the ordeal, was a Swiss student who had never before seen the sea. It was a cruel introduction, but he forgave me for having persuaded him to embark with me and he invited me to join him at some future date for a climbing holiday in the Alps. Unfortunately we never managed to arrange this, but it was at his suggestion that I attended a course on German literature at the University of Vienna.

The course, which included excursions on the Danube and rambles in the Semmering, concluded with a week of music and mountaineering at Salzburg and I fell head-over-heels in love with the mountains of the Austrian Tyrol. I returned to them with my wife during our honeymoon, which some might think a rash thing to do. But our journey extended from the Cotswolds to Bucharest, where I had been appointed as Secretary at the British Legation.

One night in Vienna I had a curious experience. I had been out all day with my sketch-book in the mountains and in the evening I went to a demonstration of ju-jutsu. I was walking back to my room in one of the dark and narrow streets of old Vienna when, a few feet ahead of me, a man suddenly sprang from a doorway with a dagger in his raised hand. I had never practised ju-jutsu in my life but, with the demonstration fresh in my mind, I grabbed a lapel of the man's coat and put my foot against his stomach, pulling him towards me. I do not know exactly what happened, for I was thoroughly frightened, but somehow the man fell over my shoulder as I ducked and I heard the dagger clatter on the pavement. Without waiting to see if he was hurt, I took to my heels and ran on to my room. I told my landlady about the incident, but she had no telephone and I did not feel inclined to venture out again in search of a policeman. I imagine that the assailant had mistaken me for someone else.

During a winter vacation in the early 1920's three of my Cambridge friends and I decided to try the art of ski-ing, for the first time. We thought of going to a Swiss resort, but we heard that, thanks to currency inflation, life in Austria would be much cheaper. So we went to Kitzbühel, then a small and little-known resort that only became popular after it had been visited by the Prince of Wales. In those days such contrivances as ski-lifts were almost unknown and we had to climb every foot of a mountain that we wished to descend on skis. "Running on skis", as it was called, had not yet been mechanized and it had not yet been converted into the form of downhill skating that is now so popular. We climbed, sometimes for hours; we broke our own trails through the snow and we picked our own routes through the silent woods. Ski-ing was a means of travelling in winter through the mountains and it gave us any amount of healthy exercise.

My attitude towards ski-ing, which I prefer in its original form still practised in Canada, would probably be regarded by members of the modern school as that of an old Blimp. I am sure it can be exhilarating to be carried up thousands of feet by a lift and to skid down on a narrow ice *piste* in a few minutes, repeating this several times during a morning. But I imagine that few of the experts who perform this rite could travel far on skis through untrodden snow: they would be unable to climb high on skis and, above all, they miss many of the greatest joys of mountain travel.

The lifts and railways which are increasing in numbers in the Alps, many of them being in use both in winter and summer, are undoubtedly a boon to numerous people who would not otherwise be able to visit the higher regions of the mountains. But they are also a source of danger to many who are not experienced mountaineers. Too often visitors on holiday ascend from the valleys wearing clothing and shoes that are quite unsuitable for high altitudes. Some of them, without the necessary physical training and with no knowledge of weather, snow and ice conditions, wander rashly among snow fields and glaciers—unfamiliar surroundings where disaster can overtake them suddenly. Occasionally they lose their lives and not infrequently they cause anxiety and trouble to others.

On a sunny morning at Kitzbühel I climbed for about two hours towards a small peak where I hoped to get a really fine view of the Kaisergebirge, the jagged and wild-looking range of mountains that dominates the valley from the north. The air was crisp and clear and my intention was to make a sketch of the range. I brushed the snow from a rock, sat down and began my drawing. It was wonderfully peaceful up there, still a little way below the timber line, and the branches of every fir tree drooped in graceful beauty under their burden of dazzling fresh snow. (Plate II.)

But presently I became aware of voices somewhere among the trees behind me, close to the precipice of rock that I had skirted on my way up. They were Austrian voices and every now and then they seemed to be raised in altercation: in fact, the same angry shouts were repeated several times.

Curious to know what was going on, I laid my sketching things aside and walked slowly through the deep snow towards the sounds. I reached a point where, looking down, I could see the cliff of bare rock that rose from the icy slope below, but there was still no sign of anyone. Yet the voices came quite clearly from just beyond a jumble of huge rocks and fallen trees above the precipice.

I stood still for a moment listening. A man was talking very fast; then another interrupted him in angry tones, saying something about his not having come all this way to be frustrated. A woman's voice intervened, apparently calling for an end to this strife. "*Bitte, bitte, ruhig!*" Again one of the men shouted. Then the woman screamed: a terrible, sharp scream that died abruptly among the snow-laden trees.

At that instant, to my horror, I saw a body hurtling from the cliff. It turned slowly as it fell, with one arm stretched out as if groping desperately for some hold in the thin air. Then, with a subdued thud, it struck the snow at the foot of the precipice and disappeared, leaving only a large black hole where it had gone through the crust into some hollow beneath.

This was no place for me, but I felt that I must wait a moment and try to see who had been responsible for this tragedy.

Almost at once I heard the voices again, this time accompanied by laughter. Then, for the first time, I noticed movement beyond the pile of rocks and a face appeared, looking in my direction. It was a horrible yellow face, with blue lips.

The unnatural colour of that face gave the show away. Slowly it dawned on me what had been happening. I went closer, to make sure.

In a hollow among the rocks there were several men and a woman, some of them wearing fur coats and caps as if travelling in a Russian winter. Their faces were grotesquely daubed with yellow. In their midst, close to the edge of the cliff, there stood a cine-camera on a tripod and several black wooden boxes bearing in white lettering the name of an Austrian film company. I gathered, from what one of the men was saying, that he was satisfied with the scene that had just been acted and that the hurling of the dummy from the cliff had been carried out to perfection. With a feeling of relief I resumed my sketching.

This holiday in Austria with my three friends was the cheapest I had ever had abroad. It cost us each three shillings and sixpence a day and, before going home, we took third-class tickets for the night train to Vienna for half a crown. In Vienna we heard Verdi's opera *Aïda* for an infinitesimal sum and we voted inflation a good thing, provided that it did not happen to us.

The Black Forest is another of the regions of minor mountains that I explored with tremendous enjoyment before tackling bigger things. Nowadays one seems to hear less about it than used to be the case. In the days when comparatively few English people took their holidays abroad it was considered the thing for scions of the aristocracy and a sprinkling of writers and painters, generally accompanied by a tutor or an older friend, to make a "grand tour" on the continent and some place in the Black Forest was often included in the itinerary. Sometimes the travellers came back with tales of brigands and wolves, both of which found good lurking places among the thickly wooded hills. A lot of old history still adheres to the outskirts of the region and I think it was that that first attracted me there. But I returned later to walk and paint and my portfolios contain several studies of some of the wonderful old wooden houses of the peasants that are a distinctive feature of the Black Forest. (Plate III.)

While I was serving for a spell at the Foreign Office after coming back from Berlin in 1927 I went back to the Black Forest for a fortnight's fishing. When I look at the sketches that I made then they remind me not so much of the fishing, which was a peaceful occupation though not very rewarding, but rather of the people who were my companions for the trip. A friend who was also going to the Black Forest persuaded me to take three car-less relations of his, while he took two more and most of the luggage. I had never met these people before. All except one were older than myself and I soon discovered that one was a source of constant irritation which provoked discord and disturbed the atmosphere. The one exception was the granddaughter of the old lady who glued herself in my car and she was a very charming girl of about eighteen. I had suggested, not unnaturally I think, that as we were going out in convoy together, there might be an occasional redistribution of seats so that we could all get to know one another. But the grandmother, who was obviously loathed by her granddaughter—and very soon by me too—insisted almost pugnaciously that the girl should remain in the other car. We could not be kept permanently apart, for we all usually sat at the same table for meals and the girl made it clear at an early stage that she would not mind a change.

I tried various subterfuges to get her into my car, at least for a day, and twice she was installed innocently in the back seat before the old lady arrived to take her usual place. But the girl was unceremoniously turned out. The second time, with my temper on the verge of a breakdown, I felt inclined to refuse to drive another yard until I had got rid of the incubus. But I suppose my diplomatic training prevailed and I weakly let the divergence of opinion drop. By the time we reached St.

Blasien, our fishing centre in the Black Forest, I had discovered that the poor girl was destined for a convent.

One memorable day, when I was fishing out of sight of anyone, she came along the river bank and literally wept on my shoulder; a touching performance that I had believed happened only in novels. I was not prepared, in the St. George tradition, to rescue her from the dragon and carry her off in my car, for at that date matrimony and the emoluments of a Third Secretary were not compatible, but I did my best to console her by suggesting that there were more fish in the river than I had been able to get out of it and that, if she showed patience in adversity, something more favourable would be sure to turn up. But the last I heard of her, many years ago, was that she was in a convent. I only hope that, wherever her grandmother may have gone, she herself will be numbered among the saints.

The bickerings that went on in my car sometimes made me feel inclined to drive into a ditch and any patch of really bad road, which tormented the passengers in the back seats, gave me malicious pleasure. The fishing gave me an excuse to get away from it all, but I could always be tracked down by anyone who cared to walk along the river bank. On several occasions an irritated male member of my crew came and stood behind me and kept up a running commentary on the iniquities of his relations, until I inadvertently hooked him with a fly while casting. This brought some severe and bitter criticism of my fishing methods. Seething with rage, I dismantled my rod in silence and returned to the hotel with the seven trout that I had landed. This was my best catch, one for each of our party, but I arranged with the cook to keep two back, so that the unjust critic and I should go without. Thereafter I spent more time sketching than fishing and I disappeared for most of the day, leaving the squabblers to squabble.

At every stopping-place on the way out to the Black Forest and on the way home again there were scenes and tantrums in the hotel lounges while the grandmother battled with the others for the best room available. There was not always much choice and, as I was usually absent during the critical stages of these arguments, putting the car away in a garage, I had to accept whatever was left over. Sometimes this was an attic. But once, after the seniors had had their pick, it appeared that the unhappy young girl and I would have to share the only remaining room. When the grandmother discovered this, she seemed to think that I had arranged it.

I decided, of course, that I must look for a room in another hotel, but, as I was the only German-speaking member of the party and had to do most of the initial arranging, I determined on the spur of the moment to see if I could for once turn the tables. I discussed the situation with the hotel manager and got him to tell the old lady himself, in his halting English, that the room she had chosen was a double room, as in fact it was, and that she must allow someone to share it with her. As I had expected, this was regarded as a preposterous idea and, as she would not even look at the other small room, I seized the opportunity to suggest that she might find a much nicer one in another hotel. Miraculously this worked. I found her a good room in a hotel along the road and I was installed in lonely, but happy, state in the double room that she had abandoned.

I walked my way into the mountains, as I suppose most climbers do. I began on the flat, walking for miles through fields and, less willingly, along roads. At school I also ran for miles, for it was only in running clothes that boys were allowed out of bounds. I remember how once, just before I was fourteen, I danced nearly every dance for five hours at a party at the Hyde Park Hotel in London and then, still in evening dress and dancing shoes, walked all the way back to Harrow, a distance of about ten miles. It was a clear frosty night early in January and, until I reached the more open country, I stopped at intervals to warm my hands at the braziers of the night watchmen at points where the road was under repair.

Later on I thought little of walking twenty or thirty miles in a day and I soon found my way to the Downs. I had very few real country holidays in England, but once I had managed to get abroad I began to learn the pleasures of walking in the mountains. I have already mentioned some of these early experiences, but many more were to come. My passion for the mountains grew, not perhaps steadily, but certainly consistently. My first rock climb and my first great Alpine peak brought new inspiration and only adverse circumstances have prevented greater ventures. It is probably the same with the majority of people who love mountain country: we enjoy the mountains when we can and are grateful for what we are able to do, but we keep on hoping for more.

I imagine that nearly everyone who enjoys mountaineering gradually develops a kind of mountain creed, though he may not actually put it into words. Probably he would find it very difficult to express his feelings about mountains, for they are bound to be complex and largely a matter of temperament. If asked why we like going up difficult rock and on steep slopes of ice and snow, merely to spend a short time on one of a thousand peaks, we should probably say that it is good, healthy exercise in beautiful and wild country, that there is always the chance of seeing marvellous panoramas and that getting to the top gives us a pleasant sense of achievement. We should refrain from saying that a climbing expedition sometimes involves a lot of tedious trudging on loose rock, shale and deep or slippery snow, that we sometimes risk falling into a crevasse or down a precipice or being hit by a fragment of rock and that quite often it is unpleasantly cold up there. At the time, we may experience both joy and anguish; but, unless we are unlucky, both of these act as spurs to keep us going. If we were not the kind of people who relish tackling arduous problems and who have the urge to persist in overcoming difficulties we would not have any taste for mountaineering.

Mallory said that he wanted to climb Everest because it was there. This seems to me a very good reason. But there are many other reasons why we like to climb mountains and, as in other fields, we have preferences and dislikes. In our youthful enthusiasm we may be ready to tackle anything, but we learn to discriminate, according to our abilities and tastes. We cannot always say, in the abstract, that we want to climb one mountain rather than another, for sometimes the desire to climb only comes when we see the mountain in front of us. Then the desire may amount to a passion; we feel that we absolutely must get to the top of that particular peak. It can be like falling in love and equally illogical.

There are, of course, among mountaineers people who might be called "peak-baggers", who like to be able to say that they have climbed so many peaks, made so many first ascents and pioneered so many new routes. Some of them make altitude a fetish and despise anything below a certain height. Others choose their routes just because they are difficult or because no one has tried them before. A few are inspired by a lust for personal fame and a rather distorted notion of national glory. But the great majority of climbers enjoy climbing as other people enjoy playing cricket or golf. It is the sport that they prefer and they play the game whenever they get the chance. I think that I have always belonged to this category: I am disappointed when a match with the mountains has to be scratched, but I hope for better luck next time.

Eric Shipton, in his book *Upon That Mountain*, advocates the small expedition rather than the large one and I must humbly say that I agree with him. He has gone in for mountaineering in a big way, having devoted much of his life to the sport, and he ought to know. A climbing expedition with two or three congenial companions can be sheer enjoyment from start to finish, but, when it is considered necessary to have a retinue of several hundred porters and a galaxy of experts with all their food and equipment, the thing becomes a kind of military operation and discipline and regimentation—and even some measure of disagreement—become inevitable. Obviously a large expedition may be necessary for a scientific purpose, but it is bound to lose a good deal of the spirit of a sporting venture. Most climbers undoubtedly prefer to be members of a small party and they find their pleasure in tackling problems that are within, though perhaps only just within, their capabilities.

In a sense it can be argued that most of the big climbs in the Himalayas have been achieved by only small parties. Only two men went to the top of Everest and the last thousand feet or so were the decisive steps to success. It took a small army, masses of equipment and a large sum of money to get them to the foot of the final pyramid, but that was the bit that counted even more than all the rest. If I went to Switzerland to climb, say, the Weisshorn, one of the highest and most beautiful mountains in the Alps, it might be proved that an army of hundreds was required to get me to its base. There would be the taxi driver to take me to the station, the crew of the train to carry me and my luggage to Dover, backed by the organization of British Railways to enable the train to run at all. Then there would be the crew of the ship to cross the Channel, not to mention the employees of the firm that built it, and so on across Europe to the Alps. Even if I went by air my transport would have to be arranged by hundreds of men. But there is, of course, a difference. The small party is not intimately involved with its background organization and, as its members march along the mountain trails, there is nothing to intervene between the landscape and their thoughts.

I do not demand that my mountains shall all be big ones. I have spent many happy days among the hills. My own personal attitude towards mountains is hard to define, but I look at them, as not everybody does, from two different points of view. One is that of the climber, at which I have already hinted. The other is that of the painter who sees in landscape some of God's most wonderful creations.

The two points of view are not incompatible; in fact they supplement one another. More than once, when nearing the summit of a mountain with my sketchbook in my rucksack, I have been tempted to abandon the final pitches in order to have time to sketch the marvellous scene from the point that I had reached. If I have gone on to the top it has been because my companion wished to go there—and because I wanted to get there too.

Pictures of mountain scenery, particularly photographs, are often disappointing. I cannot explain why without going into details that are of little interest to others than artists. But it is obvious that a great deal of the impression created by a mountain is due to its bigness and solidity and much of this feeling is lost through reduction to the size of a small sheet of paper. Then there are the moving clouds, the trees that stir gently in the wind, the continually changing lights and colours reflected from snow, ice and rocks. When these are fixed at a given moment, no matter how accurately, they lose much of their charm. It is the same with portraiture: an animated face may show endless subtle changes of expression that are fascinating, but when one fleeting expression is fixed in a photograph it may look dull and lifeless.

III. Old houses at Menschenschwand, Black Forest, Germany

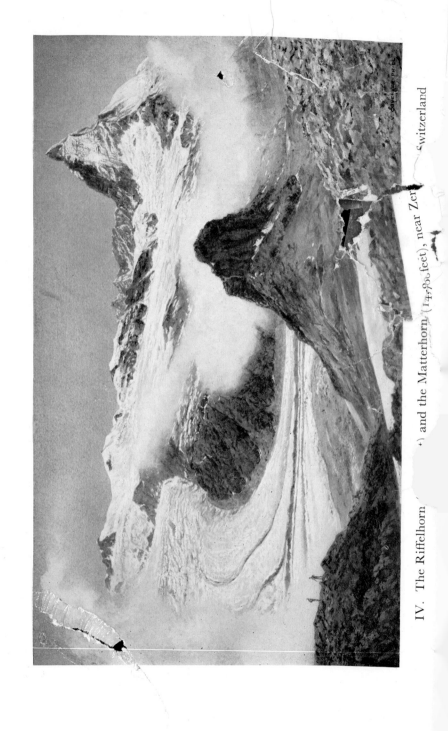

IV. The Riffelhorn (⁺) and the Matterhorn (14,780 feet), near Zer   Switzerland

A skilled photographer can make a beautiful picture of mountains by catching a striking effect of light and shadow, by avoiding a falling foreground and by printing the tones to a pleasing depth. In brilliant sunshine modern colour processes can also produce good results. But for every successful picture there must be hundreds that are unsatisfactory. Even the most sensitive plates fail to render every tone correctly and, as it is generally necessary to use a filter for mountain photography, there is bound to be some distortion or exaggeration of tones. Far too often we see photographs, not only of snow scenes, in which large enshadowed areas appear completely black. In a natural landscape the eye can see into the shadows and often they are full of beautiful forms and lovely soft colours and reflected lights. But frequently the photograph shows them only as dead, uninteresting, meaningless areas. However striking extreme contrasts of black and white may be in a photograph, they cannot fairly interpret the mountain scenery.

The most successful mountain pictures are generally those that have a good foreground: something attractive and comprehensible that indicates the scale of the scene and enhances the effect that painters call "atmosphere". Here the artist often has an advantage over the photographer, for he can arrange his foreground to ensure the correct balance of the composition. He can anticipate or recapture passing effects, for he is not pinned down to a single moment, and he can remove obstructions or unsightly objects without stirring from his stool. Unlike the photographer, who can only manipulate his effects within the limitations of his camera and printing process, the artist can make his picture convey something of his own feeling towards the landscape and, if he is also a mountaineer, he can make his mountains look climbable and even inspire others with a wish to climb them. I do not claim always to be able to achieve such aims, but in my approach to the mountains as an artist I try to show what I feel about them also as a climber.

CHAPTER II

MY FIRST BIG CLIMBS: THE MOUNTAINEER'S AND THE ARTIST'S DIFFERENT POINTS OF VIEW

WHO, I wonder, first used the word "first"? It is as old as the hills. It occurs with noticeable frequency in the Bible, where we read about the first-born of Egypt long before the birth of Christ. But we are told in the first verse of the first book of the Bible that "In the beginning God made the heaven and the earth", not that God first made the heaven and the earth. Everything must have a beginning before it can take its first step. We begin our lives as puny, incapable infants and thereafter anything that we do for the first time has a special significance.

I began to take long walks among the hills long before I made my first climb and that first climb was different from anything that I had done before. It was only a little climb, but I was roped between two men who had experience and I was shown how to use footholds and handholds on steep rock. This was the Riffelhorn, a small peak near Zermatt rising above the Gorner glacier to an altitude of about 9,600 feet and commanding views of both Monte Rosa and the Matterhorn. It was not a difficult ascent, by the route that I followed that day, but I found the experience exhilarating and when I reached the top I was entranced by the beauty of a panorama such as I had never seen before. (Plate IV.)

Thousands of people must have been on the Riffelhorn and I have no doubt that it has served as a nursery climb for many. Climbing for the pleasure of climbing has a history going back only about two hundred years, but it seems certain that the first ascent of the Riffelhorn must have been made long before that by some Ancient European. In the autumn of 1873 two Americans were on the mountain and they apparently thought it would be amusing to watch a fall of rock. Having thrown down several chunks, they pushed and heaved at a much larger block until it too went crashing down. Then, in the place where it had been poised, they discovered a bronze javelin or spear-head, of admirable workmanship.

The story of a first ascent—that is to say, the first time that a particular mountain has been climbed to its summit—often makes good reading, but it can be very boring listening to someone telling the tale of his own first ascent of a well-known mountain. There are, however, plenty of stories, mostly to be found in mountaineering journals, about climbs that have been repeated again and again and many of them are well worth reading; but this is because they are really well told. The route followed by successive climbers may be the same, but weather conditions vary from day to day, even from hour to hour, on a mountain and individuals often feel differently about the same thing. Such differences may be worth recording. If I say any-thing at all about a few of my own climbs it is only because, while I was making them, I had the sensations of an artist as well as those of a mountaineer.

After the Riffelhorn I made two or three other climbs near Zermatt and then what seemed to me a colossal walk through St. Niklaus and over the Augstbord Pass to Gruben, a hamlet in the Turtmann valley. I went back to Zermatt feeling as fit as a fiddle and immediately set covetous eyes on the Matterhorn. The Matterhorn has become a symbol; or, rather, it used to be a symbol until it was displaced by Everest, which is just about twice as high. But altitude is not everything and for a very long time the Matterhorn defied every attempt to scale it. Now that it has been climbed by a kitten we can look forward to the first ascent of Everest by a dog. Incidentally, the suggestion that Everest may some day be scaled by a dog is not as far-fetched as it may seem. Several dogs have climbed Mont Blanc, the highest mountain in Europe, and at least one has been up Monte Rosa. In 1933 a Tibetan mastiff reached well above 21,000 feet on Everest itself and another dog is said to have climbed to 20,000 feet in the Himalaya.

The Matterhorn, 14,780 feet, should not be underrated. None of the hundreds of people who have climbed it would say that it was easy, even by the ordinary route. Many of them would be ready to confess that their Swiss guides got them up and down again. A sad proportion of those who went without guides were killed. It remains a good climb and its north face is one of the most difficult and dangerous that has ever been achieved. As a spectacle—a gigantic pyramid of rock rising from the surrounding glaciers—it is magnificent.

Nearly every writer who has referred to the Matterhorn has considered it necessary to describe the fatal accident that overtook the party who made the first successful ascent. Since Edward Whymper, the leader of the party who survived owing to the breaking of the rope, published his own account the story has been repeated innumerable times and often embroidered with criticism and speculation. I do not propose to add to this almost excessive spate of narrative. But not everyone remembers that Whymper himself was an artist who made a number of sketches of the Matterhorn, including a fine engraving of the mountain as seen from the Riffelberg. John Ruskin, who was no climber, painted the Matterhorn long before it was conquered and it was he who took the very first photograph ever made in the Swiss Alps—a picture of the Matterhorn. Since then the mountain has been photographed, painted and modelled probably more often than all the "Stars" of Hollywood put together. In my own collection of mountain sketches I have at least eleven of the Matterhorn.

In spite of all that has been written about it and in spite of all the pictures, good, bad and indifferent, one's first impression of the mountain, on seeing it fairly close on a lovely day, is overwhelming. I do not suppose that any artist has succeeded in conveying the full force of that impression, which depends not only on the shape and grandiose proportions and on the many subtleties of light and shade and colour, but also on intangible influences that pervade the atmosphere surrounding a great mountain. As we stand below and gaze up at the towering summit, which perhaps appears to swing against its moving background of clouds, we feel that we are in the presence of majesty; awe certainly has a part in our appreciation of the spectacle.

Immediately after returning to my hotel in Zermatt after my

ascent of the Matterhorn some thirty years ago I wrote a detailed description of the climb in my notebook. It is a pedestrian account, for I was quite incapable of putting into words all that I had felt during this, my first big climb. But the snapshots that I took and the few little sketches that I made, usually in haste and in a precarious position, bring back to my memory many indescribable impressions and I know now that the Matterhorn experience actually had a lasting influence on the course of my life. After this I could not leave the mountains alone. The call to return to them was irresistible and I knew that up there, thousands of feet above the plane on which our normal lives are lived, there lay a world of magic beauty, of uplifting inspiration and sometimes even of fear to which I must go, at least occasionally, to readjust my sense of proportion.

I set out alone with a guide, Alexander Pollinger, who had been my mentor during the period of preliminary training. He was still a fairly young man and, like many of the best Swiss guides, a delightful companion. He died only a few years ago and I went to look for his grave when I was last in the Nikolaital. I remember how, after walking for some hours through a landscape spangled with wild flowers, we reached the hut near the base of the mountain and, like the proud owner of a splendid estate, he took me by the arm and pointed to the other great peaks surrounding that magnificent arena: the Dent Blanche, the Weisshorn, the Ober-Gabelhorn, the Breithorn, the Lyskamm and, highest of all the mountains of Switzerland, Monte Rosa. He loved them all, though they did not belong to him, but his heart belonged to them.

At that time it was customary to start a big climb during the night in order to reach the summit at dawn. This also had the advantage that the ice and snow remained frozen hard, so that avalanches were unlikely and fragments of loose rock were less liable to fall than they are after the sun has been on them. There was one other small party at the hut and we heard that they intended to set out some time after 2 a.m., so we decided to get away first in order to be above any rocks they might dislodge during the ascent.

I slept for about three hours and at a quarter past midnight Alexander Pollinger told me that it was time to get ready

When I looked out of the window the moon was shining and all was still. The dark form of the Matterhorn, very close now, was silhouetted against the dreamy grey-blue sky. The lower slopes and the whole of the east face were lost in inky darkness; but, high up, patches of ice and snow reflected a cold, uncertain shimmer of light from the moon. There was a chilly bite in the air.

I soon had my clothes on and I put an extra warm sweater and gloves into my rucksack. Carrying my freshly-nailed climbing boots in my hand I went quietly into the front room, where the guide was making tea. We ate something, drank the warming tea and then pulled on our boots, taking special care over the lacing. Having adjusted our rucksacks, we stepped outside into the shadow of the great mountain. While we roped up in the flickering light of a candle-lantern I looked all round me.

The landscape was a symphony in black and moonlight colour. The mountains that I had seen so clearly before sunset were almost invisible, but, as my eyes grew accustomed to the darkness, vague ghost-like forms began to detach themselves from the black background and soon I could detect the pallid spectre of Monte Rosa and the more substantial presence of the nearer glaciers below us.

I followed Alexander's swinging lantern as we picked our way along a ridge and crossed an area of crisp snow, until we came among the massive rocks that buttress the base of the mountain itself. Here all was pitch darkness except for the little pool of light from the lantern. Keeping close together, we groped for holds for our hands and feet and hauled ourselves steadily upwards from ledge to ledge. Presently, coming on to the ridge that leads to the shoulder, we emerged into the light of the moon. On account of thin cloud the illumination was not strong enough to show up the ledges and crevices in the rock clearly and we still had to grope for them, but Alexander extinguished the candle and we went on without pausing, moving one at a time.

It was the first time that I had looked down from such a height in moonlight into one of the most impressive mountain arenas in Europe. The cold air tingled in my nostrils. There was no sound save the click and scrape of our nailed boots on the rock. We could hear nothing of the other party, who must have started soon after us, and the whole world seemed to be asleep. Outside the areas of intense darkness the soft intangible shimmer of what I can only describe as moonlight colour indicated, by its varying intensity, the presence of snow-fields and glaciers. The moon itself, softened by the film of cloud, seemed to shrink from revealing too much loveliness.

As we passed back into the shadow I became aware of a suffused lightening above the eastern horizon and I realized that dawn could not be far away. But we were still in the grip of night among the rocks. From afar the Matterhorn appears to have been chiselled from a solid mass, but up there we were climbing on a vast mound of huge fragments, piled, jammed or nicely poised where they had fallen. As Alexander led the way I appreciated how difficult it would be to choose a route, unless there was enough light to reveal scratches left by the boots of previous climbers, for often the confused jumble of rocks prevented our seeing more than a few yards above us or a few yards below. I could not guess how far we were from the summit, but at an exposed point on the ridge, with a precipice on either side, I judged that we must be at least half way there. Here my guide stood out in black silhouette against the sky. Beyond him a cold steel sword pointed down the mountainside: it was the glint of moonlight on the edge of an ice-coated rock.

Gradually the sky turned from blue-black velvet to a soft grey-blue that brought a feeling of intensified cold. I could see the Theodul glacier quite clearly, a broad and silent river of ice now very far below. The surrounding snow-peaks appeared to hover at an uncertain distance, waiting to be brought into focus when the sun rose. We were again in the moonlight and now the climb became much steeper.

Sometimes we were hauling ourselves cautiously up almost vertical walls, sometimes we stepped rapidly across rock-strewn couloirs carved into the precipitous face of the mountain. A thin coating of ice made the rocks perilous and we reached up with anxiously probing fingers for the most secure holds we could find before moving a foot. I was tackling a problem that absorbed all my faculties and I had no time to feel afraid. When

I stopped and belayed the rope while Alexander went higher I sometimes looked down the dizzy precipice towards the glacier thousands of feet below, but I had no sensation of vertigo and I knew that I should be able to face the descent without undue anxiety.

The sky became lighter and the pale beauty of the moon began to fade. Over the eastern mountains a vaporous limpid green, tinged with cerulean blue, rose like a faintly luminous mist and the mantle of the night withdrew slowly before its advance. Soon the colours changed, becoming tinged with dull brick-red which gradually warmed in tone until an orange veil fluttered along the horizon. A scarcely perceptible reflection of this colour tinted the highest snow summits, but all below still lay dim and cold as if seen through the water of a coral sea.

Now that we could see more clearly our progress became more assured and the reflection from the east began to warm the colour of the rock. Suddenly a suffusion of rosy light spread above the horizon and the cliffs that we had yet to climb became alive. But the direct light of the sun had not yet reached the summit and I was anxious to be there when it came.

We had spent a few minutes in the Solvay Refuge, a small wooden cabin perched at 12,526 feet, where we refreshed ourselves with sugar and lemon. Then we had climbed on upwards to the great shoulder of the mountain and were now well above it on one of the steepest parts of the climb. On some of the pitches there were fixed ropes attached to iron rings set in the rock, but we decided not to rely on these and we climbed without their aid. Spreadeagled against the rock, we used exiguous foot and hand holds to haul ourselves up to the sloping snow-covered roof of the mountain. I was panting now, from exertion and the altitude. After a short pause to readjust our rope we advanced slowly over the icy surface.

I had hardly noticed how quickly night had slipped away during those last fatiguing minutes. We came suddenly upon the summit, which had been hidden by the steepness of the rock. At that moment the sun broke cover and the rock and ice beneath our feet glowed like an ember. Alexander Pollinger held out his hand and I grasped it.

Standing within a foot or two of the summit ridge, with its

overhanging cornice of snow, I put my hand on the iron post that marks the Swiss peak and looked down the precipice that falls thousands of feet into Italy. This summit ridge is rather more than a hundred yards long. At the far end another post marked the Italian peak, for the Matterhorn, like Monte Rosa, stands astride the frontier. In a notch in the middle there was the iron cross erected in memory of the four men who fell to their deaths on the way down from the first ascent with Whymper.

Although the wind at the summit, which had now dispelled the clouds, was not strong it was bitterly cold up there and Alexander and I remained only about twenty minutes. But this was long enough to survey the whole panorama, which seemed to embrace half Switzerland. It was a magnificent landscape, spread out under a cloudless blue sky. The summits of many famous mountains glowed with the rosy touch of the rising sun while their lower slopes and the deep valleys remained dark and mysterious, as if flooded to a great depth with liquid moonlight blue. Gradually, while we watched, the pink glow crept downwards, forcing the last dregs of the night to drain away. Out of the dim distance there emerged range after range of mountains and, in the gaps between them, numerous glaciers began to reflect the slowly deepening blue of the sky.

Alexander stood beside me and, like the master of ceremonies at a royal reception, named the great peaks in succession as they came into prominence. Last of all he pointed to a huge snow-covered massif thrusting up from the far-off petrified ocean that surrounded it and beginning to blush in the soft light of dawn. It was Mont Blanc, the highest mountain in Europe.

I read in a book about climbing in the Alps, published a few years ago, that "it is unnecessary" to start a big climb as early as one o'clock in the morning and I believe that it is now less usual than it was to do so. But I would not have missed my early starts for anything. From the hut near the base of the Matterhorn we reached the top in just four and a quarter hours and, although we had no wish to hurry, I believe this was fairly good time. We arrived in time to see the sunrise and it seems to me incomprehensible that anyone who is willing to make the climb should be content to forgo such a spectacle. A panorama of the Alps seen from the summit of a high mountain at dawn on a perfect morning is a world unknown to those who never climb. Even airmen, who find new worlds among the clouds, cannot enjoy such a scene in the same way, for they pass swiftly where the mountaineer can linger and they are above, but not in, the world of snow and ice.

No artist could paint such a scene: I felt indeed that it was pictorially impossible. Southwards the mountains of Italy began to gleam and sparkle and in every other direction there were beautiful forms and colours that could be individually admired. But the impression that they made as a whole was overwhelming. It was not a subject for a picture: it was an experience.

With a last look round I led the way down the sloping roof of rock and hard frozen snow and then began the vertical descent over the edge. Sometimes we faced the rock, sometimes we faced outwards and we made good progress towards the shoulder. It was not until we were nearly back at the Solvay Refuge that we passed the other party, still on their way up. When they were a few yards above us one of them stepped on a rock that gave way beneath his foot and several large fragments came bounding past us and plunged down the mountain with a sinister clatter. A moment later several more fragments fell and one of them, a flat slab as big as a soup-plate, touched a rock just above me and, ricocheting, struck my right shin just at the top of the boot, forcing my foot from its hold. Fortunately I had good holds with my fingers, but I felt a sharp pain while I hung on and watched the other fragments flying through space below me.

Alexander helped me into the shelter of a big rock where I took off the boot and found that the lace had been severed. Luckily the strong leather and thick stockings had reduced the effect of the blow on my shin, but the skin had been broken and the pressure of the boot was painful during the rest of the descent.

Falling rocks are one of the chief dangers on the Matterhorn and they have caused a number of fatal accidents on this and other mountains. Apart from those inadvertently disturbed by climbers, rocks cracked by the action of sun and frost often become loose when the ice that binds them thaws and they may fall down precipices and couloirs without any warning. For this reason it is often advisable to get over the most exposed pitches of a climb before the sun has warmed the rocks and for the same reason we were anxious to climb ahead of, rather than behind, the other party. Even during the night we heard a few small falls of rock and on the way down we saw several that would have annihilated any party in their path.

A long descent on steep rock is often more tiring than the climb on account of the continual jarring as one steps or jumps from ledge to ledge. Although the injury to my leg was not serious, it throbbed all the way down and I was glad when at last we reached the hut at the base. It was then only nine o'clock in the morning and several people who were there seemed surprised that we had managed to return so early. We had been lucky with the weather. Sometimes parties have been overtaken by a sudden storm and have spent many more hours on the mountain, either among the rocks or in the little refuge.

After having some refreshments and bandaging my leg, which soon began to feel better, we continued down the path to the Schwarzsee, which we reached in two hours. By now the day had become very hot and we discarded our warm clothing. While we ate our picnic lunch outside the hotel I looked back at the Matterhorn, towering against the blue sky in all its perfect majesty, and, although the scene had been photographed count-less times, I made a rapid sketch.

The pause restored my energy completely and, at Alexander's suggestion, we set off on a two-hours' detour through the wild valley of the Furggbach, a stream issuing from the Theodul glacier. The steep grassy slopes were carpeted with alpine flowers and the sweet scent of the hay drifted from the wooden barns on stone stilts in which it was stored. As we strode along through this paradise of colour I felt supremely happy and I was almost sorry when we entered the picturesque little village of Winkelmatten and I knew that Zermatt was not far beyond.

We passed near the Zermatt churchyard, which contains the graves of three of Whymper's party and of a considerable number of others who perished on the mountains and I asked Alexander whether there had been any recent accident on the

Matterhorn. Only then did he tell me that, a few days before my arrival in Zermatt, he was leading a party on the mountain when they came upon an Austrian and his wife, on holiday from Vienna, endeavouring to find their way up a steep pitch at some distance to one side of the normal route. They were climbing without a guide and were known to have very limited experience. Alexander warned them that they were in a dangerous position and advised them to descend to a point on the route below him. They began to move in his direction and were within ten yards of him when suddenly one of them slipped and they both fell hundreds of feet down a precipice. Alexander and a number of other guides recovered their bodies later in the day.

Many people, having witnessed such a tragic accident, would have taken any opportunity to talk about it. It was typical of Alexander not to refer to it or to the grim and difficult task that he had undertaken.

On the day following my own climb yet another guideless climber fell to his death on the east face.

I had already asked my guide if he would lead me on Monte Rosa and he said that, if I went well on the Matterhorn and was not tired afterwards, it would be a good thing to go there without delay, before the weather changed. Before we parted that evening he suddenly asked me if I would like to start for Monte Rosa next day.

"Do you think I could do it?" I asked. The Dufourspitze of Monte Rosa is the highest peak in Switzerland, 15,217 feet, and the Swiss side, which presents a fine spectacle to observers on the Gornergrat, is a long climb mostly on ice and snow.

"Of course!" said Alexander, smiling. "We will see what the weather is like to-morrow."

When I looked out of my window in the morning the sky was overcast with dull grey clouds and the Matterhorn was invisible. During the next few hours I went several times into the main street of Zermatt, where the guides foregather, to try to get an optimistic weather report. All I could hear was that it might get finer or it might not. At intervals a part of the Matterhorn appeared through a window in the clouds and I was told that it was not too bad in that direction. But reports from the Gornergrat said that it was still thick around Monte Rosa and my spirits fell. I could not afford to wait more than two or three days. I went a little way down the valley to make a sketch of some old wooden houses.

In the early afternoon I had a talk with Alexander Pollinger. He suggested waiting another hour or two, but advised me to have my rucksack ready, with food and warm clothing. I went back to the hotel to make my preparations and after tea I found Alexander again. He had been watching the sky and was still doubtful, but he thought there was just a chance that the wind might blow the clouds away before the next dawn. If the weather got no worse we might take the seven o'clock train up to Roten Boden near the Gornergrat, about an hour by the rack and pinion railway, and then walk across the Gorner glacier to the Bétemps hut which stood on a rock island in the midst of the ice.

The views from the Gornergrat, which is encircled by some of the highest mountains in the Alps, are among the finest in Switzerland and thousands of people who never climb go there every year to see them. But I found it hard to concentrate on the scenery, for I was constantly watching the sky and trying to detect in the wind some promise of a fine night. As the train climbed slowly up its steep and winding track I noticed that the clouds that had engulfed the Matterhorn were rapidly dispersing. At Roten Boden we jumped from the train and set off at a rapid pace through the dusk. The clouds were still thick above us and Monte Rosa lay hidden. All around us the steep ground seemed almost luminous with its multi-coloured carpet of alpine flowers.

We passed near the Riffelhorn and followed a rough pathway that dipped sharply down towards the immense Gorner glacier. In the shadow of the rocks it was already nearly dark and only the crunch of our boots disturbed the silence. It took a long time to reach the glacier, but when at last we stepped on to the boulders of the lateral moraine we paused for a moment to study the sky once more. The clouds were lifting. A vague shimmer of cold grey-blue ahead of us showed where they had risen from the lower flank of the mountain.

The line that we had to follow across the glacier was not difficult; there were no séracs and few crevasses, but the distance was at least a mile and a half. I had been on the glacier before and I knew that, whereas from afar it appeared as flat as a river, it rose steeply from the lateral moraine, like a colossal mound, so that it was impossible to see from one side to the other. The surface was hard ice or compacted snow, but it was deeply furrowed all over with pools and rivulets that drained away to the sides with a continual tinkling sound. At the bottom of every puddle and hollow lay black sediment composed of glacial earth and rock fragments. These were still visible in the dim light and we avoided them because we knew that they were covered with clear icy water.

Until we reached the middle of the glacier we were climbing steadily uphill, but we went on as fast as we could, constantly stretching or jumping over the streams and twisting and turning among the pools. The central moraine, that had appeared from the Riffelberg like a thin black line, was a great ridge of tumbled boulders quite a hundred yards in width. When we had climbed over this formidable obstruction we began to descend gradually and presently we could just make out the rectangular shape of the Bétemps hut. I looked down along the course of the glacier and could see dimly the upper part of the Matterhorn rising above dark billowing masses of cloud. All around me the ice extended, an expanse of dim blue coldly slumbering.

As we drew nearer to the hut we had to cross the tongue of the confluent Monte Rosa glacier and here we came among a considerable number of large crevasses, great black gashes in the ice of unknown depth. We picked our way cautiously between them and into one I tossed a stone, hearing it ricochet from side to side until the sound died away. When I peered down into the depths the vertical walls showed sombrely green for a few feet and then plunged into blackness.

It was quite dark when we reached the rocks below the hut and it was no easy matter to clamber without slipping among the wildly tumbled boulders and over huge slabs polished smooth by the ice of centuries. Several times I thought I saw the hut in front of me, but it was only a vast boulder on a patch of snow.

At last we came to the hut, mounted the wooden steps and opened the door. It was pitch dark inside, but we heard the sound of snoring. We were not going to be alone on the mountain.

Alexander struck a match and lit a candle, placing it on the wooden table. By its yellow flickering light I saw two figures wrapped in dark blankets in the wooden troughs that served as beds. We took off our boots and crept into the kitchen, a space divided from the rest of the hut by a partition. Alexander lit a small wood fire in the stove and presently we sat down to hot soup, tea and some of the food that we had brought with us. While this was being prepared I took out my sketch-book and, in spite of the dim light, managed to make a rough sketch of the scene. It was typical of the interior of alpine huts, although often they are more crowded. I wished that we were quite alone, for I felt that, for the next few hours, Monte Rosa belonged to Alexander and me.

When we had finished our meal we tip-toed back into the sleeping-room, where I rolled myself in a blanket and lay down in a wooden trough. Alexander said *Gute Nacht!* and went quietly up the ladder to the floor above, to the guides' quarters. It was half past eleven.

The snoring revived, but I was soon asleep.

Exactly two hours later I was awake again, watching three climbers preparing their rucksacks by the dull light of a lantern. One of them, a guide, brought tea while the other two sat quietly talking in Saxon-German. I wondered vaguely if they had ever climbed in so-called "Saxon-Switzerland", where I had been. Soon they rose, put on woollen caps and gloves, extinguished the lantern and went out into the night. The door creaked on its hinges and for a moment I saw a cold grey rectangle of sky. Then I heard the faint clatter made by their boots on the rocks.

I was on the verge of sleep again when Alexander came with his candle and told me that it was two o'clock and time to get up. I wondered if this sort of thing was really worth while. But I stood up, folded the blanket and went sleepily into the kitchen. We soon had some more tea ready, with a cold hard-boiled egg and bread and jam. I asked Alexander if he had looked outside.

"Yes," he said. "It's still all cloud. One cannot tell yet whether it will improve or not."

I felt like someone waiting for a train during a railway strike.

The chances seemed to be against us. But I went to the door and looked out. The sky was mottled all over with grey clouds, moving fairly swiftly before the wind. The glacier, a hundred feet or so below, faded away into mist and darkness.

"Isn't it worth starting?" I asked. I wished I could make a picture of the two of us standing there in the hut, tinged with the light from the candle. All around outside there were rocks and ice and it was the coldest hour of the night.

"We can start," said Alexander. "But we may have to come back in an hour or so, if it is not better."

We pulled on our boots, shouldered our rucksacks and went out. It was bitterly cold. We began clambering upwards in the darkness over giant boulders and then patches of hard snow. More rocks, piled in black confusion, then more snow. I cast anxious eyes at the sky, but there seemed to be no change. Still that procession of clouds, without a break.

Presently we were on the Monte Rosa glacier and we paused to rope together. My eyes had grown accustomed to the gloom and now everything except the rocks and ourselves appeared blue-grey. On our right rose the Lyskamm, a gigantic wall of ice and snow. I looked back at the vague grey buttress of the Gornergrat. The lines of moraine on the glacier were just visible, like pencil smears on dirty grey paper. Long low streaks of mist lay over the Riffelhorn and the Leichenbretter and seemed to be advancing in our direction.

"Look there!" said Alexander suddenly. He was pointing at the sky far behind us.

At first I could see no change. Then I realized that I was looking at the shoulder of the Matterhorn, barely visible through the clouds. It might be the herald of a break.

From now on we remained on hard snow and ice, proceeding at a steady pace. There was no sign of the other party who had preceded us. The slope became steeper and we made many detours round yawning crevasses. Our boots crunched the frozen surface; occasionally our ice axes clicked on ice. Otherwise the silence was complete, uncanny.

Then, among the clouds above our heads, I thought I saw a patch of pale green. Perhaps it was a gap, but I said nothing. A little later there seemed to be an answering shimmer far away

V. The
Italian side
of Monte Rosa
(15,217 feet)
seen from
Macugnaga

VI. "High Endeavour". An oil painting based on this subject was exhibited in the XIVth Olympiad "Sport in Art" Exhibition in London, 1948

beyond the Zwillinge. We reached higher and higher up the glacier.

Soon I felt sure that the all-pervading blue-grey had become a little paler. There were definite rifts in the clouds and Alexander had certainly noticed them. He said nothing about turning back.

The greenish-grey pallor became tinged with yellow, spreading upwards from the east. Dawn was coming, but how could all these clouds be cleared away? Soon we would be up among them.

The general slope of the glacier was becoming steeper, but at several points it levelled a little before plunging again, like an enormous wave. On surmounting one of these waves we saw far ahead, in the midst of a vast new snow field, the three tiny figures of the German party moving very slowly. We kept on steadily in silence, watching them as they climbed a ridge that cut into the snow field. They disappeared beyond it, but soon they came in sight again, zig-zagging up a steep slope with heavy deliberation. We were gaining on them rapidly.

At the top of the rise they stopped to rest for a few moments, perhaps half a mile away. We began to close the gap. They halted again more than once before we drew level and Alexander called across to the guide, asking for his views about the weather. They agreed that it was improving. For a short time they remained level with us, fifty yards away, then we drew ahead.

Every now and then we looked back. Twice more the others halted. The slope was now very steep and every step had to be secure. Dawn was on the way; the clouds were thinning and the pearly light was growing warmer in tone. To left and right great crevasses yawned, as if waking from too short a slumber, their cold lips reflecting the heartless green of deep ice.

Our route swept in a wide curve to the left and the cold wind rushed down to meet us. Isolated clouds, caught between the higher walls of the mountain, came tearing down the glacier and past us like express trains. Several times they enveloped us so that we could not even see one another and we were compelled to halt.

Some minutes later I looked back over my shoulder and saw

4

that a faint pink glow was beginning to tinge the snow peaks of Castor and Pollux, while the neighbouring rocks showed dark rich brown. Lower down all was still black or grey. A flake of pink appeared on the Lyskamm; then dawn touched the top of the Gornergrat with a shaft of rose. The next moment a great sweep of snow above us blushed with the same warm colour, only to be blotted out by a racing cloud.

We were now attacking some of the severest slopes of the climb and at intervals Alexander chipped out steps with his axe. The fragments of hard ice slid away with a glassy tinkle. A slip here might be fatal. Hitherto exertion had made me warm, but now the cold seemed to bite through my clothes and especially through my boots. Occasionally I glanced up at the slopes above where the glow became intensified every minute.

We could see the final ridge clearly ahead, mounting in great curves towards the summit. At a point where it was possible to halt we stood still for a moment and looked back down the perilous slope. Hundreds of feet below us the other party had stopped again, this time close together, not strung out on the rope. As we watched one of them separated and began to descend. The others followed. Now we should have the mountain to ourselves.

"On! then," said Alexander. "*Langsam aber sicher.*" Slow but sure.

The angle of ascent was now precipitous and every step had to be cut in the ice. If either of us had slipped it would have meant a swift slide of hundreds of feet, ending in all probability in a deep crevasse.

We reached the arête and we paused, panting. It was a knife-edge of ice, sloping down sharply on both sides for thousands of feet. We were now looking down into Italy, with a fresh panorama of mountains and glaciers, but we still had at least half a mile to go to the summit. The ridge rose in a pronounced curve, like a sagging telegraph wire, and we could see nothing beyond the peak at its far end. This was followed by another loop, rising higher to another rocky peak; then another and another in exasperating succession. Each in turn looked like the top, but we were not there yet and I began to wonder whether we should ever arrive.

I think that this part of the long climb was the most dangerous. Alexander told me, a little wryly, that if one of us slipped down one side of the sharp ridge, the correct technique would be for the other to throw himself instantly down the other side, hoping that the rope would not snap and that our weights would balance. I could not imagine myself making such an heroic gesture, but one never knows what one might do when life depends on swift action.

A strong wind was blowing from the east, driving the last clouds away, but it was bitterly cold and its force increased the difficulty of maintaining balance. The knife-edge was hard ice, shining like glass in the slanting rays of the sun, and we had to proceed with extreme caution, cutting steps just below the sharp crest. At every stroke of our axes, for we both used them in order to make the best possible steps for our return, the ice splinters fell away with a musical tinkle. At intervals we had to clamber over rock, often overhanging on one side, and we moved only a few paces in turns.

Higher and higher we went. *"Langsam aber sicher"* kept repeating itself in my mind. On one of the final outcrops of rock Alexander stopped and asked me to rub his hands. Three fingers of his right hand and two of the left had lost all sense of feeling. My own, in spite of two pairs of gloves, were nearly numb, but for two or three minutes we stood there in the icy wind, vigorously rubbing our hands together and stamping our feet to restore the circulation. It was a bad moment, for there was not much room for this performance and the menace of frost-bite was not to be taken lightly.

Gradually warmth was restored to our hands and we went on, up the last section of the arête. It ended in rock and, with a final effort, we stood on the highest summit of the highest mountain in Switzerland at 15,217 feet. I grasped the iron stanchion that was embedded in the rock to mark the top of the Dufourspitze and we shook hands. Despite the cold, Alexander was smiling happily and so was I. (Plate V.)

It would have been impossible to remain there for long, but we crouched in the lee of an ice-coated rock and gazed out over the stupendous panorama. It was a perfect morning and the time was a quarter to eight. We had taken only five hours and five minutes from the hut, though I had been told that we could expect to take seven or eight hours. There was scarcely a cloud in the blue sky above our heads, but thick masses were still billowing among the mountains of Italy. The Lyskamm gleamed like an immense white wall and far, far away, beyond numerous overlapping ranges, the spotless head of Mont Blanc was clearly visible. On the Italian side of the mountain the Marinelli hut stood out distinctly on its rocky ridge.

But I was even more interested in the view looking back, where the receding lines of moraine on the Gorner glacier directed my gaze to the Matterhorn, the stately pyramid on which Alexander and I had stood little more than forty-eight hours ago. To its left the great mass of the Breithorn was glowing in the early light and low down on the right, at the far end of the Gornergrat, the little black hump of the Riffelhorn stood out prominently against the snow fields beyond. I wondered if there had been any early risers at the Gornergrat hotel, watching the dawn break over Monte Rosa and perhaps seeing, through the telescope, our two minute and lonely figures ascending to the summit.

Now began the descent, myself leading the way and Alexander holding the rope short behind me. All the way back along the wind-swept ridge and then down the awe-inspiring wall of ice where we had cut steps we made our way steadily, with extreme caution. I felt that the utter loveliness of the landscape was being wasted, for the way down demanded all our attention. When we reached a patch where the snow crust was less slippery we paused for a moment to eat some lumps of sugar. Then on again, down and down, until we emerged from the shadow of the great mountain into the full glare of the sun. In spite of my dark glasses I was almost dazzled by the reflection from the snow and it was often hard to see the tracks that we had made on the way up.

Gradually the slope eased and we no longer had to use our ice-axes as brakes, but the jolting at every downward step continued. At the place where the exhausted German party had turned back we took off our rucksacks and stopped for refreshment. All around us the glacier gleamed with a whiteness that only snow can produce. In a very few minutes we were off again, faster and faster as the slope eased. I could hardly believe that here, where the sun was already warm on my head, we had been trudging upwards in the dark cold night only a few hours before.

We passed some magnificent cliffs of pure ice and I took off my glasses to appreciate the indescribable beauty of the deep blue-green where the sun penetrated their glassy surfaces. I asked Alexander if he would mind waiting a few minutes while I made some colour notes in my sketch-book, but he would have none of it and I had to obey.

"We must get off the glacier before the surface melts too much," he said. "There are two or three snow bridges to cross and already they will be getting dangerous."

The softening of the snow crust was noticeable; frequently a foot broke through with alarming suddenness and the crust cut painfully against the instep. In a short while the sore place where my leg had been injured by a falling rock on the Matterhorn was throbbing again. At times we ran, deviating in great curves round the ends of crevasses, like skiers on a *slalom* course. As we passed hastily over one of the snow bridges, I glanced down into the crevasses. Crystal-clear icicles twenty and thirty feet in length hung in the half-light from the green and blue walls. From far down in the black depths, seemingly hundreds of feet below, there came the faint sound of running water.

The sun was softening the surface snow rapidly and soon we were sinking in at every step. The perpetual jarring was tiring to knees and ankles. Constantly we had to wind in and out among crevasses. But at last we reached the island of glacial boulders on which the Bétemps hut stood.

When we entered the hut the Germans were just leaving, having returned at leisure and had a meal. We were more than ready for our hot soup and picnic lunch. Then we recrossed the Gorner glacier and, in the heat of the day, climbed up the long path to the Gornergrat. At the Riffelalp hotel a German family came out to congratulate us. They had been up very early to watch the dawn and they had observed our progress almost continuously through a telescope, from the moment when the other party turned back until we stood on the summit.

Surprisingly, I did not feel tired: indeed I felt full of energy.

We decided to walk straight on down to Zermatt instead of returning by train. All the way up from the glacier I had noticed in particular the myriad colours of the rock fragments that flashed and glittered beside the path. Now the kaleidoscopic effect was multiplied by the flowers that peeped from every nook and cranny. No picture could convey the impression of such a sight. Even one little clump of star-gentians pushing through fragments of sparkling schist had more beauty than a sapphire set in diamonds.

Before three o'clock we were back in Zermatt. I had two more days before I was due to leave for Italy.

"Have you any suggestions for to-morrow?" I asked Alexander.

He smiled. "A nice little chimney on the south side of the Riffelberg. It's a difficult one, that, but you could do it. How would you like that?"

The Matterhorn had been mostly a rock climb, Monte Rosa chiefly snow and ice. Each was a good example of its kind. On the whole I preferred rock, where one could really get to grips with the very substance of the mountain.

"If the weather is good, I'll try," I told him and we arranged to meet again in the morning.

The Matterhorn Couloir, as that southern route up the Riffelberg is called, is a real climbers' climb. It is approached from the Gorner glacier after a walk which entails springing from one enormous boulder to another for a considerable distance along the lateral moraine. The ascent itself is a matter of only a few hundred feet, but it took us about four hours to work our way to the top. Some of the holds were barely large enough for the tips of our fingers or even for a nail at the edge of a boot. At times we jammed our bodies in a broad crack or "chimney" and wormed our way slowly upwards by outward pressure of the back, arms and legs against the rock walls. In some pitches there was a good deal of moisture and ice and there were not many opportunities to relax. I confess that I felt thankful when we eventually emerged safely at the top and went up the Riffelhorn again for a final look at the view.

Since those wonderful experiences with Alexander Pollinger I have done a good deal of climbing in different parts of the world and I have learnt a little about mountains and about the nature of different kinds of rock, snow and ice. Without such knowledge it is foolish to climb, unless accompanied by an experienced mountaineer, and a great many of the accidents that occur in the Alps and elsewhere are due to the lack of it. A climbing story that includes an accident may make exciting reading and of course some accidents are due to bad luck. But most of the best tales of climbing tell of successful achievement rather than failure. They deal not so much with a mountain as a whole, but rather with the details and problems of the different pitches and they describe even particular holds. They are stories of skill and endurance, not of incompetence. (Plate VI.)

The climber has his own point of view. While he appreciates the beauty of the mountain scenery as much as anyone, he also looks at the structure of a mountain, not quite as a geologist might do, but with something of the consideration of a cat-burglar who contemplates scaling the wall of a house. He is interested in the different kinds of rock and their angle of slope, in the ridges and couloirs and ledges and in the condition of the snow and ice. He senses the wind and watches the sky, not only for the beauty of cloud formations but because he may see there indications of a change in the weather.

The artist, that is to say one who studies mountains for their pictorial qualities, has certain interests in common with the climber, but he also develops a feeling for mountain scenery that is a part of the basis of his art. His appreciation of form and structure is acute, for he does not paint a mountain scene with one all-embracing stroke, as the camera seizes the whole in a single blink of its shutter. He builds up his subject plane by plane and, by the use of subtle differences of tone, emphasizes the prominence of a ridge, the steepness and direction of a slope and sometimes even the very quality of a rock. Whereas the camera accepts without argument the effects of light and shade at a given moment, the artist absorbs more slowly an impression of the "atmosphere" of a scene and he consciously arranges the chiaroscuro in the way that seems best to convey that impression. The degree of detail that he may add is a matter of secondary importance. His colours must be true, but he will not necessarily apply the particular tints that he sees at the time of painting, for they change rapidly in nature and an ugly moment is one to avoid. There is no merit in distortion, but he regards distortion as legitimate where it helps to impress on the mind of another his own particular feeling about the scene. He should, if he lives up to the normal conception of what an artist is, seek beauty in all that he beholds and endeavour to put quality into all his works.

If the artist who paints mountain scenery is also a mountaineer he has an advantage over others who have never climbed. While he studies his subject he is aware, not only of the colours and shapes and tones, but also of the practicability or otherwise of the rock faces and snow fields that he is trying to depict. He stands up there on the ridge that he is painting. He feels the cold wind, he sees what lies beyond, he knows the effort required to take him there. And this knowledge, born of experience, flows through his brush and mingles with the paint.

In the daily press and in many books and periodicals there appear quite often pictures of mountain scenery. Some of them are advertisements. Few of these are works of art, still fewer would satisfy a mountaineer. We see rocks that are wooden stage-props and snow that is clearly paint. We see a climber with an ice-axe curved at an angle that would make it almost useless: he stands against a background of mountains that have neither solidity nor weight. Obviously the creators of such drawings know little about mountains.

There are technical difficulties in painting mountain scenery to which I shall refer later on. When painting in the open, in good conditions, I explore the mountains with my eyes and I feel my way among them as I compose them on the paper. I am rarely successful in obtaining the result at which I aim, but if I can reveal a little of what I feel about mountains and can convey a hint of their beauty and fascination, I know that I have taught myself something more about them. I do not believe that mountains, in themselves, have a spiritual influence, but to be among great mountains is to be in surroundings that are propitious for spiritual experience. If we believe in God we cannot help feeling His presence there.

CHAPTER III

I EXTEND MY TRAVELS AND BECOME
A DIPLOMATIST

I SUPPOSE that every artist hopes to visit Italy at least once in his life and in my case the desire to do so was extremely strong. As long as I was at Cambridge, studying modern languages, the ostensible object of my journeys abroad was to learn to talk them fluently. But sometimes I strayed from the narrow path, once getting as far as the Dardanelles. As an excuse for going to Scandinavia I attended a course of lectures in Danish, there being none available in Swedish or Norwegian, but that plan had to be suspended until after I had taken my degree. Later on the little Danish I had learnt came in useful as one of my extra subjects in the examination for the Diplomatic Service—an examination which, at that period, lasted about twenty-one days and covered most of the subjects under the sun.

When I came down from Cambridge in 1924 I was in a perplexed state of mind, for I had been reading languages and literature for several years but had not yet been able to decide what to do with the knowledge. I think that I wanted, most of all, to become an artist and I had recently shown that I had some aptitude by getting two oil paintings hung at the Royal Academy while I was still an undergraduate. But it had been argued, up to a point that almost persuaded me, that I should never be able to earn a living as an artist and I yielded to the advice of others instead of following my own inclination. I reached the decision—to abandon painting as a career—with considerable hesitation, but I am glad now that I allowed myself to be deflected, for eventually my experience was widened and enriched in a way that it never could have been if I had gone to an art school.

The habit of travel had grown on me to such an extent that, almost as soon as my last term at the University was over, I went off to the Alps. A climbing holiday is a good cure for excessive study and I soon felt ready for anything. It might have been better if I had been ready for one particular thing, a definite profession. Diplomacy had been suggested as a possibility, but the possibility depended on success in what was considered to be one of the stiffest competitive examinations in the world and I was in no mood to face another examination just then.

After the bout of climbing described in the last chapter I went over the mountains into Italy, first to Milan and then on to Venice where I had agreed to meet a Cambridge friend. My pilgrimage to Italy was in some ways similar to the "Grand Tour" that young gentlemen of leisure used to make in the eighteenth and early nineteenth centuries, though in my case there was nothing grand about it. I travelled as cheaply as I could, always in the cheapest class, and some of the odd *pensions* where I stayed did not bear close inspection. I made the longer train journeys at night, in order to save the cost of a night's lodging. It had been the same in Spain and I was used to it.

Of course I thought of Goethe's *Italienische Reise* and of the experiences in Italy that had helped to ripen his ideas of art. I remembered also the letters that Heinrich Heine had written from Italy and, like him, I felt that "The lack of knowledge of the Italian language distresses me greatly. I do not understand the people and cannot talk to them. I see Italy, but I do not hear it. Yet often I am not entirely without conversation. Here the stones speak . . ."

The first thing to do was to fill this gap. The Berlitz School of Languages provided vouchers that enabled me to take one or more lessons at any of their schools. As their method followed a standard system I could take Lessons 1 and 2 in Milan, Lessons 3 to 5 in Venice and so on in other towns where I might be staying only a few days.

From Venice I went by steamer to Trieste, chiefly to see some extraordinary ice caves in the mountains behind the port. On the evening before I left to go back to Venice I was sketching on the heights overlooking the harbour when a ship arrived from Egypt. This gave me the idea of going there, though not before I had seen Florence and Rome and a good many other places with world-famous art galleries.

If I had been able to decide about my future I might have returned to London from Rome or Naples, but the travel demon drove me on. After a long and uncomfortable journey I reached Brindisi, on the heel of Italy, and embarked in a little steamer for the Piræus. I snatched sketches of the Greek islands —Leukas, Cephalonia, Zante and others—as I passed and was sketching the Acropolis even before I had found a room in Athens.

Not having studied Greek I could, like Heine, converse only with the stones until I found someone who could speak French or German. If I had had a classical background every ruin and monument would have been redolent of history and mythology, but nothing like that came between me and the artistry that had created them. I tried one evening to paint the Acropolis against a flaming sunset, but my sketch never approached the beauty of what I saw. I might have done better if I had had the Greek gods at my elbow, reminding me of things unseen. But it is only in the mountains that the spirits of the subject prompt me.

I cut short my visit to Greece on hearing of a small Greek steamer in which I could travel as a steerage passenger to Alexandria for thirty shillings. I bought some chocolate, a loaf of bread and three tins of sardines and these, with a little soup scrounged from the ship's kitchen, provided sustenance for the two days and nights at sea.

This was my second experience of steerage—I had already tried it on the Black Sea—and, as it was a short voyage, it was not too bad. There must have been about a hundred of us of various nationalities, nearly all from south-eastern Europe, and we were confined to the fore part of the ship. A good many, particularly the women, went down into the hold, but one sniff at the hatch was enough for me. During the day there was nothing to do but to sit on the deck in the hot sun, but I had a book to read and I amused myself—and possibly some of the passengers—by sketching the others lolling about all round me. At night the wind was cold and a good many of the passengers wrapped themselves in the rugs or blankets that they had

brought with them. I had only a few things in a rucksack, so I
put on my mackintosh and curled up on a coil of rope right in
the prow of the ship, which gave a little shelter. The rucksack
made a good pillow. At about five o'clock in the morning some
of the crew brought hoses and washed down the deck until it
was swimming with foaming sea water. During this operation
the steerage passengers were deemed not to exist and those of us
who could stood on anything that would get us out of the way.
I put on my rucksack and stood on the rail at the side of the
ship, but did not escape a partial wetting.

It was difficult to get into conversation with anyone because,
although families were voluble enough among themselves, they
seemed disinclined to speak to strangers. But one old Greek
who spoke French and had been in Egypt before talked to me at
great length about the Moqattam hills that command a fine
view of Cairo and extend into the desert. His description made
me imagine that they must be a considerable range of mountains
and I got quite excited at the prospect of seeing them.

After a week in Cairo, where I stayed at the Y.M.C.A. and
visited innumerable mosques, I fell in with some Arabs who
were about to set off on a camel journey through the Libyan
desert and I conceived the idea of making a part of the journey
with them. At that time I spoke no Arabic, but I found another
Arab who could speak English and hired him and two camels
and a small tent so that I could join the party. We travelled in
the desert, at the camels' leisurely pace, for about ten days,
much of the time miles away from anywhere, and eventually
my hired mentor and I separated from the others and headed
back for the oasis of Fayyûm. It astonished me to find what a
lot there was to paint in the empty desert, where the rising and
the setting of the sun and moon were events of the first magni-
tude. Ever since that wonderful journey I have regarded a
certain passage in Kinglake's *Eothen*, where he speaks of riding
a camel in the desert through the whole of a long hot day, as one
of the truest things in English literature.

From the Fayyûm I went to Luxor, where I was allowed to go
inside the tomb of Tutankhamen which had been opened only
about a year earlier. At Thebes there seemed to be a tempting
rock climb up the high orange-coloured cliff behind the temple

of Queen Hatshepsut, but the insecure nature of the rock and the terrific heat of the day defeated me. I made a sketch of the temple against the cliff with the deep blue sky above and the picture still bears signs of the temperature, which was over 120° F. in the shade. To get my view I sat on a donkey saddle placed on a rock full in the sun. The rock was almost too hot to touch. As I painted, the water-colours dried instantly in hard lines and perspiration dripped from my hand.

Before returning to Cairo I made a short excursion from Sakkara into the hills where it was possible, though not very rewarding, to scramble at some risk to one's neck. Farther south there is a real chain of mountains running parallel with the Red Sea. One peak, named Shayib, is the highest in Egypt and exceeds 7,000 feet.

Back in Alexandria I took a third-class ticket, there being nothing cheaper, in an Italian steamer going to Genoa. I carried with me a large collection of Egyptian sketches and a determination to visit Africa again.

I had been back in London only two days when I met in Oxford Street a friend who had been with me at Cambridge and who was now working at a crammer's with a view to entering the Consular Service. He persuaded me to go and talk to Monsieur Turquet, who ran the establishment known as "Scoones", located in some almost completely bare rooms in Great Russell Street, near the British Museum. M. Turquet, a skilful teacher who had successfully prepared many candidates for the Civil Service competitions, forced the pace and in ten minutes he had persuaded me, with a torrent of French logic, to return at nine o'clock the very next morning to begin preparing for the Diplomatic Service examination in barely ten months' time. Even if I managed to reach the very high qualifying standard, there was every chance of failure in the competition for the very few vacancies: then I should once more be in the wilderness and past the age limit for a second attempt. But M. Turquet's forceful manner convinced me that I ought to try.

There followed ten months of concentrated hard labour and when the examination was over I was exhausted. It was then that my thoughts turned again to the mountains, but this time I felt the need of sunshine and warmth as well. Without delay I took a train to Marseilles, crossed the Mediterranean to Tunis and travelled slowly from there towards the Atlas Mountains in Algeria. I was too tired to organize any sort of climbing expedition, but I sat in the sun and painted by the hour. There is something in the atmosphere of Africa that draws me there almost irresistibly and, although I have now been in north, south, east and west Africa and have visited several places in the middle of the continent, I have not yet had enough of it. The sights and sounds and smells are not always attractive, but there are so many things that appeal to the artist in me that it is these that I chiefly remember and want to experience again.

In Algeria I passed through the gap in the mountains known as "The Gateway to the Sahara" and went to Biskra beyond the edge of the desert. The sun was hot and I revelled in it for a week or so. Then I turned once more to the mountains and finally went to Algiers before returning to England. The sunshine and the mountains had done their work and I felt so refreshed that I was ready to accept failure in the examination almost with equanimity. There was an ominous pause: then I heard that I had been successful and I was instructed to report for duty at the Foreign Office.

In 1928, after serving in Berlin and at the Foreign Office, I planned another holiday among mountains and this time I went to Corsica. Before starting from Antibes I watched one of the little ships, that made the passage to Ajaccio in about twelve hours, tossing like a cork on the rough sea and I preferred to risk the flight in a rather dilapidated-looking flying-boat. The risk was greater than I thought, for, after I had flown back in the same aircraft about three weeks later, it crashed in the sea on its very next flight, having apparently disintegrated in the air.

Corsica has a romantic history, freely peppered with stories of bandits who, when pursued by the forces of authority, took refuge in the *macchia*—the wild hills covered with scrub and trees. The French word *maquis*, applied during the last war to the underground movement in France, was derived from this Corsican word. Napoleon Bonaparte was born at Ajaccio and Nelson lost an eye during the bombardment of the citadel at

Calvi. (Plate VII.) There is a house at Calvi in which Christopher Columbus is said to have been born, but I believe that Genoa is more generally accepted as his birthplace. The island was once occupied by the British, from 1793 until 1796, when Napoleon urged us to quit.

I had gone to Corsica chiefly to paint among the mountains, where Edward Lear painted in 1868. Unluckily my first few days in Ajaccio were a disappointment, for it rained unceasingly. Most of the time was spent in reading books about the island and floundering in the rain, looking for possible subjects to paint if the weather ever cleared up. It did so at last and, after sketching in and around Ajaccio, I shared a car with two elderly Americans and drove over every possible road in the interior.

There were not many roads and they were the kind on which most temperamental drivers of the Latin race seem to take a delight in scaring their passengers out of their wits. We had some hairbreadth escapes, but we reached most of the places that I had wanted to see and the Americans, who seemed, uncharacteristically, to be in no particular hurry to get anywhere, were quite content to spend leisurely days while I went off sketching. I painted at Calvi and at other places, but I think the most picturesque setting was that of Corte in the very heart of the island, where the highest mountain, Monte Cinto, rises to nearly 9,000 feet. There were mountains all round the little town, whose houses were scattered over a rocky hill, precipitous on one side, in the midst of the valley of the Tavignano river. Olive trees abounded and it was among the mountains of Corsica that I first saw cork trees and pepper trees. In some districts there was rich sub-tropical vegetation and a wonderful growth of flowers.

During the course of my official career I was lucky to be generally within easy reach of mountains where I could go to stretch my legs and eyes after too much reading in the Chancery. The only exceptions were Berlin, where I was kept almost perpetually hard at work and Sundays were often indistinguishable from other days, and The Hague, where I was extremely busy as Head of Chancery until the outbreak of the last war and where there were no mountains within range. But at

Bucharest in Roumania, where I was sent in 1932, it was quite easy to drive to the Carpathians in Transylvania and, although I sometimes went down the Danube in pursuit of duck, I generally preferred to make for the mountains whenever I had a free week-end.

On my arrival in Bucharest, having just returned to Europe from South America, one of the first things that I did was to look for a certain café where I had a good laugh over a cup of coffee. It was not the coffee that produced my hilarious sensation, but the memory of the last time when I had sat there, about ten years previously while I was still an undergraduate at Cambridge.

That Long Vacation began with some climbing in the Alps and then I went off on a rather rapid tour of the Balkans, extending it as far as Constantinople, as Istanbul was still called. From there I took passage as a deck passenger in a ship sailing the Black Sea and I landed at Constanza on a Sunday morning. The *Autorităţei Sanitoarei*, which I translated as "Sanitary Authorities", had apparently picked up a rumour that there were cases of plague in the once "Sublime Porte" and, although they did not make this clear at once, they decided to keep passengers coming from there in a sort of quarantine-on-bail. They took my passport away and told me that I could recover it from the police station in Bucharest on the following day. This statement was misleading, to say the least of it. I stood for hours in the corridor of an overcrowded train in a temperature that killed one of the passengers until I found myself in the Roumanian capital. When I went to the police station they declared that they had never heard of my passport and I was given the impression that I was some sort of criminal on parole, for I was told to obtain from a doctor, every day until further notice, a certificate stating that I was free from plague. This document was to be delivered, daily, at the police station.

I had imagined that Bucharest might be an interesting place and that was why I had come to see it, but now I began to have doubts. I consulted the British Consul and told him that I was due back at Cambridge in a few days' time. He could get no news of the passport, so he agreed to issue an emergency one

VII. Calvi, Corsica

VIII. Camp in the Carpathians, Roumania

IX. Mount Demavend (18,605 feet), Persia

X. Wetherlam and Elterwater in the English Lake District

that I could use for the journey home, if I could get away. Nearly the whole of my time and a good deal of the little money I had left went in getting fresh visas for Yugoslavia, Hungary, Austria and the rest of the route back to England. The first and second days passed without any attempt to obtain a doctor's certificate and I thought that arrest might be imminent. On the third day I spent all the morning waiting for a single visa. Then I went to a doctor who found my predicament highly amusing, for he said that the plague scare was utter nonsense. He gave me the required certificate without any kind of examination and I rushed off with it to the police station and pushed it under the door.

For half an hour I sat at a café—the one to which I had now returned—sipping coffee to calm my nerves. Then I took a car to the airport, which seemed to offer the quickest and perhaps least supervised exit. I was just in time to get a seat in a small plane leaving for Belgrade. The man who examined my passport did not notice that there was something unusual about it, but I was not entirely happy until the Iron Gates of the Danube had passed astern and I was outside Roumanian territory.

Back in Bucharest once more, I wondered if my name had been kept on a list of plague suspects who had evaded quarantine; but it was good to know that, if I were to be picked up by the police, I could now claim diplomatic immunity.

In those days King Carol was more or less enjoying a spell on the throne in succession to his son Michael, who later succeeded him, and it was fashionable to visit Sinaia, a mountain resort with one of the royal palaces amidst picturesque woodland scenery. But my wife and I travelled much farther afield and we soon found that Roumania was a land of infinite variety. The peasants' costumes, beautifully embroidered, indicated the regions from which the wearers came. Unusual forms of ecclesiastical architecture, often built largely of wood, attracted us to widely scattered parts of the country and we saw several examples of the old fortified churches where the people of the neighbourhood used to take refuge in times of stress. Some of the many churches and monasteries were decorated with mural paintings both inside and out or, like the houses in certain districts, ornamented with carving. Almost every region

5

seemed to have a distinctive form of peasant art, such as pottery, embroidery or wood carving.

The mountains of Roumania, composed largely of limestone, form a loose and irregular chain of more or less separate ranges. Some of these are jagged and precipitous, others are more rounded and show signs of glacial action. From the climber's point of view the rock is not generally as good as that of the Swiss and Italian Alps, but we enjoyed some good walks and scrambles and there were plenty of ski runs in winter. The winters, however, seemed to me extremely cold; the plains between the mountains and the Black Sea were exposed to the icy winds from Russia and I very seldom even thought of trying to sketch out of doors when there was snow on the ground, although I have done so in other countries.

Fortunately I can enjoy mountain scenery without feeling an impetuous urge to climb every peak in sight and I think some of our most pleasant days in the Carpathians were spent in camp. (Plate VIII.) Occasionally we took a small tent and camping equipment by car to some secluded valley where, if the weather was fine and warm, I could paint without being disturbed by a crowd of onlookers or we could walk through the woods and climb as far as we felt inclined.

While I was serving in Roumania I drove my car at least three times across Europe, between London and Bucharest and, during one of these journeys, I spent a week-end in Munich. It happened to be the week-end at the end of June in 1934 when Hitler had news that an insurrection was being brewed by General von Schleicher, a former Chancellor, and Captain Roehm, Leader of the Storm Troops. During the night Hitler descended on Munich to scotch the snakes. Within a few hours Schleicher, Roehm, several other ringleaders and a considerable number of their supporters had been summarily executed. One would imagine that such a holocaust must create a local disturbance, but in fact I heard nothing whatever about it in Munich, where everything appeared as normal as when I arrived there. A day or two later, when I was crossing the Kehl bridge over the Rhine to enter Strasbourg, a French Customs official asked me for the latest news about the Munich massacre. I had to confess my complete ignorance of anything unusual

and I first learnt details of the event from the French newspapers.

Some newspapers "blow up" quite minor incidents to alarming proportions, as every diplomatist knows. Once an organization in Roumania known as "The Iron Guard" became involved with the police. I was in Bucharest at the time and I
knew that it had been little more than a brawl. I was therefore
astonished to receive a telegram from my mother inquiring
after my safety, as she had read in certain London newspapers
that Roumania was in the throes of revolution.

I had been told by some joker before I went to live in
Roumania that the people in Bucharest society were great
sticklers for etiquette and that if I slipped up I might one day be
challenged to a duel. I soon discovered that the business of
exchanging visiting cards had been developed to an extent that
I had never experienced in any other capital and I was anxious
not to be caught out if the printer failed to deliver my latest
order for cards in good time. It could hardly be supposed that
a single omission to leave cards on a hostess on the morrow of a
dinner party would involve me in a duel, but, in order to be
prepared for any eventuality, I went to a fencing school and
inquired about lessons. It appeared that a rifle and revolver,
the only weapons that I could handle with any degree of skill,
were not likely to be required and fencing lessons would cost
only a moderate sum, so I signed on without further delay.

The elementary movements of fencing necessitated the use of
a number of muscles that I had not known I possessed and their
development was a painful process. But I persevered throughout my first winter in Bucharest and at last began to make some
progress. Once the prolonged initial stages had been passed I
found the art quite fascinating, but I continued with it chiefly
because it was good exercise for the winter months.

During my second winter a Roumanian colonel who, my
instructor told me, was an expert with both the *fleuret* and the
épée and had acted as second at several duels, came in occasionally to watch the efforts of the learners. One day he asked me if
I would like to have a few bouts with him once a week and of
course I was delighted to accept his offer. We met regularly
at the barracks and before long I was able to match him

reasonably well. He did not always defeat me. Then he asked me one afternoon to take on a girl pupil of his who had been making good progress and would like to try a bout with a fresh opponent.

I had never before crossed swords, or even foils, with a lady and I was a bit alarmed at the prospect; but, after being introduced, we put on our masks and became almost indistinguishable. Normally every bout begins with certain formalities—a salute with the foil comparable to the handshake in the boxing ring—but this girl was apparently so eager to get on with the fight that she disregarded the preliminaries and, while I was drawing on my glove, made a sudden lunge at my chest. Her foil snapped off short and the broken butt gave me quite a nasty jab. The colonel disqualified her forthwith and nothing that I could say would persuade him to allow us to resume in the proper manner. The fencing code is a strict one and I suppose it is a good thing to deal severely with infringements, for they can have serious results. A French fencing master whom I knew slightly years ago in Biarritz was accidentally killed by a pupil who had not made sure that the "button" on the tip of his foil was secure. Luckily I had nothing worse than a bruise.

I began learning the Roumanian language as soon as I arrived in the country and at first I found the medley of Latin, Slav and Turkish words extremely confusing. Gradually, by dint of reading innumerable newspapers with the aid of a dictionary and supplementing this with a daily lesson, either in the lunch interval or late in the evening, I began to get the hang of the unusual construction. My teacher was an expert in detecting forgeries and the government employed him to solve many such problems. We worked in his laboratory among cameras, enlarging apparatus, equipment for X-rays, infra-red rays, ultra-violet rays and endless other devices. My vocabulary soon became highly technical, but after some months I passed an examination in the language.

I think I could have passed the examination without any subterfuge, but I remembered that one of the teachers at the crammer's where I had worked in London always advised his pupils to prepare three or four talks on different subjects— enough to last about five minutes each—if they were to be examined *viva voce*. I had prepared two such talks, one about my first visit to Roumania and the other about life at an English university, when by a stroke of luck I learnt who my examiner was to be. I found out that he was extremely fond of fishing and so, during the week before the ordeal, I got my teacher to help with the preparation of a talk on that subject, which I more or less committed to memory. I waited my chance and, when the examiner asked a question about my hobbies, I launched out on the topic of fishing and we were soon engaged in an animated discussion of the subject, about which I really knew little. However, it filled in the rest of the quarter of an hour allotted to the *viva* and got me through with a good margin.

Some years later, during the last war, when I was serving for a year and a half as a Political Adviser on the staff of the Minister of State in the Middle East, I thought I might again make use of this device to help me to qualify in an examination in Arabic. Things looked black from the start because it was not easy to find time for lessons and, when one is past forty, learning a new and difficult language requires a lot of concentration. However, I managed to go fairly often to the School of Oriental Studies in Cairo, either early in the morning before office hours or at lunch-time, when most sensible people were either eating or taking a siesta.

I had two alternating teachers; one an "Effendi" who could speak a little English, the other a "Sheikh" who spoke only Arabic. I nearly gave up after a few weeks because hardly a single word bore any resemblance to anything I had met before and the Arabic characters, written from right to left, made me feel quite dizzy. I persevered for two reasons. One was the language allowance that I hoped to earn by passing the test and that would be granted as long as I remained in an Arabic-speaking country. The other and more potent inducement was my dislike of not being able to talk to the people of the country in which I am living.

As soon as I could decypher enough of the script I was never without a phrase-book in my pocket and I took every possible opportunity to study it. But during the war Cairo—and Egypt as a whole for that matter—was crammed to overflowing with British troops and officials and, of course, Egyptians and it was almost impossible to find a place where one could be alone and in peace. I thought I had discovered the one and only peaceful spot on the top of the Great Pyramid of Cheops, but within a few minutes of my arrival there half a dozen young soldiers came up to join me.

This pyramid, incidentally, is not at all a bad rock climb, although the stepped arrangement of the blocks of stone makes it easy. Most of the blocks are too big to be taken in a stride and a certain amount of agility is required to get up and down. Before a few layers of stones were removed from the top the pyramid was 481 feet high and its base covers twelve acres. During my first visit to Egypt twenty years earlier I had photographed this and the second pyramid at dawn. Both were surrounded by low clouds which made their projecting tops look very like the summits of mountains. Several people, descending carelessly, have fallen and been killed on the Great Pyramid. Normally it takes about a quarter of an hour to get to the top: my own record is seven and a half minutes.

Somehow or other I contrived to learn enough Arabic to feel prepared to face the examination and I did not worry about possible failure. At least I could talk to the people who crowded round me while I was sketching and even crack a few feeble jokes, taught to me by the Sheikh, to keep my audience amused. But when I asked the Effendi to help me to prepare a talk about some topic that might interest the examiners, I found that he had no ideas about anything except the iniquity of certain Arabs in the quarter where he lived who, according to his story, constantly raided British army dumps and got away with a lot of swag. He seemed to think that, if I talked about this to the examiners, something would be done to stop it. His were admirable sentiments, but I felt that it might be excessively difficult to drag such a topic into an oral examination conducted by members of the Sudan Civil Service.

In the end I prepared a short talk, entirely off my own bat, about painting in Cairo, for I had made sketches all over the place. I passed the examination and a week afterwards one of the examiners commissioned me to paint a picture of his favourite view from the window of his flat. I received the language allowance for the remaining months of my time in

Egypt, but the total sum barely paid off half of the amount that I had spent on lessons. In the end I got my own back when, after the end of the war, I arranged an exhibition in London of my paintings of "Egypt and the Middle East". Some thirty pictures were sold and several were bought by the Egyptian Institute.

I had no opportunity during the war to climb anything much higher than the pyramid of Cheops, but I did this several times and painted a picture of the view from the top on the eve of flying back to England. However, I made two flying visits to mountainous country where I made a good many rapid sketches to remind me of what I had seen. At first I felt rather nervous about painting in the open at all, for in war-time a pencil and paper were apt to be regarded as the insignia of a spy. When I wanted to make sketches in London for exhibition in some of the galleries I had first to obtain a special permit: then I took the pictures to the censorship where they were stamped on the back as "passed for publication". In the Middle East I had none of this business to cope with, but I was, of course, extremely circumspect.

When I accompanied the late Lord Moyne on a mission to a number of places in East Africa I was always with other officials, who could see that I was not up to mischief. But I went to Palestine and then on to Persia alone and there was always a chance, I imagined, that some busybody might start a scare when I produced my sketch-book. As things turned out, I think I must have contributed to the entertainment of quite a lot of people, for I seldom sat down to sketch without a small crowd collecting to watch. If there happened to be a policeman about he usually bagged the best position beside me and saw to it that enough space was kept clear in front so that I could see my subject. But one of these guardians of the law and self-appointed defenders of art became a bit too enthusiastic and I had to protest when he began using his baton to keep the audience at bay.

The official talks that were the object of my journey to Palestine and Persia usually took place in the mornings and left me a fair amount of time to explore. I found it intensely interesting and indeed very moving to be sketching the ancient walls of Jerusalem and the Mount of Olives. I could not help feeling that Our Lord must have found in the silent loneliness of a mountain-side a propitious atmosphere for prayer, for the Bible records a number of occasions when He went up into a mountain to pray and both the Transfiguration and the Ascension took place on mountains.

Although my visit to Persia was for an official purpose, for transport I was left to my own devices—a happy-go-lucky arrangement that added considerably to the interest of the journey. I got a passage without great difficulty in a civilian aircraft from Lydda to Baghdad, flying over the mountains that enclose the deep valley of the Jordan and on across the deserts to the fertile valleys of the Euphrates and Tigris. From there on it was a matter of hitch-hiking, a rather irregular procedure that I had never tried before but which had to be exploited by military and civilian officials alike in the exigencies of war-time. After a short delay I was given a lift to Teheran in a Royal Air Force aircraft with temporary wooden seats which were not designed for comfort. The long flight over the mountains was at times almost alarmingly bumpy, but we landed safely with a jaunty kind of flourish that would not have been allowed by B.O.A.C., but which I found rather elating.

After doing what I had to do in Teheran I visited Gulhek, the mountain resort where the staff of the British Legation had their summer quarters, and made a sketch of distant Mount Demavend, the highest mountain in Persia with a beautiful snowy summit rising to about 18,600 feet. (Plate IX.) From Teheran I had to go to Isfahan and Shiraz, where I was to meet the Persian general who was responsible for maintaining peace in the surrounding tribal areas.

I made the journey as far as Qum by night, seated next to the driver of an army lorry, and stayed for a day to talk to some British military authorities who were stationed there. This gave me a chance to make a painting of the remarkable Golden Mosque, which I managed to do without arousing suspicions that I was a spy. Another lorry took me on to Isfahan, through lovely mountain scenery, but the most spectacular part of the journey was yet to come. For two days I thought that I might never get a lift beyond Isfahan, but three enormous petrol tankers suddenly turned up and the Armenian driver of one of them agreed to take me with him to Shiraz.

The journey was a fascinating experience, for the road lay entirely among mountains and, from the high seat beside the driver, where I felt as if sitting on the front of a railway engine, I had a splendid view. So far I had only been able to snatch quick sketches at any short halt during the day, but when I showed these to the friendly Armenian he told me to let him know if I saw a good subject and he would be pleased to stop for ten minutes or so. I had seldom seen anything to compare with the rich golden lights on those bare yellow mountains at dawn and at sunset, when the long shadows assumed a deep blue colour that seemed almost unnatural. I was tempted to call for a halt at frequent intervals, but I was careful not to abuse the privilege and we only stopped for a short time when I saw something that was quite irresistible.

Night fell long before we reached Shiraz and we came to a place where the Persian military authorities had put a barrier across the road. No traffic was allowed to pass this point during the hours of darkness on account of the danger from bandits who were lurking among the mountains overlooking the road. We pulled up before a small roadside café not far from Deh Bid, where we had a little refreshment. The driver and I both agreed that the interior of this establishment did not invite slumber, so he put his camp bed on the top of the huge petrol tank and I made myself as comfortable as I could in the driver's seat. It was a cold night, but I managed to sleep for an hour or so and the bandits kept their distance. At dawn we went on again and I was deposited at the entrance to the British Consulate in Shiraz before the driver went off to his depôt.

The journey back to Teheran was a good deal more adventurous. It began on a lorry, but half way through the day the lorry broke down and I had to wait nearly four hours for another. The driver of this vehicle was under the influence of opium, a common failing in those parts, and twice he drove off the road into a ditch. I was contemplating how I might persuade him to hand over the wheel to me when, half a mile short of a military post where he had to report, he drove into a crumbling wall and demolished it. I found the officer in charge of the post and told him that it was my duty to get back to Teheran, but I absolutely refused to go another yard with that driver. The officer was full of understanding and sympathy and he told me that, if I would not mind staying the night, he would provide me with a jeep in the morning.

A young Indian driver arrived with the jeep soon after dawn and we set off along the dusty road at a good speed. I noticed that he was weaving about the road in a way that seemed to me quite unnecessary, but when I commented on this he said that he was trying to avoid potholes. We did not, however, avoid potholes and two or three times we took short cuts over the grass verge. For a few more minutes I restrained myself with difficulty from seizing the wheel, for it seemed to me that, sooner or later, we should leave the road altogether. Then, without warning, the driver slumped over the wheel and the jeep, swerving violently, struck a solid milestone at forty miles an hour, sprang over a ditch and ended up against a low wall amidst scrub about ten yards from the road.

Shaken but not injured, I got out and pulled the driver from his seat. He too was unhurt, but it was now obvious that, early though it was, he had succumbed to the effects of opium. When he had more or less recovered his senses we got the jeep back on to the road and found that, although there were some very obvious dents, it had not been put out of action. The milestone, however, had been snapped off short.

I told the driver that I would have to report his performance to the military authorities and that nothing on earth would persuade me to go on with him. I was inclined to try my hand at driving the jeep myself, but while we were standing there in the road I saw a lorry approaching and the driver agreed to take me on my way.

After a few more days in Teheran I left with a British colonel who was travelling by car through the mountains to Khanaqin, a few miles inside Iraq beyond Persia's western frontier. We went by way of Kazvin, Hamadan and Kermanshah, following the famous route by which aid was being sent to Russia, and we crossed the extremely formidable Paitak pass. Near Kazvin we were stopped, for the examination of our documents, by a young Russian woman armed with a Sten-gun and at intervals along the road we met, or overtook with great difficulty, long convoys of lorries with Russian drivers. The drivers, not unnaturally, were so impressed by the military importance of their task that they showed scant consideration for anyone else on the road. Our British chauffeur, whenever he saw them coming, very wisely behaved as if we had no right to be there and took the first opportunity to get well out of the way until they had passed. When he overtook them he sneaked past before they realized that anyone was sharing the road with them. But once or twice, when no evasion was possible, in a defile or on a steep slope, we had some narrow shaves.

In spite of the difficulties I managed to make a few sketches even in this part of the country, including impressions of Russian convoys on the mountain road and parked at a stopping-place. They are worth nothing as pictures, but they remind me clearly of my journey along an "aid to Russia" route during a momentous period and of how I made them sitting in the car with a newspaper to conceal what I was doing. Some of the Persian sketches were in my exhibition of paintings of Egypt and the Middle East and several, including that of the Golden Mosque at Qum, an impression of the ruins of Persepolis and another of strange Yezd-i-Khast, were sold.

Fortunately I can still remember such sights without the aid of my sketches: Yezd-i-Khast in particular would be hard to forget. It stands on a bare rocky plateau at an altitude of about 6,500 feet in sight of mountains between twenty and thirty miles to the west that rise to 14,000 feet. The approach to it reveals only some uninteresting-looking mud houses in dreary surroundings, but suddenly you come to the brink of a deep chasm where probably a river once flowed. In the midst of the chasm rises a rugged island of bare rock and on this the curious balconied houses are perched.

When I think of Persia the memory of these places and of the mosques and gardens of Isfahan and Shiraz returns. But my most vivid impression remains that of the mountains in the golden light of the setting sun.

Chapter IV

HAPPY DAYS WITH A PAINT-BRUSH AMONG
THE BRITISH MOUNTAINS

WHEN we have been abroad for a long time we are nearly always glad to get home again. As an undergraduate I was always pleased to be back, even though I had been away for only six or eight weeks. In those days the periods of absence seemed more significant than in later years, for they broke into my normal existence at home and were spent in unfamiliar surroundings. During these periods abroad there was always some consciousness of restriction, because I could only talk to the people among whom I was living in proportion to the progress that I had made with their language. Later on my profession kept me abroad for years on end and it was my normal life to be in a foreign land, speaking or trying to speak a foreign language.

While at Cambridge I went two or three times to France, Germany and Spain and, having returned to Folkestone or Dover and passed through the Customs, I invariably bought a bun and a copy of the *Daily Mirror* before getting into the train for London. I have no idea why these two very different things, each costing a penny, became symbols of England, but I still like buns.

For about fourteen years I lived almost continuously abroad and did not always return to England when on leave. Sometimes three years passed before I got back. I saw more of several foreign countries than I had ever seen of the British Isles and it seemed as if my own country would be the last bit of Europe that I should explore. Friends found it curious that I had been to Japan but not to Wales, to Peru but not to Scotland and to South Africa but not to Ireland. Even the north of England was almost unknown to me. I lived in Chelsea and worked at the Foreign Office for the greater part of the last war, excepting the period of my service in Egypt, but even then most of the British mountains remained unknown to me, though I managed to make one visit to the Lake District.

After the war, when the Diplomatic Service and the Consular Service had been merged in the new Foreign Service, retirement became a possibility. Conditions had changed drastically and an officer might find himself transferred from a consular to a diplomatic post, or vice versa, or even seconded to work under a different department. The more I thought about retirement the more I felt that an independent existence as an artist and writer would give me the kind of life that I had imagined for myself long ago. My wife shared my feelings and together we took the plunge into country life.

It was a cold plunge, for on the very day on which we moved into our house among the Surrey hills snow began to fall. It was early in 1947 and for many weeks the snow lay thick in our garden, high up on a hill with a view towards the south. When we went for long walks it was almost like following mountain trails in Canada, with the heavily laden trees drooping across the path and icicles glistening in the sunshine. From my studio window I could look out across the Weald of Sussex and the South Downs and, on a clear day, even catch a glimpse of the sea through Shoreham Gap, thirty miles away.

Our first holiday after the war was spent in the Alps with skis. Then it seemed high time to give attention to the mountains of the British Isles. In a few years I had climbed and walked and painted among nearly all of them.

Although the mountains of Westmorland and Cumberland are only little mountains, like the Harz and the Black Forest in Germany, no climber would despise them. What we call the foothills of the Andes and the Himalaya are, generally speaking, very much greater than anything in the British Isles, yet the English hills provide a practice ground for climbers that, being easily accessible, is second to none. Scafell Pike, the highest summit in England, is little over 3,000 feet, but it commands a magnificent view embracing some of the best climbs in the district. There is an easy walk up every mountain, yet there are also some stiff rock pitches that demand real mountaineering skill.

The charm of this region lies largely in its infinite variety, with lakes in many of the valleys radiating from a centre like the spokes of a wheel. The lakes have given the district its name, but it might more appropriately be called the Lake and Mountain District. For my wife and myself, as for many who prefer a walking holiday, the Lake District is primarily a walkers' paradise where the lakes are mirrors reflecting the hills we love. Each mountain and lake has its own personality, with moods that change with every passing hour. If the weather is kind there is little more exhilarating, more conducive to peace of mind, than to walk for twenty miles or more over the high fells, passing from summit to summit and generally within sight of a placid expanse of water tinged with the blueness of the sky.

Once during the last war, with a rare spell of leave in prospect, we took our bicycles to Ambleside at the north end of Lake Windermere, an obviously good centre from which to explore the heart of the district. In my rucksack I carried my usual light sketching equipment: sketch-books, water-colours in tubes, a porcelain palette, a water-bottle and a few brushes. I never use an easel for water-colour sketching as I like to hold the book on my knees so that it can be tilted at any angle.

We had booked a room in a small hotel that had been recommended to us, but the room provided was depressing and none other was available. While riding beside the lake I spotted a much more attractive hotel and suggested that we might look at it. The entrance hall and lounge were so comfortable that we decided at once that, even if there was a bedroom free, it would almost certainly cost more than we were prepared to pay. We were about to slip away when one of the staff appeared and we felt obliged to ask if there was a room. To our surprise we were offered a choice, including one of the best rooms facing the lake, and the price of this was more moderate than expected. Better pay a little more and enjoy our holiday, we felt, rather than return to our dull room in Ambleside.

Our stay there was delightful; on the whole the weather was fair and we bicycled and walked for miles. I sketched the Langdale Pikes from at least three different directions and painted the magnificent view from the top. We went up many of the surrounding mountains, basked on sunny summits or beside heavenly blue tarns while we ate picnic lunches, and covered so much ground that, on a later visit when we went by car, we were astonished by the extent of our activity. Two of my sketch-books were nearly full in a fortnight, but there were still countless subjects that I had to leave for another time. (Plate X.)

In the warm evenings I painted in the grounds of the hotel and, while I was doing this, the finishing touch was put to our holiday. One of the guests came to watch me at work and afterwards asked if I would sell the picture. I had been painting solely for pleasure, trying to catch something of the harmonious colouring and ever-changing light on Wetherlam and the Langdale Pikes seen across the lake, but I named a reasonable price and the purchaser carried off the painting almost before it was dry.

I was returning to the hotel to tell my wife of this unexpected transaction when a lady who had just seen the picture met me on the doorstep and wanted to know if I had any more. While I was showing her some of my sketches in the lounge, several other people gathered round and in a short time I found that my paint-brush had all but paid off the cost of our holiday.

It has been said that many artists are poor salesmen and I can make no claim to be any better than the worst. I have often failed, presumably through sheer lack of business sense, to take advantage of an offer that some might describe as a golden opportunity, if gold were still used for currency. I was once sketching some ships at the quay at Yorktown, Virginia, the place where, in 1781, General Lord Cornwallis was forced to surrender to Washington and Lafayette and the American colonies gained their freedom. A man stood watching me for some time; then he said that he was the owner of the large shed that stood near the quay and he had a fleet of three large lorries. Would I, he asked, paint him a picture of his lorries in front of his shed?

I suppose that, had I been business-like, I should have agreed and named a stiff price in dollars. I had promised to take my wife to see Williamsburg, a gem of a place not far away with perfect examples of American colonial architecture, and there was a view that I badly wanted to paint in the Alleghany Mountains, then in their best autumn colouring. But I might have changed that plan and stayed on to paint the three hideous lorries and the revoltingly ugly shed, all inscribed with the owner's name in huge letters. Instead I told the man that I was sorry, but I was leaving that afternoon and had no time to accept his commission.

Quite recently, when I was sketching in the main street of an English village, a lady with two children stood watching me for some minutes. I noticed that the children were very plain. Presently, without any preamble, their mother asked me if I would paint their portraits. It was perhaps rash to turn down such a commission, but I find it hard to paint subjects that do not attract me and I excused myself by saying that I doubted if I could do them justice. Only a Velasquez, I felt, would have accepted the challenge.

Two or three years ago I was asked to write and illustrate an article about the Outward Bound Trust's Mountain School at Eskdale, for publication in *The Sphere*. This was a task after my own heart, for it took me to a lovely part of the Lake District, that I did not yet know well, to roam in search of subjects. The school was established in 1950 in the former home of Lord Rea of Eskdale, a fine house overlooking a lake in about fifty acres of woodland. All around it are mountains and sparsely inhabited valleys which invite exploration. The highest mountain in England is only five miles away and still closer lies Wastwater, the deepest lake.

The origin of the school is interesting, for it arose from the hardships endured by merchant seamen during the last war. When ships were sunk by enemy action and the crews had to take to open boats their survival often depended upon their having sufficient knowledge and experience to cope with such an ordeal. It was realized that many young entrants into the Merchant Navy had no training in the handling of open boats and could not improvise in emergency. A Sea School was therefore established at Aberdovey, by Mr. Lawrence Holt of the Blue Funnel Line and Mr. Kurt Hahn, the headmaster of Gordonstoun, to give the necessary training. This experiment was so successful that it was decided to continue it after the war.

On the cessation of hostilities the scope of the training could be widened and it became one of the principal objectives to give boys from all walks of life an opportunity of training through the sea, the mountains and other natural elements, as a

XI. Cader Idris from Maes-y-brynar, near Dolgelley, Wales

XII. Loch Affric, Inverness, Scotland

means of developing their capacity to face hazards, difficulties, hardship and emergencies of all kinds. In 1946 the Outward Bound Trust was formed to carry these principles into the future and the first great development was the inauguration of the Mountain School at Eskdale. Since then a second Sea School, at Burghead on the Moray Firth, and a second Mountain School, at Watermillock on the Cumberland shore of Lake Ullswater, have been added and it is hoped eventually to provide enough courses to train five thousand boys a year.

Mr. Geoffrey Winthrop Young, the President of the controlling body of the Mountain School at Eskdale, has expressed the belief that "everyone in his youth should pass through some test of adventure and hardship and the adventure must be real". Although a course at the school lasts only twenty-six days, it provides ample opportunity for the boys to have such experience, as I saw for myself. But the undeniably valuable results are not achieved merely by a process of toughening: the schools are based on a Christian foundation and they introduce boys to some of the finest aspects of nature and of human behaviour. The mountains, like the sea, command respect and there could be no better setting for the "character training through adventure" which is the purpose of the Outward Bound Trust.

We arrived in Eskdale at the time when the Warden of the Mountain School, Adam Arnold-Brown, was handing over his duties to his successor, Eric Shipton, the distinguished Himalayan climber, and I was able to discuss the activities of the school with both of them. I watched the boys at work and play and followed them, or rather overtook them, on a walk over the Styhead pass, where some of them were going to camp. I also saw them receiving elementary instruction in climbing on Great Gable, a part of the training which gives some of the boys their first love for the mountains, though a few were obviously finding it a struggle. I remembered my own early efforts on rock and had no doubt that several of these boys would feel the urge to add to their mountain experience whenever an opportunity occurred.

But the teaching of mountaineering technique is not an objective of the school; it is merely one of many activities, in-

6

cluding swimming, canoeing, camping, fell-walking with map
and compass, forestry and athletics, which are designed to
develop character, self-reliance and a sense of responsibility,
to encourage the spirit of team-work and to promote self-
knowledge through experience. This the mountains can do
most effectively and in a remarkably short space of time.

During our stay in Eskdale we explored the whole of the
surrounding area and I made many sketches, not only in the
school grounds but on Scafell and other mountains, beside the
deep water of Wastwater and in the lovely Duddon valley, which
was the subject of no less than thirty-four sonnets by the poet
Wordsworth.   It is all wonderful country for the water-
colourist, full of subtle contrasts and gentle colouring, with
continually changing atmospheric effects. Even on a rainy day,
of which there are many, there is beauty in the rounded forms
of the hills, in the cold glint of moist rock and in the subdued
tints of green. When the sun shines and great white cumulus
clouds come riding in from the sea, deep shadows glide over fell
and dale, concealing and revealing pictures in endless succession.

High up on a fell, far from any road, the enchantment of the
region grows in the lonely silence. Sometimes a gentle wind
combs the tussocks among the grey, ancient rocks and a little
blue tarn reflects the soft clouds as they pass. You stretch your
eyes to the far, hazy horizon and through a gap in the hills you
catch the shimmer of a drowsy lake. You lie on your back in the
warm sun, sinking luxuriously into the grass, and high above
you see a pair of buzzards wheeling slowly with searching eyes.
The sound of traffic cannot reach you, but a curlew calls beyond
the tarn and, with your ears close to the ground, you can detect
the faint hiss of the wind in the tufted grass. It is a place to
dream, a moment to snatch from the turmoil of the world
around. A sketch made in such a place will recall—better than
almost any other kind of record—the pleasure of the miles of
walking over the fells, the descent to the little white farmhouse
where you had tea and the peace and beauty of it all.

When we first went to Wales together it was agreed that our
dog, Sandy, must go with us. He had had many good walks on
the Surrey hills, but he had not yet been up a mountain, though
he had Highland blood and just the build for a mountaineer.

Often near our home he scampered up the steepest slopes, where we could not easily follow, in pursuit of squirrels and he tackled rough ground with a combination of caution and fearless decision. But he still had a few things to learn and, if we had had reason to climb with a rope, we should have put him in the middle.

The Welsh language daunted me and I left its interpretation to others, but the charm of the Welsh mountains, despite the unattractive drabness of villages, made me wish that I had been able to visit them many years ago. In order to get the best general impression of the region we began by going up the highest mountains in north Wales and Sandy generally led the way. Cader Idris was nothing to him. While we followed a route that gave us quite a good climb he made excursions in every direction, probably adding several miles to the walk. We returned to the bottom and had our picnic tea while Sandy, refreshed by milk, investigated the rabbit situation. Routine now demanded that he should return to the car and settle down on his rug for a sleep, but instead he made for the track by which we had started our walk and, calling to us to follow, headed once more at a good pace for the top of Cader Idris. Obviously he had qualified for bigger things. (Plate XI.)

When we went up Snowdon, at Whitsun, there was still a lot of snow on the summit and the building at the railway terminal was buried to the roof. The railway itself was completely hidden, so that only pedestrians could reach the top. Some of these ought not to have been there, for their costumes were unsuitable for an icy cold mountain and their footwear was fit only for walking on pavements. It is regrettable when accidents occur to such improvident people, but sympathy is more justly due to those who have to rescue them or to recover their bodies. There are now a considerable number of first-aid stations and mountain rescue teams among the British mountains, but there is not much cause for the exercise of their skill except the recklessness and stupidity of tourists. Few of the mountains are dangerous, though fog and bad weather may make them so, and such conditions are generally predicted in time to warn walkers and climbers to avoid them.

While looking for a place to eat our lunch in shelter from the cold wind we heard voices beneath the snow and discovered that someone had burrowed down to a window of the buried building. We crawled through this tunnel and got inside, where several other people were already having a picnic and one was trying to make a fire with scraps of wood. A few more hikers arrived before we left. There were icicles even inside the building and no one was tempted to linger long.

From the point of view of an artist, I think the most attractive subjects are in the Welsh valleys and among the woods, rather than on the hills. I found many delightful spots for sketching scattered about Wales and most of them were beside rivers or mountain torrents. I remember a lovely day on the Dovey near Mallwyd when I settled down to paint at a bend of the river. The water foamed white among the rocks and the varied foliage of the trees cast shadows on a dark pool. It was just the place for an angler and, sure enough, before I had been there long, a man with a rod arrived from the nearby Brigands' Inn and began to fish along the more open bank. Soon another arrived and I put them both in my picture. At lunch-time I joined my wife beside a tumbling waterfall, where great boulders in the stream provided precarious foothold for at least two more fishermen.

During the afternoon I made another painting, with the water swirling round a bend and plunging into a cauldron from a ledge of steeply tilted rock strata. I watched the fishermen casting indefatigably, but not once did I see a rise. When the time came to leave I packed up my things and strolled along the bank to where the first arrival was still hopefully flogging the water. As far as he knew not a single fish had been landed, but he agreed with me that it was a beautiful place in which to spend a peaceful day. His bag was empty, but there were two paintings in my satchel and I felt that I had had the best of it.

Years ago, in the days when the walls of the Royal Academy still offered space for long-haired Highland cattle standing in bogs and breathing blue vapour against a background of heather-covered hills and mist, I wanted to go to Scotland. Pictures had made these woolly creatures familiar and had almost convinced me that shaggy sheep and bellowing stags were to be seen on every Scottish hill. Some forebears of mine

were Scots and I ought to have been inducted into that country
at an early age, but somehow those relations, like the cattle, disappeared in wraiths of mist and I never got north of the border.
Never, that is, until in my thirties I paid a brief visit to Glasgow
and came away with a rather dreary impression. But I just had
time to discover that Loch Lomond and the hills I had been
taught to sing about really existed, suggesting that something
even better might lie in the more distant north.

But as time went on and I saw more of the world I felt less
and less inclined to risk a holiday in Scotland, for by all accounts
the mist and the rain were inescapable and I had grown to love
the sunshine and the warmth of tropical countries. It seemed
that the Highlands would remain for ever out of reach, for the
price of ten days' holiday was a lot to spend on one day of sunshine and nine days of rain.

In the late summer of 1952 a telephone call from London
asked if I would like to go to Scotland to draw some special
pictures to illustrate an article in *The Sphere*. First I said yes,
then I asked what was the subject. I was told that in October
the Duke of Edinburgh was to inaugurate the Glen Affric Hydro-
Electric Scheme and that it was desired to publish, a few days
before the opening ceremony, an article about the scheme by a
well-known author. It was to be accompanied by ten illustrations
painted—if I agreed—by me. I took the night train to Inverness.

I have seldom felt more apprehensive than I felt during that
journey. I had no doubt at all that, given suitable conditions,
I could produce the pictures required, but adverse propaganda
about Scottish weather had made me extremely doubtful
whether the subjects would be visible.

During the drive from Inverness to Glen Affric I had my first
sight of the real Highlands: to my surprise it was quite a fine
day and I could actually see the mountains. From the hotel
I walked to see Neil Gunn, who was to write the article, and we
had a chat about the hydro-electric scheme and the subjects
that he thought might make the most suitable illustrations.
Then I was entrusted to the care of the engineers and trans-
ported in a car from one part of the landscape to another until
I had a good general impression of the whole scheme. During
the next four days I was hard at work, snatching every fine

moment to make drawings of the various dams, the power-house and the new houses for the staff, all in a mountainous setting.

In almost every instance when a new scheme of this kind is contemplated there are protests against the assumed ruination of the scenery. In Scotland great fears were expressed about the future appearance of Loch Affric and the glen. Often such protests are justified, but in this case it must be hard to maintain them now that the dams have been built. When I was there the great Mullardoch dam, the largest in Scotland at that date, spanning Glen Cannich across a width of nearly half a mile, had barely been completed and some of the equipment and débris left by the builders was still there. The river, not yet harnessed, remained very low. But it was obvious that the beauty of the landscape had not been destroyed. The dam itself, a great white wall making skilful use of the contours, had a dignified beauty of its own, particularly when the sun broke through the clouds and revealed it against the background of rolling heather-covered hills. I could visualize—and was able to show in my painting—the enhanced beauty of the long valley above the dam when the water would have risen to its destined level and a new loch would take the place of the straggling, powerless river.

The power station, a ferro-concrete building of severely practical design, had been placed where it could offend no one on a bend of the Affric river between the wooded slopes. I was told that, when completed, it would be entirely faced with sandstone quarried near Burghead on the Moray Firth, the site of the second Sea School of the Outward Bound Trust, and I was asked to show this finish in my drawing. The sandstone has an attractive golden-yellow tint which, with the effects of weathering, will help the building to blend well with its surroundings.

The weather was much kinder than I had been led to expect and the sunshine, alternating with sudden showers, allowed me plenty of time to finish my task. Besides the drawings of the actual power scheme I made sketches in a wild and lovely part of Glen Affric, on an unspoilt fishing reach of the Cannich river and at the eastern end of peaceful Loch Affric, which remains entirely unaffected by the scheme. (Plate XII.) Birch trees and pines, heather and bracken combined to soften the contours of the hills and to remind me of the Surrey hill on which I live

In Glen Affric Lodge, half hidden among trees at the end of the loch, I was shown some mural drawings in charcoal of fishing and hunting scenes which, it was said, had been made by Landseer whose "Monarch of the Glen", widely reproduced a century ago, still adorns the wall in many cottages in the Highlands. I personally have some doubt whether these drawings are the work of Landseer; they are certainly not Landseer at his best. But I share Neil Gunn's opinion that the view over Loch Affric is probably the most lovely and impressive piece of natural scenery in the Highlands.

A few months later a similar commission took me once again north of the border, but this time I was to write the article as well as to produce the illustrations. The subject dealt with the gipsies of Kirk Yetholm, a village cradled in the Cheviot Hills about two miles beyond the border of Northumberland. It is at the northern extremity of the Pennine Way, much of which my wife and I followed on our way north. On the village green at Yetholm the last Queen of the Gipsies was crowned in 1861. The Gipsy Palace, a tiny and unpretentious cottage, still stands there in a street that used to be known as Tinkler Row.

Yetholm is divided by Bowmont Water, a tributary of the Tweed, into Town Yetholm and Kirk Yetholm and gipsies have been associated with the latter at least since the end of the seventeenth century, though they came to Scotland, possibly from Ireland, long before that time. The gipsies have nearly always been wanderers, but restrictions on their movements gradually induced some of them to settle, though they still travelled for part of each year.

It was delightful to have an opportunity to sketch in this hilly border country and I was tempted to paint subjects that had nothing to do with my article. But much of my time was taken up with inquiries at the Manse, at cottages where some of the old gipsies lived and anywhere that seemed likely to lead me to more information about the gipsies of the past. I picked up many tales of gipsy life and gathered that, in the early days, the gipsies of the border had little respect for the law. The fights in which rival clans were occasionally involved were not without bloodshed, caused sometimes by a horrible barbed weapon called a "jagger".

There is a tradition that in 1695 a gipsy from this region accompanied the Laird of Kirk Yetholm to the Low Countries and saved his life at the siege of Namur. As a reward this man and his family were allowed to settle in Kirk Yetholm. The next Laird became the patron of the gipsies and his favourite, a man named Will Faa, was acknowledged as the King of the Gipsies throughout most of Scotland and the north of England. When he died his son's right to succeed was contested by another gipsy chieftain who enjoyed the title of the "Earl of Hell". They and their respective supporters fought a battle on Yetholm green in which the Earl was defeated. The victor, who lived to be ninety-five, was a good violinist, as many gipsies have been. He was also a good shot and an expert fisherman; gipsies were in fact among the first to fish with the fly in Bowmont Water. Unluckily for him he was once caught smuggling by Excisemen and, in the ensuing skirmish, he received a sword-cut in the hand that put an end to these more peaceful pursuits.

The last Queen of the Gipsies to be crowned at Kirk Yetholm was Esther Faa Bligh, who was proclaimed at the town cross with the customary formula, "Challenge who dare". Her coronation on the green produced a large and colourful gathering of her subjects and of other onlookers and the ceremony was a skilful travesty of the coronations at Westminster. The Queen appeared in a purple jacket and the purple hood that she wore habitually, even when asleep, and the scarlet robe of state was draped round her shoulders. The crown was made of tin by the village blacksmith, who had the honour of placing it on her head. The sword of state was a weapon that had been captured in a skirmish with Excisemen and another important item of the regalia was an old sword that had been picked up on Flodden Field, about six miles from Kirk Yetholm.

Esther was a widow who had had twelve children and she only settled in Kirk Yetholm after many years of wandering. She was a pipe-smoker, but it is not recorded whether she smoked while seated on the throne. In her old age she was flattered when members of the Hungarian gipsy band came from Paris to pay their respects to her and there is a story that Queen Victoria once visited her at the tiny palace. She died in

1883 and was buried, among other gipsy kings and queens, in Yetholm churchyard. Before the present church was built in 1837, to replace a much smaller thatched building, the sexton was a gipsy. Occasionally he used to lie down to rest among the graves and one day someone remarked to him that it was a strange place to lie. His retort was "It's a' richt if ye can git oop when ye lik'!"

In the course of my travels about the world I have accumulated a great many sketches and, incidentally, learnt a lot of interesting things about a wide variety of subjects. At one time I used to take snapshots and some of these found their way into an album, but most of them were put away in envelopes seldom, if ever, to be looked at again. Snapshots of landscape, even good photographs, cannot often revive the feelings that we had when we took them. They are cold and impersonal and, if they represent mountain scenery, they are often disappointing. The grandeur of mountains is not merely something that we see, depending on size and shape and colour; it is something that we feel. Many factors contribute to produce that feeling of grandeur, such as the warmth of the sunshine or the cold tang in the air, the movement of the clouds, the contrast between the tiny twinkling flowers and the glint of ice on a peak. Still more effective may be our own mood at the time.

A photograph, if it is a reasonably good one, records the amount of light reflected from every object within its field; but, except in a cinema film, there is little sense of movement. All the details of the subject appear in the picture, including many that you had not noticed in nature. Unimportant details are as clear as the rest. Yet the significance of what you admired in the scene is largely lost and, when you look at the photograph years afterwards, you may find it hard to recall what you felt.

In making a drawing the artist notes what is significant to him and rejects or subdues much that is not. He studies each detail as he decides how much to indicate on the paper and in this way the scene becomes embedded in his memory. He not only sees the view; he absorbs it. While he draws, for example, a great rock buttress running out from a mountain mass he is conscious of the kind of rock, of its bulk and weight and solidity. He is aware, not merely of the rock face that he sees, which is

all that a camera can note, but of the space behind the buttress.
If he is a mountaineer he may even analyse the construction of
the buttress, considering how it could be climbed. All this will
make his impression far less fugitive than that of an observer
who has only looked at the mountain, taken a snapshot with his
camera and gone on his way.

Among my sketches there are many that were made solely for
the pleasure of making them. For many years they have lain
unused in a box or portfolio, ready to recall half-forgotten
pleasures but otherwise serving no purpose. But now and again,
when I have been asked to make a drawing of a subject over sea,
I have been able to disinter a sketch of the essential setting and
to relive my experience as if I were there again. Some of the
sketches are only slight: a glimpse of Lake Trasimene from the
foothills of the Apennines, an outline of Teneriffe from the sea,
the silhouette of a volcano in Guatemala. Others are detailed
studies, such as the summit of the Lenzspitze from the Nadelhorn, the decorated costume of a Cambodian dancer, the roof
of a temple in Kyoto or a cave among the ice on Ixtaccihuatl.
Several of these old sketches have been put to use in recent years.

Most of the great modern hydro-electric schemes, such as
that in Glen Affric, are situated among hills or mountains and
at various times I have been asked to make drawings of several
of them. More than once drawings have been required in advance, before the construction of the scheme had even begun.
The pictures were to show the dams and reservoirs, the power
stations and all the ancillary buildings as they would appear in
full operation when completed. Such a requirement poses
difficult, but highly interesting, problems.

As a rule photographs of the site, some taken from the air,
are supplied, but these are not always clear. They show the
ground encumbered with forest and mountain débris which
will have to be removed before construction can begin and the
viewpoint is seldom the best one for a comprehensive view of the
most important parts of the scheme. Great imagination based
on experience and a knowledge of the type of terrain is required
to visualize the future appearance of the site and it is in this
connection that I have found some of my sketches invaluable.

In the past two or three years I have drawn pictures of the

hydro-electric schemes which were being designed to supply power to Northern and Southern Rhodesia. One, if finally approved, would be in the gorge of the Kafue river, a tributary of the Zambezi in Northern Rhodesia; the other and probably more important of the two would be in the Kariba Gorge of the Zambezi itself. Fortunately I had been on the Zambezi in that region and could turn up sketches that reminded me vividly of the nature of the country, the type of rock and the kind of vegetation. In London the engineers and architects responsible for the schemes gave me copies of their large maps and plans to study and they explained to me in detail the working of the different parts of the schemes.

It was essential to have, for instance, the exact dimensions of the dam that I was to depict so that I could work out its shape, how it would be sited between the walls of the gorge, the water levels above and below and the relative sizes of lamp-posts, railings, motor-cars and people at different points along the dam. But there were difficult problems of perspective to solve in order to show, in one of the pictures, what the dam would look like to an observer at a precise point on the mountain-side a little downstream from and a hundred feet or so higher than the dam. In one case, where the dam was to have a slightly concave face, with a subtly changing curve throughout its length, I made a small scale model in my garden so that, when the sun was in the right quarter, I could note the shapes and direction of the shadows that the dam would cast at a different time of day in the southern hemisphere.

In such pictures, which are intended to show non-existent scenes with what might be called almost photographic precision, great attention has to be given to numerous significant details. The surrounding landscape must be made convincing to anyone who knows it. The mountains and vegetation have to be built up, as it were, detail by detail, with lights and shadows in keeping with the rest of the subject. There may be glimpses of existing native trails and of the new approach roads that will have to be constructed. Cuts and embankments, reflections in the water and all the incidental minutiæ of a natural scene must be thought out and correctly blended into the whole. It is a taxing procedure, but extremely interesting.

CHAPTER V

CLIMBING, WALKING AND PAINTING
IN THE ALPS

A STORM at night in the high Alps can be terrifying: the reverberation of thunder among mountains is a threatening, persistent sound. As it comes nearer you feel that the demon of the storm has discovered where you are. He fires his lightning darts about you, like star shells in no-man's-land, so that you cannot stay hidden for long. He beats on the door, he rattles the windows; it seems that there is no escape, that he will batter down the walls in thunderous turmoil. Rain, heartless, icy rain, threatens to wash away the foundations beneath you and each louder crash must surely set loose the avalanche and bring down the rocks.

The contrast between a storm and a perfect morning seems greater than the change from night to day. A storm sets our nerves jangling; it is an experience that we have to endure, an event to remember. But when the dawn brings peace and relief our gratitude soon fades, like that of a man who receives what he regards as his due. A lovely day is a wonderful thing to enjoy, but it rarely affects us like a storm. Yet I have known perfect days in the high Alps that affected me deeply and that I can never entirely forget.

Above the snow-line there is a world unknown to millions. Sometimes fine weather continues for days on end. Morning after morning the landscape, more beautiful and impressive than almost any at lower levels, is displayed to the smallest audience that any great spectacle ever had. Here and there, on a peak or a glacier or on the wooden balcony of a mountain hut a few tiny figures stand—perhaps only two or three together—to watch the dawn unfolding. Never, as long as they live, can they forget the sight.

It was on such a morning that I stood with a guide on the

summit of the Fletschhorn, one of the peaks overlooking Saas-fee from the north-east. Recently I had passed my fiftieth birth-day and, not having climbed high for several years, I was pleased to find that I could get above 13,000 feet without exhaustion. This peak had been chosen, after plenty of training walks, because its south-west ridge, a moderately difficult rock climb, was too steep to hold much snow. Recent heavy falls of snow had made most of the other peaks for the time being un-approachable.

My guide and I were alone on the summit and we arrived just at dawn. When the sun began to strike the numerous high peaks that can be seen from there the scene was quite incredibly lovely. There it was—miles of snowy mountains and glaciers in every direction—but I could hardly believe it. No words could describe how the sun plucked each peak in turn out of the cold blue-greyness that lingered after the night had ebbed away or how, as the seconds passed, the pink glow increased steadily in intensity until it seemed impossible that it could become brighter. Nowhere, not even lurking in the dim valleys, was there a single cloud in the whole panorama. I had never before seen such a view so utterly unblemished. It was cold up there, but we could not turn to go until the valleys too were filled with light. My guide said it was the clearest dawn he had ever seen.

After leaving the ridge on the way down we descended over a long and steep snow-field, skirting round crevasses and keep-ing as far as possible from couloirs where rock fragments were liable to fall. The tracks made by some of these extended far down the mountain-side. The snow was soft and deep, getting softer as the sun warmed the surface, and occasionally one or other of us plunged up to the thighs in a deep pocket. When we got back to the Weissmies hut it was pleasant to remove our rucksacks and to stop for twenty minutes for refreshments. My wife had come up to meet me here—a walk of about four hours from Saas-fee—and we could now talk about the mountain as a mutual friend, for she had climbed it, by a different route, more than twenty years before. Then we went on down through the woods at a good pace.

It was only on the lower slopes that I was once again able to think in terms of pictures, when the dark trees framed in turn the peaks of the glittering Mischabel group on the other side of the Saas valley. There could be no question at present of attempting any of those climbs, on account of the deep snow, but we had already made several lesser excursions and we decided to add a few more before leaving Saas-fee for Zermatt.

One of these was a glacier walk to the Britannia hut, which stands at an altitude of nearly 10,000 feet close to the Klein-Allalinhorn. This hut was presented in 1912 to the Swiss Alpine Club by its British members and is much used by climbers and skiers. The proprietor of the *pension* where we were staying, a Swiss guide now more or less in retirement, insisted on going with us and, in view of his age, he proved to be a startlingly jovial companion. Even on the glacier he burst into song, though we found that we had little breath to spare for such vociferation. But the views up there were enough to make anyone feel lighthearted and it was not long before we had caught his spirit. We went back to Saas-fee by the narrow and rather exposed path that skirts the east flank of the Egginerhorn and the Mittaghorn and all the way down, for two or three hours, the three of us sang English, German and Swiss folk songs with joyful abandon.

I had kept the *bonne bouche*, my half-century celebration, until last and we went over into the next valley to Zermatt in the hope that the Zinal-Rothorn, one of the finest rock climbs in the Valais, would be in good condition for climbing. My wife had climbed so many of the peaks visible from Saas-fee that I was glad now to be able to point to some of my own climbs.

The guide who I had hoped would lead me on the Rothorn was unfortunately already engaged, but he introduced me to Edmund Biner, a member of a well-known family of guides. This young man, who had not even been born when I first climbed the Matterhorn, already had a good record, but he seemed to think from the very start that there was no reason why I should not be able to go as fast as he did. He certainly put me through my paces and, thanks to my previous training, we soon settled down to a good steady pace, overtaking several other parties who were on their way up to the hut.

Until recent years the climb was made from the Trift Hotel,

only about two hours above Zermatt, but now there is a hut in a much better position at the head of the moraines two hours higher up. The track up the moraines is steep and laborious and it reminded me how tough and persistent were the pioneers in the Alps, who climbed their mountains direct from the valleys, without any huts in which to snatch a few hours' rest and often without even a bivouac. We reached the hut sooner than I had expected, in time to watch the glorious sunset fading from the surrounding summits.

There were half a dozen other climbers in the hut and, after the usual bowls of hot soup with the food that we had brought with us, we turned into our bunks. Some people find pleasure in spending a night in an alpine hut, but I am not one of them. Were it practicable, I would prefer my own tent or just a sleeping-bag. A hut can sometimes be as impersonal as a railway waiting-room and the pause of a few hours that it offers may seem rather like the period of waiting for a train in the middle of the night. You hang up your rucksack and such clothing as you care to take off in a room dimly illuminated by a candle or a lantern, you wrap yourself in a coarse brown blanket and you lie down, on a straw paliasse if there is one, in a wooden trough which you may be sharing with half a dozen other people, like sardines in a tin. If there are several parties you have to pick your way carefully in the confined space; someone is sure to have a cough and someone else is certain to snore. I sleep badly in such circumstances, being keyed up for the coming climb and knowing that I shall have to get up again at some unearthly hour. A hut, sometimes a substantial building of stone constructed at great expense and labour, is a tremendous boon to climbers, but I prefer it as a place to return to after the climb has been accomplished.

At a very early hour one of the parties was preparing to leave and shortly afterwards my own guide came and told me it was time to get ready. He and I, he said, were going to have most of the long south-west ridge to ourselves, for the other parties were going by the "ordinary route". The ridge is a difficult rock climb, one of the finest in the Alps, and I fear I was selfishly pleased to know that there would be no competitors that day.

Outside, the night seemed pitch dark, but gradually the rock and the snow became distinguishable in the blue-black ambience. Edmund Biner carried a lantern and for a short time there was a clatter of nailed boots as we and another party moved off. But soon they disappeared and we began to climb up a steep part of the glacier where the snow that covered it was frozen hard. Presently, as we drew nearer to the great wall of rock, it became necessary to cut steps in the ice and this continued until we crossed the bergschrund and climbed through a narrow couloir where the rocks were coated with ice.

From a distance the ridge appears jagged, like the blade of a badly-used saw, and it might be thought that the teeth could be stepped over without much difficulty. But up there they present a very different aspect. Many of the teeth are quite large pinnacles or "gendarmes" rising abruptly from the knife-edge of the ridge itself and each of them has to be scaled or turned in succession. There are points where the rock actually overhangs a sheer precipice plunging hundreds of feet to the glacier. It would not do to be in such a place without a good head for heights. The climb demands complete concentration and there is no time to meditate on the artistic qualities of the situation.

There have been several fatal accidents due to falls from that awe-inspiring ridge. It was at an exposed spot of this kind, high up on the mountain, that the great climber Geoffrey Winthrop Young nearly lost his life. He lost a leg in the 1914 war, but the call of the mountains was so insistent that he trained himself to resume climbing with an artificial leg and made many remarkable ascents with guides. At the age of nearly sixty, having with difficulty reached the summit of the Rothorn, he decided that this must be his last great climb. On the way down he fell. The rope held him dangling from an overhang and only the superlative skill of his companions, particularly of the guide Josef Knubel, brought him back to safety.

It was a beautiful, though bitterly cold, morning when we reached the top—at 13,855 feet—and there was no real shelter from the wind. We spoke little. My mind was fully occupied with the dazzling panorama. It embraced several mountains that I had climbed and I asked Edmund Biner to name others

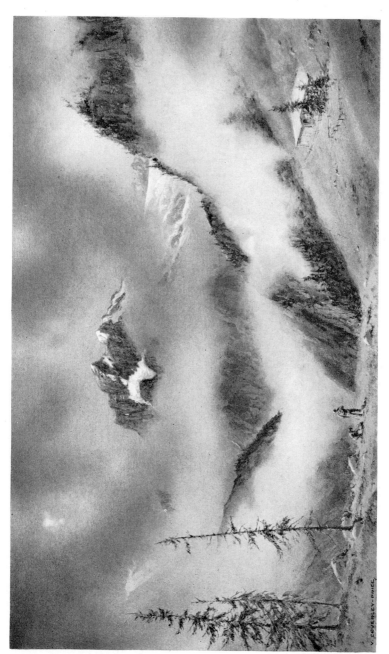

XIII. Storm over the Wetterhorn (12,149 feet), Bernese Oberland, Switzerland

XIV. Grimentz,
Canton Valais,
Switzerland

that I could not identify. But the grandest of all, from that marvellous viewpoint, was the peerless Weisshorn, cold and gleaming and eternally lovely.

During the first part of the descent, which is as tricky to negotiate as the climb, we waited above a huge slab of rock sloping at a steep angle to allow a later party to pass us on their way up. The slab had a rough surface, but it was devoid of any adequate hold and there were patches of ice on it. It had taxed all my energy, for it bulged outwards and there was little but the friction between the rock and our hands and the nails at the edges of our boots to take the place of holds. When the ascending guide was half way up the slab he suddenly slipped back and for a moment I thought he must have gone over the precipice. Luckily his feet landed precisely on the sharp ridge where the next man on the rope was able to steady him. A few inches either side might have proved fatal. His hands and fore-arms were badly grazed and he was shaken. Satisfied that nothing worse had happened, we went on down with extreme caution and I heard later that that party had decided to go no farther.

When we were back on the glacier we found that the sun had softened the snow to a considerable depth and it was tiring to keep plunging in well above the knees. But the climb on the excellent rock, spiced with hazard, had been the very best in my experience and I was now ready to make a drawing of the mountain with real understanding of its nature.

Although Zermatt and Saas-fee are two of the best climbing centres in Switzerland I find it extremely hard to decide whether I really prefer that region of the Alps above all others. I have been to so many, both in winter and summer. But as I no longer use skis the mountains attract me most in summer and my wife and I both like to choose a high starting place, right in among the mountains. There is more than enough to fill a short holiday, walking and climbing and painting, but it is always tempting to go and see what is in the next valley. Then, once started, we go on from village to village, from valley to valley, until time or money runs out. But first we explore all round our base.

One of our bases was Wengen, where for several days the

weather was bad. (Plate XIII.) The continual downpour did not prevent our making long excursions on foot, even through the clouds, but at last my old climbing boots wore out. I have never been so attached to any footwear and I discarded them with great reluctance. They were heavy, ungainly objects, well studded with nails. The rubber composition soles that many now prefer are much lighter, but they are not suitable for all conditions and it is still wise to have a few nails in addition. My original boots were made in Zermatt and they served me well, with many renewals of the nails, in the Alps and other mountainous regions of Europe and in Mexico and Peru.

I had already made friends with a local cobbler and his wife, who were themselves keen climbers, and on a rainy day I went to the shop to ask if he could make me a new pair in time for use before I had to go home again. The cobbler, surrounded by boots and the instruments of his trade, sat at work near a window looking out on the mountains and he sighed for a chance to go out for another climb. Quite recently, he told me, he had made himself a new pair of climbing boots, but there were so many demands for his services that he had not yet been able to use them. I told him how badly I needed a new pair, but it looked as if I should have to go without them, as I had only another week to spare. He then showed me the pair that he had made for himself—perfect in workmanship and admirably supple—and said that he could let me have a similar pair in about a month's time.

"Try them on," he said.

I pulled off my battered veterans and slipped my feet into the cobbler's boots. They fitted precisely.

"They look as if they were made for you!" exclaimed his wife.

The cobbler examined the fit, laced them up carefully and gave them a fond pat.

"You can have them," he said. "I can make myself another pair when there is time. These will serve you well."

Those boots, in turn, have become old friends and, to remind me of that lucky transaction, I have the sketch that I made of the cobbler, sitting there in his blue overall, surrounded by climbing boots and tools.

Two or three years ago we flew to Geneva and went to the

Canton Valais for a walking tour. We had planned to start at
Fionnay in the Val de Bagnes, but, hearing that the valley was
encumbered by work on a new hydro-electric scheme, we made
for Arolla instead. The excitement of arriving at a place that
was new to me was increased by our doing the last lap of the
journey, from Les Haudères, in a jeep. I remembered my experience in a jeep in Persia and thanked my lucky stars that on
this occasion the driver was not an opium addict. We arrived
safely after a spectacular climb by a narrow road and bundled
out with our rucksacks and ice-axes in full view of lovely Mont
Collon. In ten minutes we were out of the hotel again, feasting
our eyes on the snow summits. Less than twenty-four hours
after leaving our home in Surrey I had made a sketch of the
Pigne d'Arolla rising above the glaciers, with a foreground of
the foaming river winding between larch woods.

After several training walks we stuffed our rucksacks with
everything we thought we might need for a few days and set off
on a long walk from Les Haudères up the Ferpècle valley. The
idea was to find out how much we could conveniently carry.
The day turned out to be one of the hottest of the year and at
intervals during the first few miles we mentally discarded item
after item from our rucksacks. But we did not actually lighten
the loads until we ate our picnic lunch.

The wild flowers in the Ferpècle valley were growing with a
tropical luxuriance that I have seen nowhere else in Switzerland. A few peasants, wearing local costumes, had begun to
scythe the hay, but the steep slopes were smothered with
flowers, often of unusual size. Beyond the head of the valley,
where the track became much steeper, we were tempted to
dump the rucksacks, but we felt that we had not yet made a fair
test of our ability to carry the weight. When we reached a
point above the Alpe Bricolla, having climbed nearly 4,000 feet,
I could no longer resist the temptation to make some sketches
and we agreed that there was no need to go any farther to convince ourselves that the weight of the rucksacks must be reduced
by a good many pounds. We took them off and sat down in the
brilliant sunshine. Below us lay the Ferpècle glacier, above rose
the Dent Blanche and the Grand Cornier. Here was glorious
scenery, but I was looking for a better composition.

I walked back down the track to the point where the Ferpècle glacier met the Mont Miné glacier, named after the dark mountain that stands like an island between the two rivers of ice. A ridge of rock cut diagonally across the Mont Miné glacier, which broke off here in towering cliffs of solid ice. In the background rose the Pointe de Bertol and deep shadows emphasized the steepness of the glittering icefall. It was an interesting composition.

I had nearly finished my sketch of this subject when suddenly an enormous mass of ice broke from the cliff in the midst of the glacier and plunged among the deep crevasses below. A great white cloud of snow and ice particles rose like steam high into the air and the noise of the fall echoed and re-echoed through the valley. I just had time, before the first impression faded, to indicate the avalanche in my sketch, with the shadow of the dense cloud lying across the glacier and the sunlight gleaming through its thinner fringe.

Another beautiful walk took us to the Plan de Bertol, at about 8,600 feet overlooking the Arolla glacier, and there we were close under the massive head of Mont Collon. I made a drawing of this splendid mountain, with the Petit Mont Collon on its right and a glimpse of the upper part of the Otemma glacier, which is more than eight miles in length. Another sketch shows the Pointe de Bertol from this south-eastern side, with the hut perched on rock above the col.

On the way down I found an impressive subject in the Aiguilles Rouges d'Arolla, towering above the tremendously deep valley. A day or two later three British climbers who were staying at our hotel set out to climb the Aiguilles. They failed to return within the time expected and there was great anxiety about them that night. Before dawn a small party set out to look for them and eventually met them on the way down, tired and all but frostbitten. Owing to the condition of the snow they had had great difficulty in finding a safe route down and had been obliged to spend the night on the mountain, waiting for daylight. They had been about forty hours on the climb.

The surroundings of Arolla were so fascinating that we were reluctant to leave, but we had come with the intention of walking eastwards across the Canton Valais amongst some of the

finest scenery in the whole of the Alps and we hoped to cross the
Monte Moro pass into Italy for a view of Monte Rosa from that
side. Early one morning we went down into the Val d'Hérens
and began the ascent to the first pass, the Col de Torrent, at
about 9,600 feet. This time the weight of the rucksacks, though
considerable, was not excessive and the rest of our things were
posted on ahead, for collection some days later.

Marmots whistled shrilly among the rocks as we climbed in
sunshine, but otherwise we seemed to have the world to ourselves. We had lunch just below the pass and looked back
over the western panorama, which included at least ten splendid
peaks. That was the world in which we had been living : in a
few minutes a new world would open out before us.

We climbed the last steep zig-zags and there it was. This
was a magic moment, when an even more magnificent array of
snow-covered peaks came into view and the old world slipped
away. Our flight from London to Geneva, our arrival at Arolla,
even the walk that we had enjoyed only yesterday seemed to
have receded into the distant past. New impressions crowding
into the mind often produce this sensation of prolonged time
and we were to experience it at each new pass that we crossed.
Days acquired the value of weeks and it was hard to remember
that things that we had seen and done only twenty-four hours
before were so recent. This is one of the advantages of moving
from place to place instead of going out from and back to a
single centre; a short holiday seems much longer than it is.

We went down steeply from the Col de Torrent into the
Moiry valley, where we were obliged to walk for some miles
along a road that was being constructed in connection with
another new hydro-electric scheme. We had enjoyed coming
down among the rocks and over the tufted grass, with occasional pauses to examine alpine flowers, but the unfinished
road was disagreeable and tedious. It is extraordinary how
unpleasant it can be to walk in climbing boots on a level road,
whereas scrambling for hours over the roughest ground pro-
duces no discomfort.

It seemed a long way to Grimentz, but at last we were in the
narrow main street between tall wooden houses with overhanging balconies. To right and left tunnel-like gaps between the

buildings, curious old doorways and window-boxes gay with flowers suggested many more pictures than I would have time to paint. We passed a group of women and children washing colourful clothes in the clear water that flowed ceaselessly through a stone trough, while a tall crucifix—a feature of most alpine villages—looked down on the scene. (Plate XIV.)

Grimentz became our headquarters for two or three days and I was continually busy with my sketch-book. This mountain village found a place in the news not long ago on account of its being the first place to have a pipeline installed to convey milk down to it from the alpine pasture 1,300 feet above. From Grimentz we walked over into the Val d'Anniviers, where I sat on a rock in the river to sketch a bridge with the Besso rising above the larch woods behind. At least a score of butterflies settled on me and my book while I worked. Then we went on up to Zinal and, from a point above the head of the valley, looked across at the Weisshorn, the Zinal Rothorn and other great peaks embedded in their vast glaciers and now seen from a fresh angle. The summit of the Rothorn appeared so remote and aloof that it was hard to believe that I had been up there.

I make no pretence to be a great climber, though I would have climbed much more had circumstances permitted. Some mountaineers are only satisfied by first ascents, others find their satisfaction, though surely little pleasure, in going to the greatest possible altitude. Perhaps I would join them, if I could; but I regard mountaineering primarily as a sport to be enjoyed and if a climb promises no pleasure I would rather not attempt it. Mountains are no less wonderful because they have been climbed before and I can enjoy being in their presence, whether they are great or small, if they are lovely, mysterious and endowed with personality. It is a great experience to climb two or three of the finest peaks in a group, but I have found as complete satisfaction in walking among them, exploring their valleys, crossing the passes and merely looking at the mighty ramparts above me. I like to be free to stop and sketch a view that strikes me, without feeling that it is of paramount importance to reach a summit or some other destination. If a summit is the goal, I will go for it. But mountain scenery is so infinitely varied that I can also find satisfaction lower down.

When we left Grimentz we again went down into the Val d'Anniviers, climbed to the village of St. Luc, where we could see the tip of the distant Matterhorn, and went on steeply upwards to the Meiden pass which leads over into the Turtmann valley. Nearly all the way down we had before us the stately beauty of the Weisshorn. (Plate XV.) As we came in sight of the houses of Gruben, an isolated hamlet on the floor of the deep valley, old memories of thirty years ago revived in me. I remembered how, coming from the opposite direction, I had made the long and tedious crossing of the Augstbord pass and had descended steeply among trees and tumbled rocks, in almost pitch darkness, to spend a night at Gruben. The hotel that had stood there then had been burnt down, but a comfortable new one had taken its place.

The Turtmann valley can be reached only on foot and it is relatively little known. For that reason it is quite unspoilt and I found there delightful subjects for painting, both at the head of the valley, which is filled by the magnificent façade of the Turtmann glacier, and at the lower end where the river foams and gurgles through the forest and down into the Rhône valley.

We began the climb to the Augstbord pass early one morning and a short way above the hamlet we paused to watch a fascinating family of young stoats popping in and out among the rocks as if trying to coax us to play hide-and-seek with them. For a long way beyond the pass the route lay high up among masses of huge boulders, but on the brink of the Nikolai valley there suddenly opened up the grandest panorama of snow-peaks that we had yet seen, including the giants of the Mischabel group. Thousands of feet below the white water of the Mattervisp came foaming down from Zermatt.

At St. Niklaus, beside the river, we refreshed ourselves with delicious peaches and red wine and then made our way to Stalden, where the Nikolai and Sass valleys meet, for the night. At six o'clock in the morning we were awakened by the vibrations of an earthquake, a reminder that the mountains are not as stable as they look. After breakfast among vines and oleanders, we went on up the Saas valley to Saas-fee, where the temptation to climb again assailed me fiercely.

We had, however, decided that the crowning glory of our walking tour should be a view of Monte Rosa from the Italian side. Saas-fee must wait until we were on the way home. After a picnic lunch among the ancient larches outside the village, some of them six or seven hundred years old, we continued up the valley to the isolated hostel at Mattmark. In the evening I made a drawing looking towards the Monte Moro pass into Italy, which lies at about 9,400 feet. During the last war many escaping prisoners took this route into Switzerland. A considerable number of them, unused to mountains and without suitable clothing, perished in the snow and ice. In the foreground of my picture was a gigantic serpentine boulder, as big as a hotel, known as the "Blue Stone". It is believed to have been carried down from the Strahlhorn on the back of a glacier.

The next dawn looked unpromising, with much low cloud, but when we reached the top of the pass, which was covered by recent snow, the clouds parted and we found ourselves gazing with awe at the whole of the upper half of Monte Rosa. Very soon the clouds closed in again and we went on down through deep snow to the Italian frontier post. From there it was a steep and rough descent to Macugnaga, the name given to the group of fourteen villages and hamlets scattered through the upper part of the Anzasca valley.

Staffa, the largest village of the group, looked inappropriately sophisticated, with a formal main square and modern hotels, but we found a room facing the head of the valley in a delightful little hotel at Pecetto, the highest hamlet of the group. Monte Rosa was still invisible, but we were prepared to wait.

I woke up at five o'clock in the morning and went to the window. Quickly I called my wife. Directly in front of us, in the clear cold light of a perfect dawn, the mighty mass of rock and ice that was Monte Rosa was framed in the window. It was one of the most exciting moments of our lives. While we watched, the first pink glow touched the Dufourspitze, the highest of the peaks on which I had stood on just such a perfect morning more than thirty years ago. An artist or a mountaineer would have been thrilled by such a sight. As I had something of both in me, I was almost overwhelmed by the impression that it made on me.

Steadily the first warm flush crept downwards, illuminating the Nordend, Zumstein and Gnifetti peaks and flowing like molten gold towards the glaciers that were still enshrouded in the blue-grey residue of the night. We did not move from the window until the whole valley was flooded with the full light of morning. As soon as the spectacle began I snatched my sketch-book and drew a rapid impression of the mountain and, when the direct light of the sun had seeped a third of the way down, indicated the different areas in colour. But mere pigment could never cope with that vivid fire on ice and rock, advancing steadily downwards in a silence that seemed uncanny.

For two days we walked and I sketched in the valley. There was a perfect view of Monte Rosa from a point in the hamlet of La Villa and I sat in the sunshine on a rough stone wall to paint that wonderful scene, with the old German church and some wooden houses in the foreground. (Plate V.)

When we arrived back in Saas-fee it seemed incredible that we had passed through there only four days earlier. The rich experiences of the past few days had prolonged time beyond the bounds of reality.

The next evening, with the guide who had led me on the Fletschhorn three years before, I walked up to the Mischabel hut five thousand feet above the valley. Long before dawn he and I set out to climb two of the four peaks exceeding 14,000 feet in the Mischabel group. The Lenzspitze culminated in a very steep slope of ice and snow, but there was some good rock-climbing on the higher part of the Nadelhorn. The two mountains are connected by a sharp, jagged ridge more than half a mile in length, which affords little foothold but plenty of opportunity to fall several thousand feet on either side. When we were half way across my guide, who sometimes revealed a macabre sense of humour, said that, if he slipped down one side he would whistle three times as a signal to me to throw myself down the other. At the moment I was leading along a particularly tricky knife-edge and I wondered whether the rope would be cut if I slipped and he jumped off to balance me. As soon as we reached a safer position I asked if he had ever had to do such a thing. He laughed. Yes, he said; he had done it once when he was a young guide. Unfortunately he had been too quick. The other man had slipped, but had managed to check his slide almost immediately. By that time he himself was over the other side and only a miracle and his ice-axe had saved him.

Although it was cold up there, I managed during a short pause to make a sketch from one of the gendarmes on the ridge. On the way back to the hut we were enveloped in a sudden snowstorm, which imposed extra caution among the crevasses, but in a few hours we were down in the valley again.

This walking tour was such a pleasant experience that we decided to make another in the following summer, starting at the end of May in order to see the alpine flowers at their best. This time we chose the valleys and passes of the Ticino, the only Italian-speaking canton of Switzerland. This promised to be very different from what we had done before. Although there are few peaks above 10,000 feet, the heart of the canton is exceedingly wild and rugged, with numerous waterfalls and cascades plunging hundreds of feet over sheer precipices of solid granite. The vegetation is quite different from that in the Canton Valais and there are dense woods of chestnut, beech, walnut, birch and alder. The fir and pine forests that are so characteristic of other parts of the country are rare. The architecture of the scattered villages shows strong Italian influence, but the region is thinly populated. There are roads through the main valleys, but not many well-used footpaths and very few visitors explore this mountain area. Foreigners are attracted instead to the well-known resorts in the south, such as Locarno and Ascona on Lake Maggiore and Lugano on the lake of that name.

We arrived in Switzerland with rucksacks nicely calculated and an insatiable appetite for mountain scenery. On the way south from Zurich we stopped at Brunnen on the lake of Lucerne and I made a sketch of the Rütli meadow where, some six hundred and fifty years ago, representatives of the three forest cantons, Uri, Schwyz and Unterwalden, took an oath to drive out the Habsburgs. This incident led eventually to the formation of the Swiss Confederation. At Bellinzona, the capital of the Ticino, I sketched the three medieval castles that were built to guard the northern passes—the Gotthard, the Lukmanier and the San Bernardino. Their puny defences, once thought to be impregnable, are toy-like in comparison with the formidable bastions of the mountains.

In many parts of Switzerland the abundant paths are so well marked—with signposts and dabs of coloured paint on the rocks—that it is simple to find the way from one place to another. But in the mountain region of the Ticino, which is much less frequented, maps are indispensable and compasses sometimes useful. The main rivers flow in a southerly direction to Lake Maggiore and it is easy enough to get to the villages in their valleys by road, but we intended to walk across the mountain passes from west to east and to explore some of the little-known tributary valleys. All that we had read about the canton made it obvious that we could expect to see some very fine scenery, but it was too early in the season for going high and we wondered whether we should be able to find our way once we had left the main valleys.

We made our headquarters at Bignasco (Plate XVI), where the Val Bavona and the Val Lavizzara join at the head of the Val Maggia, and began by walking through these lovely wild valleys, where I made several sketches. The Maggia river is subject to sudden floods and there are records of its having wrought great destruction in its lower reaches. We had an indication of this after a day or two of heavy rain, when the numerous cascades falling from great heights into the higher valleys increased enormously in volume overnight and the river turned from a moderate stream, forming rapids among the rocks, into a broad tumultuous flood.

The Val Bavona was liberally strewn with gigantic boulders, some of them larger than houses, that had fallen in times past from the towering walls of the valley. It was no uncommon sight to see a massive boulder serving as one wall of a house that it completely dwarfed and protected against further landslides. The water power available in these valleys must be enormous and in the Sambuco valley, beyond the village of Fusio, a new lake is being formed behind one of the largest dams in Switzerland. But it was sad to see this beautiful valley, which contained Fusio's best pasture lands, given over to a hydro-electric scheme. A guide book published in 1948 said that "the cattle of the

people of Fusio graze there and throughout the summer months
the air of that remote and sunny little retreat is filled with the
peaceful tinkling of their bells". All that we heard, after due
warning, was the detonation of blasting charges and the crash
of falling rock.

The Ticino is a land of contrasts. It is only about twenty
miles, in a direct line, from the white summits of the Basodino,
the Campo Tencia and other mountains to the sub-tropical
gardens on the shore of Lake Maggiore. It is less than that
distance from some of the lonely passes, miles from the nearest
tiny village, to the car-infested waterfront at Ascona. On a
sunny day the murmuring streams of crystal-clear water pick
their way daintily among the rocks; the next morning, after
an all-night storm, they may be turgid, raging torrents. At
dawn the lacy frills of a cascade are dispersed by the wind
before they can reach the ground; by midday a foaming flood
pours from the precipice and shatters into a vast cloud of spray
on the rocks hundreds of feet below, filling the whole valley with
its roar.

The day on which we crossed the Cocco pass on the way from
Bignasco to Brione in the Val Verzasca was hot and sunny. We
set out early, by a path that climbed a wooded slope, but it soon
became encumbered by undergrowth and appeared to have
been little used. I stopped to make a drawing of a lovely old
stone bridge in the Val Lavizzara, high arched over the foaming
river; then we followed a track that ascended more steeply
towards the east. When this faded out we tried to follow the
course of a mountain torrent coming from the snow-fields high
above, but we had to pick a way among boulders, patches of
bog and scrub. As the slope became steeper and steeper we got
very hot and our heavy rucksacks were a considerable burden;
but at last the jagged ridge where the pass lay came in sight,
still more than a thousand feet above us, and we sat on a grassy
mound to eat lunch.

Mountains surrounded us, forests filled the valleys and deep
snow extended far down from the pass—a notch between two
prominent peaks of bare rock. We had seen no sign of a human
being since leaving the bridge. We could find no track and
none of the usual marks on the rocks, so we headed for a rocky

shelf that cut across the end of the snow-field and that seemed to offer the best line of approach. But for a long time we had to force our way upwards over damp rock smothered in a tangle of stunted alders that constantly caught in the straps of our rucksacks and gave way beneath our feet.

Then, suddenly, I was attacked by cramp in both legs. This had never happened to me before and it was probably caused by the loss of salt through perspiration. For some minutes I wondered if I should be able to go either up or down, but luckily I found a tiny packet of salt in my rucksack. I dissolved it in water and drank it and soon I was able to go on again.

On the last steep slope before the ridge the snow was frozen so hard that I had to cut steps with my ice-axe and it seemed certain that no one else had used the pass this season. It was a great relief to reach the crest at last and to find that there were red marks at intervals on the rocks to mark the route down into the Val d'Osola. Unfortunately they failed us several times at crucial points where we had to cross broad gullies filled with snow, domed and hard like glaciers, and we lost time searching for a safe way through the tumbled mountain débris.

When we reached the bottom of the valley, where we expected a small stream with a path along the bank, we found a swift torrent at least a hundred feet wide, full of boulders and rapids throwing their spray into the air. There was a red mark on a large rock in midstream and another on the opposite bank, but no bridge. The guide books had not warned us that the river had to be crossed and presumably it would not be such a formidable barrier later in the season. It was now late in the afternoon and we knew that we could not possibly get back over the pass before dark.

Fortunately I had crossed many rivers of this kind in South America and I told my wife that, if we hung on to one another and kept three of our four feet on the bottom, moving only one foot at a time, we ought to be fairly stable in the violent current. We stepped into the river and at once the pressure of the water made it difficult to maintain balance on the slippery rounded boulders. The water reached well above our knees and in midstream we felt that our feet might be frozen before we got to the other side. But we arrived there safely and marched off down the valley as fast as the rough ground would allow.

Presently, with some five miles still to go before we could reach Brione, we came to a narrow road of loose stones. I pulled out of my rucksack the old mouth-organ that has cheered us on many a long tramp and we squelched along in our sodden boots to the music, very imperfectly executed, of the familiar marching songs. An hour later, not far from our destination, we met an old woman carrying milk to a hut, the first human being we had seen since the early morning.

The inn we had read about did not seem to exist, but a charming old lady and her daughter-in-law, who were chatting outside their house in the dusk, welcomed us in for the night. We had been on our feet for thirteen hours. While they prepared a meal we changed out of our wet clothes and afterwards we sat outside, exercising our Italian and sipping an excellent local wine, until the moon rose above the dark mountains.

We explored other valleys to the east and, a week later, I was sketching in picturesque Gandria on the lake of Lugano. One day we sailed luxuriously round the lake in a steamer while a mannequin parade on board, organized by an enterprising local store, did its best to distract us from the mountain scenery. Such is this land of contrasts.

The mountains of northern Italy and especially the Dolomites have been described in numerous books and the motor-roads that cross many of the passes between the main groups enable thousands of tourists to see something of the unique Dolomite formations. But I doubt whether more than one in five of those who visit them actually explore the crags and pinnacles or climb the higher peaks in the region of eternal snow and ice. It is a fascinating experience to drive for a day or two among these abrupt and colourful mountains, provided that you are not yourself at the wheel with all your attention concentrated on the dizzily twisting road; but their peculiar charm can only be fully appreciated by walking and climbing far above the fertile valleys to the solitude of the precipitous rocks. Hidden among trees on the lower slopes there are blue-green lakes that reminded me of others in the Rocky Mountains of Canada, but the fantastic ramparts and pinnacles that dominate them have, in my experience, no counterparts in other mountain regions.

During our walking tour in the Dolomites in July, 1956, we crossed at least eight passes, made a complete circuit of the Marmolata, the highest Dolomite that rises to nearly 11,000 feet, and were caught in a thunderstorm while descending from the Catinaccio whose German name, Rosengarten, seems to me more appropriate. An autumn sunset can turn its rugged face of grey and ochre rock into a glowing wall of colour that has been compared with that of the "Rose of the Alps"—the small rhododendron which grows abundantly in many parts of the region. Among the prolific wild flowers we identified several that we had never found before in the Alps, including the graceful white Soldanella minima which has a very restricted range. We saw many species of orchid, but the handsome "slipper orchid" (Cypripedium Calceolus) was rare. It was an exciting moment when we first came across the stately Martagon lily or "Turk's cap" with at least half a dozen buds on each stem, but we did not see it in full bloom until the very last day of our tour. Then we found numerous specimens, one with no less than eleven of the graceful magenta flowers.

I hoped before returning to England to do one or two bigger climbs, so we moved westwards from the Dolomites to Solda, within reach of the Ortler group. For some days the weather had been unsettled and the coveted summits remained concealed in heavy clouds. My zeal was damped by the news that, just before our arrival, two Germans, unroped and without a guide, had rashly attempted to climb the Ortler in these unsuitable conditions when the warm *Foehn* wind was blowing from the south-west. High up on the mountain an avalanche swept one of them into a crevasse where he was buried under such vast quantities of ice and snow that all hope of recovering his body had to be abandoned. Occasionally the sun broke through, but fresh snow fell on the summits and for three or four days we waited in vain for better conditions. In a gloriously sunny interval we went together to the summit of the Beltovo, an easy climb of nearly 11,000 feet which commanded a magnificent panorama of all the surrounding peaks, but soon the snow-laden clouds closed down again. With only four more days to spare I reluctantly abandoned my designs on the Ortler and the Grand Zebru and we went off to seek compensation among the mountains of Liechtenstein, the delightful little Principality on the Rhine between the borders of Austria and Switzerland.

By this time my sketch-book was nearly full. In spite of cloudy days, I had captured impressions of the mountains that no camera could have snatched. Sometimes, in the Dolomites, I waited patiently while the billowing clouds drifted from one part of a mountain to another and I completed my picture piecemeal as each crag and pinnacle appeared for a few fleeting moments. In Liechtenstein there were castles as well as mountains to sketch and it was on our way down from one of the highest mountains in the Principality that we found the Martagon lily in full bloom.

XV.
The Weisshorn
(14,804 feet)
from below the
east side of the
Meiden pass,
Canton Valais,
Switzerland

The new Quaker settlement and Friends' Meeting House (1909-1911 feet) in the background

W. COVERLEY-PRICE

CHAPTER VI

AN AMBITION REALIZED: ADVENTURES ALL ROUND NORTH AMERICA

FEW of childhood's ambitions outlive school days, but two of mine were somehow kept alive until they were achieved many years later. The earliest and most vigorous ambition was to become a painter, but it was kept under by the sheer weight of Education and very nearly died of frustration. The other, inspired by a large photograph of Lake Louise which hung in the dining-room of my preparatory school, was to see the Rocky Mountains of Canada and to paint a picture of that perfect lake.

In early boyhood I saw no prospect of foreign travel, yet I suppose the germ of what the Germans call *Wanderlust* must have been there. I developed an early interest in geography and, although the school curriculum kept history and geography strictly apart, I never studied the one without reference to the other. This—to my mind—eminently sensible combination led me into the entrancing realm of exploration and I read numerous books about the adventures of the pioneers in all continents. It was a proud moment when I carried off the School Geography Prize at Harrow, success being largely due, I believe, to my associating historical events with geographical information. One of the questions, for example, concerned the eastern part of the United States of America where the Civil War had been fought and it happened that I had read a good deal about that prolonged campaign. But geography, like geology, has practical applications and before long I made up my mind that I wanted to travel.

As an amateur dabbler with paints I needed no urging. In fact I had to be restrained from drawing in class, from decorating my books and from producing over-elaborate maps that occupied time intended for other purposes. But I won the art prize at the age of nine, in competition with many older boys,

and added several more art prizes at Harrow. These achieve-
ments failed to convince anyone that I ought to be encouraged
to study art: on the contrary, it seemed that almost any sort of
job would be regarded as a wiser choice. But when at last I had
a chance to go abroad the most important item in my luggage
was the paint-box. It was cheaper to use than a camera and it
certainly gave me more satisfaction. Always thereafter I
painted in my spare time, but there were many long years to
wait before I could, without equivocation, call myself an artist.

While that ambition was in cold storage, or perhaps I should
say simmering, the hope of getting to the Canadian Rockies
never left me. The years passed and it seemed unlikely that I
would ever be able to afford the journey, but in 1929, when I
was working at the Foreign Office, the prospect looked a little
rosier. With sixty days' leave in hand I began to calculate the
possibility. Then one day I was advised to take my leave as
soon as I could, as I was shortly to be transferred to Mexico.

Even in my wildest dreams I had never contemplated going
to Mexico. I had read Prescott's accounts of the conquests of
Mexico and Peru and I knew that, as a member of the Diplomatic Service, I might some day be sent to a Latin-American
capital; but somehow Mexico had never occurred to me as a
likely destination. Now I was delighted at the idea of going
there, to see mountains higher than any in Europe and to enjoy
sunshine nearly all the year round. Furthermore, Mexico was
a part of the North American continent—the continent that
contained Canada—and this fact helped a new project to
crystallize. If I could get enough leave when over there, I
would make a dash to the Rockies.

Abruptly I switched my immediate leave plans to South
Africa, a less expensive journey outside the dollar area. In
haste, I worked out an itinerary that would take me from the
Cape as far north as the Victoria Falls on the Zambezi river
and I put a good stock of painting materials in my luggage.
The ship sailed from Southampton in April.

It was a delightful voyage, both there and back, and I saw
all that I had planned to see, including gold mines, diamond
mines, the Victoria Falls, Zulu war dances, native kraals and,
of course, the mountains. Little did I dream, while sketching

on the Zambezi, that twenty-five years later some of my sketches would provide useful information for drawings to be published in *The Sphere*. I still have a number of those paintings, but one, made in Capetown, was bought and presented to the South African High Commissioner in London. (Plate XVII.)

Ten days after I got back from South Africa I sailed again from Southampton on the way to Mexico. Countless thousands of people have crossed the Atlantic in ships and now even the air passage has become commonplace. But this was my first crossing to what used to be called the New World and I had all the appropriate sensations, except that of seasickness. I could now pace the deck like a hardened seaman, for I had recently spent thirty-four days at sea.

During the voyage I had ample time to read more about the country to which I was going and I made exciting plans to visit as many as possible of the scenes of the exploits of the early explorers. The making of American history began only a few hundred years ago, but I was just as eager to touch the living stones of its foundations as are many Americans to explore the sites of their origins in Europe.

As the ship approached the West Indies, on a calm blue sea under a hot sun, I spent most of the time on deck on the look-out for whales, porpoises and flying fish. One morning there appeared a belt of white foam extending for miles across our course and it seemed that the ship was heading straight for a reef. But with binoculars I discovered that the foam was caused by hundreds of porpoises, travelling at considerable speed. An old German seaman told me that it was the largest school he had ever seen in more than forty years at sea.

Next day several waterspouts appeared at intervals, when sea and clouds met in whirling grey columns that pursued an erratic course until their energy was expended. The commander altered course to avoid them. They reminded me of the "dust devils" that I had seen in the desert. The rapid sketches that I made of them record how one, a really formidable pillar, wriggled like a snake and finally contorted itself into a giant S.

One of the passengers, bored after a fortnight on the empty ocean, expressed astonishment that I could find any subjects to draw, but I think his eyes were opened when I showed him the pages filled in my sketch-book. Little studies of different parts of the ship with deep shadows cast by the tropical sun, impressions of men at work on the rigging and of stokers resting on the foredeck, sketches of passengers taking their siesta and studies of the magnificent clouds that sometimes paraded in ever-changing succession across the limitless blue sky made an interesting record of the voyage. As the ship entered Havana harbour a sudden downpour all but blotted out my first sight of Cuba; but it cleared after a few minutes and, before I went ashore, a view of Havana was added to my sketch-book.

Three days later I landed at Veracruz. As I stepped on to Mexican soil the flood of historical memories surged up once more. I felt, for a moment, like a gambler who has just staked his fortune on a single throw. I wondered to what extent the New World would enrich my experience. Disappointment, I suddenly realized, was possible.

Now, looking back, I know that my time in Mexico, getting on for three years, was one of the happiest periods of my life. There was plenty of work at the Legation, but there was also time for riding, golf, tennis, swimming and some mountaineering. New experiences came thick and fast. I soon grew accustomed to earthquakes, although one, which lasted four minutes and destroyed a large part of the town of Oaxaca in the south, threw nearly everything movable on to the floor of my flat and rocked more than half of the water out of my bath. It flung open the steel shutters of the Legation windows, which had been put there in the days of revolutionary disturbance, and it set the chandeliers swinging until they all but touched the ceiling on either side.

I was present at the inauguration of a new President of the Republic, who was fired at and wounded before he had reached his palace; but the series of revolutions that used to recur with the regularity of Cup Ties in England seemed to have ceased. The European press had led me to imagine that revolution was the national sport of Latin-American countries and I was almost surprised to find that there were so few occasions for violence. But I might have come to a violent end myself during my first week in Mexico City.

I returned late one night to my small temporary flat after

a dinner at the Legation. There was only one key to the flat and I had left this with the old Mexican servant, who promised to let me in. But I found the main entrance to the block firmly locked. Several times I banged on the doors and called to my servant on the first floor, but there was no response. I knocked again, more loudly. Suddenly a ground-floor window opened and a head appeared, followed by a hand grasping a revolver, and the irate Mexican shouted in Spanish, "Go away or I'll blow your head off!"

I had learnt Spanish in Spain and with my best Castilian accent I apologized for the noise and explained my dilemma.

Keeping me covered with the gun, the man said, "Get the night-watchman!" and promptly slammed the window.

I walked all round the block in the moonlight, but could find no one. I tried two or three doors, but all were locked. I walked round again, in vain. The situation was annoying. Greatly daring, I banged on the front door again and quickly took cover in the porch. Nothing happened. In desperation I gave several mighty bangs that echoed through the streets. I heard the nearby window open and guessed that the Mexican was ready to fire. Without showing myself, I called out that I could not find the night-watchman.

"The back door, you . . .!" the man shouted and again slammed his window.

Keeping close to the wall, I crept past under his window and round to the back of the building. I tapped on a door, but there was no response. I tried another, louder. Someone stirred inside and the night-watchman, barely awake, opened the door and asked what I wanted.

When he had let me into the building I discovered my servant fast asleep on the doormat outside my flat. She said she had left the key inside by mistake. I had nothing with which to pick the lock, so I told her to go and get some implement from the night-watchman.

I waited for several minutes, then I put my hand on the handle of the door. It opened, for it had not been latched.

During the first two years I travelled fairly widely about the country, making sketches wherever I went. In 1930 a British cruiser, H.M.S. *Durban*, paid a visit to Veracruz and I helped

to entertain the officers who came to the capital. At the end
of the visit the captain invited me to spend a month in the ship,
which was to proceed to Guatemala, Venezuela and Trinidad
before returning to the base at Bermuda. Although I had
intended to save my leave for Canada, this was too good to miss
and I enjoyed every minute of that trip with the Royal Navy.
On the way back from Bermuda I spent some days in New York
and Washington.

Incidentally, the visit to Guatemala gave me an excellent
"talking point"—in Spanish—when in 1937 I was appointed
to be in attendance on the Representative of Guatemala at the
Coronation of His Majesty King George VI. It was a busy
week, spent mostly in full uniform, for we were not only present
at the Coronation in Westminster Abbey but we also attended
a Court Ball at Buckingham Palace, a Reception given by the
Speaker of the House of Commons and other functions. On a
free day the Representative, a former Minister for Foreign
Affairs of his country, asked me to take him to Oxford. As an
old "Cantab." I did my best to give him a favourable impression of the University, but I felt that he would have fared
better under the guidance of my wife, who graduated at Lady
Margaret Hall.

There were so many interesting things to do in Mexico that
it was easy to be deflected from one plan to another, but in the
following spring I decided that Canada must come first. The
long train journey seemed uninviting; I wanted to be free to
stop at will. The more I studied the map, the more I felt
inclined to choose my own route by car, though it obviously
involved a very long drive. By joining the American Auto-
mobile Association I got some excellent strip maps for routes
north of the Rio Grande, but that was not much short of a
thousand miles away and there was little information about
Mexican roads. In fact at that time, more than a quarter of a
century ago, there were not many highways in Mexico except
near the capital.

After prolonged cogitation I resolved on nothing less than
a trip round North America by a route covering nearly 10,000
miles. I had already been to the little port of Acapulco on the
Pacific coast, three hundred miles from Mexico City, and I

decided to ship my car from there to Los Angeles as there seemed to be no other way of getting to California. From there I would drive north to Vancouver, then east through the Rockies, across the prairies and round the Great Lakes to Ottawa, Montreal and New York. I would go to Washington, then southwards in a great sweep through the mountains until I reached New Orleans on the Gulf of Mexico. Next I would turn westwards into Texas and cross the Mexican border at Laredo to join the line of the proposed pan-American highway. I knew that this road had been extended recently into Mexico, but by all accounts it had not yet got very far. Before I could reach Mexico City again I should have to find my way through five or six hundred miles of mountainous country where, in all probability, such routes as existed were little better than mule tracks. This last lap, from the border to the capital, promised to be the most difficult.

Before starting I drew up a time-table to make sure that, on paper at least, I could fit into sixty days' leave all that I hoped to do. Nearly ten days would be needed to get me to Los Angeles, for the voyage in the little coastal steamer to that starting point would take at least a week. Generally, I proposed to drive all day and to stop only for the night, but I had a list of places of special interest to each of which I allotted two nights. This list included San Francisco, Vancouver, Banff, Chicago, Ottawa and a number of other towns. I was going to have a lot of long spells at the wheel, the longest being over four hundred miles, and I calculated that, after deducting the rest days in towns, I should have to average 250 miles a day. I left a day or two in hand for probable delays during the incalculable last lap, but I could obviously spare little time for mechanical breakdowns. Luckily I had the greatest confidence in my car—and in myself as a driver.

The car that I owned during my first few months in Mexico was called The Bull. It was the decrepit residue of a once glorious vehicle that had been the pride of a famous bull-fighter and the envy of wealthy Mexicans in the capital. Dazzled by its reputation, flattered by the thought of owning a two-seater that was classified as the "American Rolls-Royce" and fascinated by its (sadly faded) colour scheme of olive green and primrose yellow, I had failed to discern that it was on its last wheels. When I tried to coax it over the 10,000-foot pass to Cuernavaca, a normal week-end excursion, it nearly blew up. My temper actually did so and I vowed that, if I could dispose of it, I would make sure that my next purchase would be an efficient engine and not a famous hulk. I soon found that I could not even give The Bull away and I had to leave it to moulder in an empty garage.

I then heard that the pro. at one of the local golf courses was going into business in California and that his little two-seater would shortly be for sale. The Bull being *hors de combat*, I hired a taxi and arrived at the entrance to the golf course just as the pro. was emerging in his car. I knew that this was exactly what I wanted. At first he said it would not be for sale until the end of the following week, but we bargained there in the gateway and he agreed to accept my offer on the understanding that he might continue to use the car until he left.

A photograph of this bargain that I still possess shows a scrubby little car of antiquated design with a dickey seat behind and a shiny silver greyhound on the radiator-cap. I christened it The Greyhound. Although of mean appearance, it had a heart of gold and for nearly two years it carried me for thousands of miles over the best and the worst mountain roads. Sometimes it was loaded with four passengers and quantities of camping equipment and baggage, besides a motley collection of unusual tools that were essential in the remoter parts of Mexico.

When I first went to Acapulco the greater part of the road had only just been cut and roughly surfaced with loose stone. Parts of it were barely passable and the lower section, through the sub-tropical *tierra caliente* of mountains and wild rivers, was a romantic and even a perilous journey. Large areas not far from the road were marked on the map as *tierra incógnita*. Bandits on the road were not unknown, petrol stations were few and far between and wild animals were sometimes seen.

The great bay of Acapulco, facing the Pacific, is big enough to anchor the whole of the British Navy. When I walked down to the curving strand I seemed to have arrived on a remote Pacific island. There were two or three buildings near the end of the road and a wooden hut on the white sand, half concealed by coconut palms. A short way along the coast a large lagoon reminded me of a stretch of the Zambezi river in the heart of tropical Africa. Strange birds fluttered invisibly among the dense foliage and I almost stumbled over several alligators as I forced a passage along the shore. Now, I have been told, Acapulco has been "developed" and its natural beauty has been tarnished by an agglomeration of hotels and all the paraphernalia that is supposed to attract tourists.

On the evening of the 18th May I left my desk at the British Legation and twenty minutes later I was on the road to Acapulco, accompanied by a friend who had never been there. As we climbed out of the Valley of Mexico, ringed by mountains and extinct volcanoes, lights began to appear in the City far below and, miles away to the south-east, the lovely snow summits of Popocatepetl and Ixtaccihuatl blushed in the glow from the setting sun.

I drove all through the night, except for an hour before dawn when we dozed in the car. After the first fifty miles much of the road, winding through the mountains towards the warmer regions of the State of Guerrero, was in poor condition and almost completely deserted. During the night we saw a few wild animals, including a large armadillo that showed up well in The Greyhound's headlights. As we passed through one tiny village a shot was fired, but we did not stop to find out if it was intended for us.

I had to wait two days at Acapulco because the cargo steamer was delayed, so we spent much of the time in the sea. The water was so phosphorescent that, as we waded ashore in the moonlight, our bathing costumes flashed and sparkled as if covered with silver sequins. On the 21st May, with The Greyhound on deck, the steamer put to sea and proceeded northwards in leisurely fashion. My companion stayed on for a day or two until he could get a lift back to Mexico City.

The mountains of Lower California looked bare and uninviting through the mist and there was nothing to hold attention except turtles floating in the sea. One of the crew told me that the captain sometimes stopped the ship and lowered a boat to catch a few turtles. It was easy, he said, to capture a couple of them when they were preoccupied with love-making on the surface. Not only turtles sometimes meet their fate in such circumstances.

It was in the days of Prohibition in America and, early one morning, we were overtaken by three "rum runners" and a United States coastguard cutter that was shadowing them. I was reminded of an occasion in New York when, arriving very late at night and wanting some coffee before going to bed, I asked a police officer where I could get it. To my astonishment, he directed me to a "speak-easy" where smuggled "hooch" was sold at fantastic prices. A girl, stunningly good-looking and endowed with persuasive charm, induced me to drink a glass of so-called champagne with her. I had sampled so much champagne at diplomatic receptions that I detected at once that this concoction had been doped. I said nothing, but prepared to leave. At once the girl and the proprietor of the establishment tried to persuade me to finish the drink, but I insisted on going. Even when I had paid the bill, equivalent to about three pounds sterling, they endeavoured to bar my exit and I practically had to force my way out. Already I was feeling muzzy in the head and, when I got back to my hotel, I was violently sick. Had I drunk any more I should undoubtedly have been robbed, even if nothing worse had befallen me, and I considered myself lucky to have escaped so cheaply. Obviously it would have been futile to inform the police. I was just another example of an innocent abroad.

On arrival at the docks at Wilmington I filled up The Greyhound with oil and petrol and drove the short distance into Los Angeles. The highway to the north, passing through the country of the famous redwoods (*Sequoia sempervirens*), the tallest and oldest trees in the world, lay before me.

I followed the chains of mountains that extend all the way from Mexico and Lower California to Alaska, forming the backbone of the continent and comparable to the Andes of South America. It was a wonderful drive through the states of California, Oregon and Washington and I longed for time to spend at the seaside resorts facing the Pacific where, incidentally, I had fleeting glimpses of some of the most beautiful women I have ever seen. Many of the gigantic redwoods, extending for miles in sombre forests, were thicker than the length of The Greyhound at the base of their unbelievably tall trunks. Every now and then the mountains beckoned through the blue haze.

As soon as I had embarked on this long drive I began to wonder whether it was not a crazy undertaking. I had been unable to find anyone to share the journey with me and I wondered how I would fare if I had an accident or a mechanical breakdown in some remote region north of the Canadian border. But it was useless to anticipate difficulties and, as I had a good understanding of The Greyhound's mechanism, I brushed any doubts aside and drove on.

Oregon is a land of roses and at Roseburg on the Umpqua river, where I spent a night, there were ramblers even on the telegraph poles. As I approached Portland I had a splendid view of distant Mount Hood, a snow-capped peak of nearly 12,000 feet in the Cascade Range, overlooking the Columbia river. I kept a sketch-book open on the seat beside me and occasionally drew rapid impressions of the constantly changing scenery.

I crossed the border at Blaine and, feeling the thrill usual on such occasions, stepped out of the car on to Canadian soil for the first time. The area around this frontier post was unspectacular, but I drove on to Vancouver with growing excitement, for I had reached the Fraser river, the western gateway to the Rockies that I had dreamed about as a little boy at my preparatory school.

Most Europeans who visit Canada arrive from the east and, if they go as far west as British Columbia, they approach by rail across the prairies. After leaving Calgary they look out for the first hazy outlines of the Rockies, rising like a great barrier from the plains. It is less usual to penetrate the mountainous region from the west and, in my experience, even more impressive.

The first railway across Canada, the Canadian Pacific, was constructed about thirty-five years before the first highway for motor traffic, which was only completed in 1922. In both cases the engineers had to solve problems that were unusually difficult, even for mountainous country, for much of the country was wild and unmapped, with many precipitous slopes and huge areas of forest that had been rendered almost impassable by fallen trees and the débris of forest fires and landslides. When I arrived I found that for long distances the road still had only a loose gravel surface, often deeply rutted.

Vancouver itself is backed by mountains and as soon as I drove away eastwards I was right in among them. The road, following the main river valleys and crossing several passes, winds in great loops that sometimes pass close to the international boundary and sometimes reach more than a hundred miles to the north. The early part, known as the Cariboo Highway, threads its way through the spectacular gorge of the Fraser river, winding continuously above precipices. At one moment The Greyhound was poised in the shadow of dark fir trees high above the river; at another it was passing through spray blown from the boiling rapids that filled the valley with a ceaseless roar. I stopped frequently and sometimes backed down the road to get a better view of a scene that had opened up suddenly as I rounded a bend. It was one of the advantages of going by car, that I could stop at will.

In the evening of the first day after leaving Vancouver I was driving up the valley of the Thompson river when heavy rain began. I reached Ashcroft, where the road turned east through a gap in the mountains for Kamloops, but the deluge was so terrific that I decided to wait there for a little while. Some people in a café warned me that, owing to the poor condition of the road immediately ahead, I should have to make a detour. But this rain would probably make even that route impassable and it would be wiser to stay in Ashcroft for the night.

The stage that I had set myself for that day ended at Kamloops, 286 miles from Vancouver, and I was determined to get there if I could. Before now, in Mexico, I had driven The Greyhound through regions that were said to be impassable and I felt that, if I did not persist in the face of difficulties, my whole time-table would be upset. Besides, experience of driving in bad conditions could only be had by actually driving in bad conditions. Ten minutes later, while rain was still falling, I set out again on the main road.

In a few minutes I reached a place where the road was flooded to such a depth that even The Greyhound could not get through. Someone told me of a rough branch road that rejoined the highway some miles farther on, but he added that there had been a cloud-burst over Cache Creek, precisely where I had to pass, and there was no hope of going any farther that night. Nevertheless, I went on.

It seemed unlikely that there would be any other cars on the detour, but, after negotiating about a mile of water and slimy mud, I found one lying on its side in a ditch. A few minutes later I came upon two cars, with their front buffers interlocked, in the middle of what looked like a lake. The drivers were sitting disconsolate inside their cars, having evidently given up attempts to extricate themselves.

The Greyhound slithered to a standstill in nearly a foot of muddy water. I took off my shoes and socks, turned up my trousers and waded out to the stranded cars. The drivers explained that, coming from opposite directions at the height of the storm, they had skidded slap into one another and stuck fast. They were not sure whether they were still on the road or not, for the water had continued to rise and now no trace of the road was visible.

I told them that I hoped to reach Kamloops. Impossible, they said. All the same, I was going to try, I declared, and waded back to The Greyhound to fetch a spade that had often been useful in the past and was to be invaluable many more times before I got back to Mexico City. In the gathering dusk I probed through the liquid mud until I found the edge of the road, tracing it for about a hundred yards until it curved to the right and eventually rose above the water level. The line passed some yards to one side of the interlocked cars, showing that they had left the road.

I went back to The Greyhound, dried my feet, put on my socks and shoes and settled into my seat. Then I lit a pipe. I cannot say that I was feeling particularly confident, but it seemed silly to give up and sit there for the night and, if I had to be bogged down, it might as well happen in an attempt to go on as in trying to go back.

The rain had eased a little, but it still made a sparkling curtain in my headlights. Concentrating on the alignment of the submerged road that I had discovered, I put the engine into low gear and expected the wheels to churn in the mud. But

slowly The Greyhound began to move ahead and I strained
every nerve to keep going in the right direction. Very cautiously
I steered past the stranded cars and vaguely heard encouraging
calls from their occupants. It was a panicky moment when I
had to decide to make the turn to the right, for I could feel a
tendency to swing sideways. But I somehow got round the bend
and out of the water. Not daring to stop, I sounded my horn in
triumph and heard an answering salute from behind. Much of
the road was still partially flooded and greasy, but I reached
Kamloops at half-past ten that night.

Now deep in the mountain region I began to appreciate the
character of these ranges: a compact archipelago of lofty islands
in a turbulent ocean of conifers. Strictly speaking, the name
"Rockies" should be applied only to the range that forms the
main watershed, extending along the British Columbia-Alberta
boundary. The ranges lying to the west of this have separate
names, such as the Selkirks and the Coast Range. The highest
mountain in Canada is Waddington, 13,260 feet, in the Coast
Range: the highest in the Rocky Mountains Range is Robson,
12,972 feet. There are said to be more than seven hundred
peaks exceeding 9,000 feet, but fewer than fifty of these rise
above 11,000 feet.

The greater part of the mountain region is composed of
stratified limestone, with intrusions of harder rock. Sometimes
the limestone strata are tilted, but the horizontal structure of
many of the mountains is a notable feature. Often, when I saw
a great mountain mass towering above the road, I was reminded
of flat-topped Table Mountain and of similar formations that I
had seen so recently in South Africa.

Throughout British Columbia—and not only in this part of
Canada—there are innumerable lakes. Some of them, occupy-
ing the north-south valleys, are considerably more than fifty
miles long. Kootenay Lake, which I had to cross with the car
by ferry, is an elongated stretch of water seventy-five miles from
north to south. Many of the smaller lakes, in their setting of
dark pines and towering snow-covered peaks, appear on a fine
day almost unbelievably beautiful. Often the colour of the
water, which is sometimes very deep, approaches that of
amethyst or the greenest kinds of jade, while the surrounding

cliffs of bare rock seem to glow with the tints of autumn leaves.

During the whole of my journey through the Rockies I had no trouble of any kind with the engine of The Greyhound. But the tyres, a new set of a well-known make, let me down far too often. The first puncture came before I had gone a thousand miles. In the Rockies I had three punctures in one day. On the following morning, in a narrow gorge, some chunks of rock fell in front of the car. There was no room to swerve to avoid them and a tyre burst. Later on, before reaching Chicago, I had two more bursts on a smooth concrete highway. On both occasions I managed to control the car, but hardly my temper. Another cause of delay in the Rockies was the burning out of the electric cables, due to overcharging of the battery. Thereafter I kept the lights on for two or three hours every day.

When I left Vancouver I was on the look-out for scenes that would make good pictures, but soon I was rejecting excellent subjects right and left. I could not spare much time for sketching, but I found myself driving on without drawing anything because it seemed impossible to choose. Occasionally, however, I forced myself to sketch some typical scene, knowing that it was but one of hundreds. With a camera I might have snapped a lot of them, but I am sure that by now they would have lost their power to recall what I felt. My few sketches, on the other hand, are still vivid reminders, for I absorbed so much in the process of drawing them.

In Kootenay National Park—one of Canada's splendid reserves—I came upon a scene that seemed to me the very essence of the British Columbian landscape and, although I was hoping, in another seventy miles or so, to reach Lake Louise, the goal of my early ambition, I could not resist stopping to make a drawing. Below me the broad Kootenay river wound in a great sweep in its valley between the Purcell Range and the Rocky Mountains Range. Dark fir trees and, here and there, pale trembling alders or poplars were clustered on the slopes rising from the water's edge. In the distant background jagged snow-peaks formed a mighty rampart of gleaming splendour. On a low gravel bank in midstream, just where the gurgling water swept round a sharp elbow, there stood a solitary moose, his great antlers prominent against the white foam beyond. He looked like the monarch of all he surveyed. While I watched, a dark cloud-shadow passed slowly across a fir-clad hill in the middle distance, emphasizing the sparkle of the river and the dazzling whiteness of the snowy summits. (Plate XVIII.)

As I approached Lake Louise I felt that I knew exactly what I was going to see, for its photographic likeness had been familiar for more than twenty years. But the reality exceeded my expectations. I pulled up in front of the Chateau Lake Louise, the immense hotel built by the Canadian Pacific Railway Company at the end of the lake facing Mount Victoria and Mount Lefroy, and I walked slowly down to the shore in a sentimental reverie.

Most of us, at some time, have probably fallen in love with a portrait but have never met the subject in the flesh. The portrait showed beautiful features, but it was a lifeless thing without a soul. At Lake Louise my vision sprang to life. The colours glowed; clouds rode majestically above the mountains, changing the subtle tints of the snow and ice with their shadows; the dark trees stood ready to whisper in the slightest current of air; the perfect reflections from the calm water enhanced the majesty of the cliffs towering on either side. At my feet little ripples came and went soundlessly, like the smile of a silent greeting.

I knew it would be hopeless to try to capture the perfect beauty of this scene in a painting, but after lunch I made a little sketch to remind myself of the colouring. Then I walked along the shore, among lofty spruce and tumbled boulders, and climbed until I had opened up a wider view of the mountains and the great ice cliffs of their glaciers. For some minutes I sat gazing, until a large mass of ice fell suddenly from the 200-foot vertical face of the hanging glacier on Lefroy, followed by a cloud of powdered snow. The sound of its fall reached me as a muffled echoing roar.

On the way back, although there was not a soul in sight, I heard a piercing whistle. It was repeated several times and I thought there must be someone trying to attract my attention. Then, guided by a whistle much closer, I distinguished a large

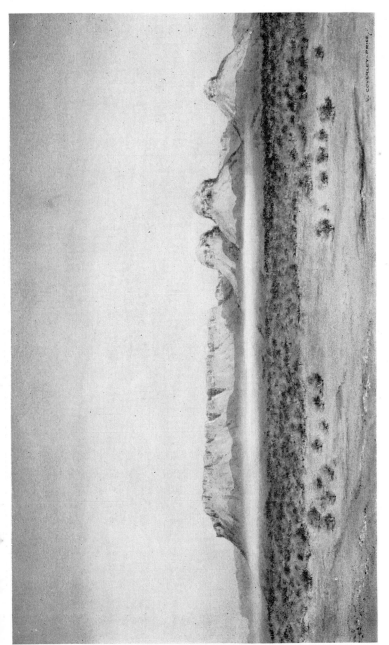

XVII. Sunset in the Great Karroo, South Africa

XVIII. Rocky Mountains landscape, Kootenay National Park, British Columbia Canada

marmot—*siffleur* the early settlers used to call it—sitting upright
on a rock not thirty yards away. It disappeared among the
boulders when I moved on, but the whistles continued until I
was back on the shore of the lake.

From Banff I drove eastwards to Calgary and on across the
prairies: I was to drive thousands of miles and to see many
wonderful sights before I returned to my post in Mexico. But
already, as the mountains faded in the mist behind me, I had
a longing to be back among them. Yet it seemed probable that
I could never pass that way again.

At about this time it was decided that a Foreign Office
official should be attached to the staff of the United Kingdom
High Commissioner in Canada, to serve as a political adviser
and to gain experience of Commonwealth affairs. A similar
appointment was made to South Africa. In 1934, when I had
been serving for about two years in Roumania, I was unexpectedly appointed to Ottawa. I was told, in official language,
that I was to be an "Administrative Assistant on the Staff of
the High Commissioner in Canada for His Majesty's Government in the United Kingdom", a title that could conveniently
be interpreted as "Secretary". Perhaps, after all, I should see
the Rockies again.

There was so much to see and to do in eastern Canada that at
first my wife and I saw little prospect of visiting the west.
I had plenty of work, but we snatched every chance, however
brief, to get to know our surroundings. At week-ends in winter
we took our skis to the wooded hills of Ontario and Quebec. In
summer we swam and fished in lakes both near and far afield
and sometimes we went camping. Two or three times we went
to New York and we explored the mountains of Virginia, where
I had passed in The Greyhound in 1931. One of my sketch-
books of that time contains impressions of the autumn tints in
the Alleghany Mountains, where the woods assume colours of
startling brilliance. But even these, far more striking than the
autumn colours we usually see in England, could not match the
almost incredible vividness of the colours of the Canadian
maples and elms. The purest reds and yellows in my paint-box
failed to reproduce the fiery quality of the Canadian woods
when the autumn sunshine was filtering through the foliage.

9

When we had been nearly a year in the Dominion I was able
to take leave for a trip across to the Pacific coast. We were
obliged to start in May, rather too early in the season for walking and climbing in the Rockies, so we decided first to go by
steamer up the coast of Alaska and to stop in British Columbia
on the way back. Travelling by the Canadian Pacific Railway,
across the prairies and through the mountain region, we took
about three and a half days to reach Vancouver. Then we
flew across the Strait of Georgia to spend a few days at Victoria
and to see something of Vancouver Island.

On the return flight the aircraft was caught in a sudden
squall and for several alarming minutes we could see nothing
at all. The pilot turned about in an endeavour to escape from
the blinding rain and then began to descend in a tight spiral
above the sea, in the hope of catching sight of a familiar island
that would enable him to check his course. The air was so thick
with cloud and rain that it seemed that we might hit the water
before seeing it, but suddenly the tops of some tall fir trees
appeared, only a few feet below, and we lurched violently
upwards, leaving our insides behind. In a few more moments
we emerged from the squall, visibility improved and the pilot
resumed his course for Vancouver.

The steamer that took us as far north as Skagway followed the
channel between the islands and the mainland and called at
several small places, where we were able to go on shore. From
Skagway we travelled more than a hundred miles farther north,
by the White Pass and Yukon Railway, to Whitehorse and we
took the opportunity to see a section of the "Trail of '98"—the
route followed by numberless hopeful, but often misguided,
prospectors during the notorious gold rush in the Yukon.
Terrible tales have been told of the hardships endured and of
the crimes committed during that reckless scamper to get rich
quickly and vestiges of the actual trail, worn by the feet of
thousands of adventurers with their wretched beasts of burden,
still remained in that bleak and inhospitable region as a pitiful
memorial to those who had sought riches before all else.

Skagway is a tiny town wedged in among the icy mountains
at the head of a long inlet from the sea. (Plate XIX.) In the gold
rush days it had a much larger population, among whom was

the famous Mrs. Pullen, who founded a considerable fortune on apple pies. Her most notorious contemporary was "Soapy Smith", the outstandingly bad man of Alaska. We visited his gaming parlour, now maintained as a museum.

Near Skagway, in heavily timbered country, we set out one day to climb "A B Mountain". The alphabetical name seemed a good one to start on, but we did not get very far. We enjoyed the approach, through a forest of hemlock and spruce—hoary trees draped heavily with lichen—but we soon got into deep snow. The ground was encumbered with fallen and rotting trees and sometimes we plunged waist-deep through snow bridges across their hidden trunks.

Presently, on a higher slope, we came across tracks in the snow and one set of these indicated unmistakably that a bear had passed that way not long before. It was obvious that we could not hope to go much farther through the deep, soft snow, but we were so eager to catch sight of the bear that neither of us would make a move to turn back. We went on steadily, pestered by mosquitoes and getting very hot.

Then, simultaneously, we stopped. There had been a sound among the trees on our right; a sound something like a grunt. My wife suggested going a bit farther to investigate, but another grunt pulled us up short. We spoke in whispers and decided that the sound probably came from the bear. The question that arose in my mind was "What kind of bear?" The small black bears that I had seen in the national parks in British Columbia were, I imagined, generally harmless. At Lake Louise one or two came fairly often to pick morsels out of the hotel's rubbish bins. But in Alaska there are big brown bears—one of the largest species in the world—and in some parts the even greater Kodiak bear is found.

We did not voice the real reason for our retreat, but, commenting that it was very hot, that the snow was much too deep and that the mosquitoes were terrible, we began to retrace our steps. Occasionally we looked back, for neither of us fancied the idea of scrambling over buried tree-trunks in an endeavour to dodge a pursuing brown bear.

In 1932—three years previously—it had been estimated that on Admiralty Island, which we passed on the way to Juneau, there were nine hundred Alaskan brown bears. I could not imagine how this estimate was reached, for it would be difficult even to estimate the number of dogs in Hyde Park at any given moment.

Most of the little ports at which we called in Alaska were constructed chiefly of wood, the buildings being clustered on the steep slopes of the mountains that rose abruptly from the water. Even some of the streets were paved with wooden planks. Dark trees clothed the lower slopes and often the smell of spruce was noticeable a long way from shore.

There is a great variety of wild flowers in this part of Alaska and, in spite of the short summer, some things seem to grow with tropical exuberance. We heard of strawberries two inches in diameter and cabbages weighing up to fifty pounds. We saw several birds that were new to us, including two bald eagles and a hermit thrush that was one of the most fascinating songsters we had ever heard. At Ketchikan, Wrangell and other places we saw collections of totem poles, grotesquely carved from whole tree-trunks. A totem pole is the crest of a clan, but it may also be used by individuals. It is a kind of Indian coat-of-arms.

During the whole journey I was busy with my pencil. Although rain and fog sometimes obscured the view, at dawn and at sunset there were glorious effects of light on the snow-capped mountains and the calm water in the deep inlets gave wonderful reflections that emphasized the peacefulness of the scene. In some parts of Alaska there are vast snow-fields and enormous glaciers that flow down to the sea. Our ship drew close to the Taku glacier, which is a mile wide at its foot with terminal cliffs from a hundred to three hundred feet high. At intervals huge masses of ice break off and fall into the sea with a tremendous roar and great disturbance of the water. The Mendenhall glacier, which we also saw, is seventeen miles long and nearly three miles wide at the face.

Daylight, sufficient to read by, persisted until half-past eleven at night. When the moon rose and the sky darkened the beauty of that mountainous coast, seen from the deck of the ship across the placid water, made us extremely reluctant to go to bed.

As the train carried us back through the gorge of the Fraser river into the rugged heart of British Columbia I remembered many of the minor incidents of my lonely drive there nearly five years before. Then I could see much more than I could see now from the railway. But at one place we spotted two moose and later there appeared no less than six black bears disporting themselves in a clearing.

Soon after three o'clock one morning, when the sun was just beginning to rise in a riot of glorious colour over Lake Shuswap, we left the train at Sicamous for two days' fishing. Unfortunately the fish were not very active, so we spent most of our time watching birds. Here, in the evenings, we heard the eerie cries of loons echoing across the lake—an unforgettable sound that we had often heard on lonely lakes in northern Ontario.

Leaving the railway again at Field, in the Rocky Mountains Range, we went by car to Emerald Lake. Here, instead of an ordinary hotel, there were some delightful little log cabins scattered about near the shore. The one that we chose was called Lone Pine Cabin. The lake is one of the most beautiful in a region of lovely lakes and I spent hours sketching among the fir trees at its edge. It is dominated by the precipitous mass of Mount Burgess and the colour of the water, which reminded me of jade rather than emerald, is a deep and most unusual blue-green.

One day we walked to the summit of Yoho Pass, but the snow was still deep up there. We came across the tracks of moose and heard sounds of their movement in the thick tangle of trees, but we could not see them. Near the top of the pass we found the prints of a bear, a hare and a large feline that we could not identify. Marmots whistled defiantly among the rocks, and chipmunks, which soon grow accustomed to human beings, came quite close to us.

The chipmunk is a delightful little rodent with black stripes down its back. Later on, near Mirror Lake and Lake Angus, we were assailed by a party of tame chipmunks that had discovered that we had some chocolate. I was about to break off a piece when one of them sprang on to my fist, pushed its head between my fingers and went off with the whole tablet.

Inevitably we went to Lake Louise and this time I had leisure to paint a more finished picture. Both here and at Banff we went for long walks among the mountains and always we were on the look-out for wild animals, birds and flowers. One evening near Emerald Lake, as we were approaching a foot-bridge, we saw some creature walking slowly ahead of us. It was about the size of a spaniel and it quickened its pace when it heard us. We followed, trying to identify it in the fading light, and every now and then, as it stumped across the long wooden bridge, it looked back nervously, like a naughty boy slinking away with stolen apples. We caught it up just as it left the bridge and saw that it was a large porcupine, much perturbed by our pursuit. It soon vanished among the trees.

At Moraine Lake we discovered a ruby-throated humming bird sitting on her nest, a beautifully made structure suspended from a low branch of a pine tree. On the summit of Sulphur Mountain, with magnificent views all round, we shared our lunch with a mountain sheep, even to the after-lunch cigarette. While I smoked mine, the sheep ate hers.

We spent a large part of one night paddling a canoe quietly about on Vermilion Lake and watching several beavers at work. While we lay still on the calm water, an exceedingly difficult thing to do when one is assailed by voracious mosquitoes, some of the beavers with their babies swam quite close to us and splashed us freely when they slapped their tails on the surface as they dived.

During a perfectly lovely walk to Consolation Lake, which lies under the towering ramparts of Mount Bident, we had some anxious moments when we heard a large animal stamping about among the trees only a few yards away. Discretion suggested retreat, but curiosity compelled us to remain. We waited and watched for some time, hoping to see a moose at close quarters, but the ominous sounds gradually receded. The reward for our patience seemed a bit niggardly: nothing but a few birds that might have been sandpipers.

We parted sadly from the Rockies, but I carried with me back to Ottawa a collection of paintings and sketches that still remind us vividly of happy days in that wonderful mountain region. Two years later I crossed the Dominion again, but the weather was dull and cloudy and I saw little of the glorious colouring that had been such a delight on my previous journeys.

Chapter VII

MOUNTAINEERING AND PAINTING IN
LATIN AMERICA: FROM MEXICO TO PERU

Mexico is probably associated in the minds of most people who have never been there with Cortes, Montezuma, revolution, big sombreros and perhaps music. To me the name recalls, first of all, mountains: some of the most beautiful mountain scenery in the world. About three-quarters of the many paintings and sketches that I made in Mexico have mountains as their subject or at least in the background.

Although the Mexican Republic is known officially as the *Estados Unidos Mexicanos*, we seldom speak of the United States of Mexico. The term "The United States" is understood to mean the central part of North America, between the Canadian border and the Rio Grande. But Mexico too is a federation— of about thirty States and Territories—and is also in North America. A friend once addressed a letter to me to "Mexico, South America". In my reply I pointed out that Mexico was not one of the South American republics. His next letter was addressed to "Mexico, Central America".

A chain of mountains, continuing the chain of the Andes of South America, trends in a north-westerly direction from the Isthmus of Tehuantepec and divides into three chains north of the twenty-first parallel. The central part of the country is a vast high plateau, cut into irregular sections by numerous deep ravines. There are at least thirty volcanic cones of considerable size, nine of them exceeding 10,000 feet. The highest mountain in Mexico is the Pico de Orizaba, a lovely cone rising above 18,000 feet that can sometimes be seen a long way out at sea after leaving Veracruz. I saw it for the first time from the railway on my way up to Mexico City.

The railway from Veracruz to the capital climbs for twelve hours through magnificent mountain scenery to the plateau at

8,ooo feet. It is the kind of scenery that keeps you jumping from one side of the coach to the other, in case you miss something. During nearly three years in the country I went down to Veracruz several times, usually to take an official bag to the ship and to collect the incoming bag from the Foreign Office, and I never grew tired of that scenery. It seemed a waste of time when I had to make the journey at night.

Once I had an alarming experience when I was in the observation coach at the rear of the train going back to the City. On a long steep gradient the coach suddenly became uncoupled. For a few moments none of the passengers realized what was happening: the coach slowed down and came to a stop. But then it began to roll back, steadily gathering speed. Several of us looked out and saw the train disappearing round a bend far above while we were moving rapidly downhill towards a curve which could not be negotiated at speed. Someone shouted, the guard grasped the situation—and the handle of the emergency brake—and soon the coach was brought to a standstill. It seemed a long time before the train came back to fetch us: long enough for me to make a sketch out of the window.

On another occasion, this time at night, the train came to an unexpected halt while skirting the precipitous wall of a deep valley. It was very dark and raining hard. For half an hour nothing happened, then a rumour went round that a landslide had carried away a section of the track ahead. A passenger got out and presently returned with confirmation. He had gathered that we were to sit there for several hours until another train arrived from the City at the other end of the gap. Meanwhile the crew of our train were trying to make some sort of footpath across the landslide, hoping that it would not move any more.

At long last we were told to get out and to walk up the line, carrying our luggage, until we reached the other train that was out of sight round a bend. I clutched my small suitcase and the Foreign Office bag and jumped down on to the track, landing in a ditch full of water. Still holding the precious bag in one hand, I helped other passengers to avoid the ditch and then we all filed up the track, between the train and the mountainside. With the aid of a lantern we were guided over the mass of mud and rocks that had cut the track, with rain pouring down our necks and threatening to set the landslide in motion again. When we climbed aboard the other train we were all soaked to the skin. I could have done with a plate of hot soup, for I was chilled in the tropical suit that I had been wearing in hot Veracruz, but there was no food on the train and we could only lie down or sit and shiver until we reached the capital in the morning.

Mexico is a land of sunshine and colour, where the people and their villages are as picturesque as the landscape. But when I was there twenty-five years ago I seldom saw a painting of a Mexican scene that showed real feeling for the beauty and charm of the country. A few topographical painters, most of them foreigners, had tried to depict the Mexican landscape, but it seemed to me that nature was far more lovely than their works suggested. They never probed far into the life of the people to reveal the rich background of colour and music and song.

On the other hand the Mexican painters of that time—Diego Rivera, Orozco, Goitia, Atl, Best-Maugard, Leal, Guzmán and others—appeared to be overwhelmed with feelings about the unhappy state of the Mexican peasants and the cruelties and debaucheries of their rulers, while their skill in handling paint had not developed far beyond that of the Mexican Indian. Many of their paintings were tendentious, expressing irony and bitterness with the directness of a caricaturist. The execution was often naïve and sometimes crude. Native ideas, derived largely from the struggles of the revolutionary period, were handled in a manner that betrayed at least some foreign influence, often on too big a scale to allow any concentration on beauty or quality. The paintings, sometimes on the walls of public buildings, seldom did justice to the Mexican landscape.

These were my own impressions: many people hold very different views. It is understandable that, when Mexican paintings are exhibited in Europe, the exotic subjects themselves convey something of the atmosphere of Latin America. Yet, apart from the subject-matter, most of the Mexican paintings that I saw when I was in the country suggested little that was peculiarly Mexican and struck me as being not particularly good. At least one writer, Ernest Gruening, has said that Rivera is "probably the greatest painter of our time". If this means that he has covered a greater expanse of wall with paint than any other painter, this may be true. There was plenty of tendentious comment in his vast combinations of distorted figures, but I could find little beauty in his work. In art I look for beauty. There was so much beauty in the Mexican landscape that I had hoped to see more of it in contemporary Mexican painting.

Mexico has a great deal of art, but the best of it is relatively old. The Maya and Toltec temples, dating from before the conquest, have great dignity both in construction and in decoration. Many of the churches, monasteries and residences of colonial times, strongly reminiscent of the architecture of old Spain, suit the climate and fit admirably into the landscape. Much of the peasant work in silver, pottery and wool, when made for use rather than for sale to foreign tourists, has simplicity and considerable charm. But already in the 1920's the increasing influx of tourists, encouraged by the development of highways and hotels, was affecting the design and quality of such products.

North of the Rio Grande standards of taste are different from those of Europe and American tourists will often buy things that few Englishmen would care to possess. The Mexican Indian's *zarape*, for example, a kind of woollen blanket used as an all-purpose cloak, can be a thing of beauty when made with wool in its natural colours of white, brown and black. But I saw *zarapes*, intended to appeal to the "*Norte Americanos*", that were a riot of hideous colours with crude designs in bad imitation of those on ancient temples. Certainly much of the contemporary Mexican art had qualities that would appeal to anyone, but it seemed to me that too often it lacked real beauty. There was beauty in Indian faces, in traditional costumes and in much of the genuine Mexican music, but the real beauty of Mexico lay —and I hope will be allowed to remain—in the mountain scenery and the wonderful flowers.

Twenty-five years ago it was not difficult to keep a horse in Mexico City and it was easy to ride out to the open country for an hour or so before breakfast. Up on Chapultepec Heights, where one could ride for miles on the high ground and among deep ravines, it was usually possible, in the early morning, to see the two great mountains, Popocatepetl and Ixtaccihuatl, getting on for fifty miles away in the south-east. Often I would rein in my horse and remain for some minutes gazing at their lovely snow-capped forms: Popocatepetl, "the mountain that smokes" and Ixtaccihuatl, "the white woman". I have been told that most of that open ground, which became so familiar to me and my horse, is now smothered with modern residences.

One of my earliest excursions to the mountains was to the volcano Ajusco, a few miles outside Mexico City, and to the Pedregal, a very ancient lava stream that is believed to have flowed from the crater. The solid, dark lava is terribly jagged and harsh to walk over and there are forbidding caves that are reputed to have been the haunts of bandits. But the vegetation —flowers and shrubs and cacti—is of great interest to botanists.

In the flat Valley of Mexico, within sight of the outskirts of the City, there are several smaller extinct volcanic cones and I climbed all of these in my search for good subjects to paint. But I never had to look far for subjects: there were plenty in the old streets of the City and innumerable landscapes outside. I think that I climbed into more unlikely places than any of my contemporaries, for I often tried to see a well-known view from an unusual angle. This quest took me on to church roofs and belfries, up trees and over walls where I probably had no right to go. If anyone appeared and objected to my activity, I usually managed to persuade him to help me and to satisfy his curiosity by asking him to watch while I painted.

Once, on the roof of a church outside the City, the guardian threw a brick at me before asking my business, but his aim was poor and the brick smashed a piece off a pinnacle instead of hitting me. He was so concerned over this mishap that he forgot to ask what I was up to and we discussed at great length how he could repair the damage. Then he settled down on his haunches and watched me at work on a picture.

On another occasion, when I was exploring the roof of a church near the town of Puebla, I found a corpse wrapped in a *zarape* in a corner. I had not often come across unattended corpses—I had done so only twice before—and I wondered what I ought to do. This specimen appeared to have been drying in the heat of the sun for some time, but I thought it best not to touch it. The interruption in my time for painting was annoying, but I went back down the obscure staircase by which I had come and tried to find a policeman or some other official. Eventually I discovered a rather sleepy man who said he had something to do with the local authorities and I told him what I had discovered. He seemed very little interested, but undertook to report the matter after the hour of the siesta. By now there was not much time left for sketching, so I got into my car and drove back to the City. I never heard any more about my gruesome find.

One of the other corpses that I came across by accident was lying on the pavement in a busy street in Mexico City and I passed it on my way to lunch at the British Club. No one gave it the slightest attention and I supposed, as presumably everyone else did, that it was awaiting collection by an ambulance. Anyway, it had gone when I went back that way after lunch.

I never counted how many paintings I made in Mexico, but some years after I had left the country a selection of about sixty of them was exhibited in London. They included architectural subjects, flower paintings and studies of Mexican peasants and dancers, but the majority of them contained a view of mountains. I must have painted Ixtaccihuatl and Popocatepetl at least a dozen times, from far and near and from many different directions, before I had an opportunity to climb either of them. They are better subjects for an artist than for a mountaineer, but they are higher than any mountain in Europe and, if altitude is an objective, that is a reason for climbing them. A better reason is to see the view, which is superb from either mountain.

With three friends I planned a week-end expedition to Ixtaccihuatl, which rises well above 16,000 feet but is the lower of the two mountains. In my little car, The Greyhound, we drove to Amecameca, the small town a few miles from the mountain, where we had arranged to have mules waiting to carry our baggage. The muleteer, a jovial happy-go-lucky Mexican, confessed that he was an ex-bandit who had settled down to a more orthodox existence. We took with us plenty of warm clothing and we improvised sleeping-bags, with blankets and some straw to line them. My bag, which reached only a little above my waist, was the largest Foreign Office bag I could find, made of stout canvas.

For several hours we followed a track through the foothills among beautiful pine woods, where many of the trees were heavily draped with lichen, and by the evening we had reached a point just above the tree-line at about 13,000 feet. The permanent snow-line was not far above and here our bandit-guide showed us a cave in which to shelter for the night. It was little more than a large hollow in the face of a cliff of volcanic rock, with an overhang of several feet, but we dumped our belongings among the rocks, made a small fire with wood that the mules had carried and prepared a meal. (Plate XX.)

It soon became extremely cold and we huddled in our wrappings on the hard ground near the remains of the fire. Before long sleet began to fall, driven by a chilly wind, and we moved under the shelter of the overhanging rock; but none of us got much sleep.

Before dawn we were up again, feeling very stiff and cold, but we made some coffee and stamped about until it was light enough to start. The muleteer said that, as we were leaving the baggage in a dump until our return, we might as well ride the mules as far as the snow-line. This struck me as a crazy thing to do, for the ground was encumbered with enormous boulders and, although mules are often remarkably sure-footed on rough ground, it was much easier to clamber here on foot. However, two of my friends took the muleteer's advice. Before we had climbed far I heard a scuffling sound behind me and, looking round, saw one of the mules standing on its hind legs with its forelegs on a large boulder that it was trying to surmount. The next instant it toppled backwards and its rider fell hard on the rocks, injuring his back.

This accident upset our programme, but the injured man insisted that the rest of us should go on while he rested at the site of our bivouac. The muleteer remained with him and later on took him slowly down the mountain on a mule.

The climb to the top of the mountain was not in the least difficult, being merely a fairly steep ascent on ice and snow, but above 15,000 feet we all felt the effects of the altitude, though we were accustomed to living at about 8,000 feet. The central and highest part of the mountain was a broad domed expanse of hard snow and ice, but in places there were cornices fringed with some of the longest icicles I had ever seen. We stayed on the summit for about half an hour and, with rather cold fingers, I made a drawing of the mighty head of Popocatepetl, about two miles away to the south. (Plate XXI.) The Valley of Mexico, shimmering in the early sun, extended far into the blue distance, ringed by lesser mountains, but owing to haze we could barely distinguish Orizaba and other great peaks in the east.

The descent to the snow-line was rapid and soon we had loaded our kit on to the three remaining mules and were making the long trek back to the car. It was nearly dark when we reached it and we were glad to find that our injured friend, who had arrived just ahead of us, was already feeling much better. I think he decided never again to try to climb a mountain on a mule, but he soon made a complete recovery.

This friend was a great walker and had twice taken part in the London to Brighton walking race, in which he was among the leaders. One day he asked me if I would accompany him on a walk from Mexico City to Cuernavaca, the lovely week-end resort in the State of Morelos forty-six miles from the capital. I dislike walking long distances on roads, but there was no practicable footpath and it was out of the question to attempt to force a passage over the lava-encrusted mountains that lay between the City and Cuernavaca. I knew the road well, having often driven The Greyhound to Cuernavaca when I felt in need of a week-end change at the lower level, about 5,500 feet. It crossed the plateau for about nine miles, climbed to the summit of the pass at 10,000 feet and then descended in continual curves for more than twenty miles, passing through wild and densely wooded country.

I agreed to make the attempt, though I had no special walking shoes like those that my friend wore. Mine were the best I could produce, a pair of ordinary black shoes that had been made for me in London. We started from the centre of the City at half-past four in the afternoon and we marched away at a good pace towards the mountains. As night approached the traffic on the road almost ceased and, on the way up to the pass, we looked back over the vast silent Valley of Mexico, where groups of lights were appearing in the town and in the outlying villages. Near the top and again in the dark woods beyond the summit we were challenged by soldiers at military posts, who were presumably keeping a look-out for bandits. Once or twice we stopped for a short time to refresh ourselves with coffee from a thermos flask, but we maintained a steady speed through the night.

The road that we were following had recently been improved by the removal of some unnecessarily sharp hairpin bends and already the abandoned curves were becoming overgrown with vegetation. At least once one of these disused backwaters furnished bandits with an excellent trap for their victims. The gang stopped a succession of cars coming from the capital and ushered them into the abandoned loop out of sight. When they had several prosperous-looking cars in the trap they allowed any further traffic to proceed down the road, in blissful ignorance of the robbery that was going on a hundred yards away among the trees. Having relieved the passengers of their valuables, the bandits let their victims depart. The nearest police or military post was a good many miles away and the bandits had time to make off with their swag.

The last few miles down the long slope into Cuernavaca were torture to our feet. My shoes fitted so well that I had no sign of a blister, but the soles of my feet, after so many hours of pressure on the hard road, were burning as if on hot iron. However, we managed to keep going and we reached the inn where we had booked rooms at half-past four in the morning, having completed the forty-six miles in twelve hours. We went to bed and slept like logs.

When I first arrived in Mexico the British Minister, Sir Esmond Ovey, who later became British Ambassador in Moscow, had a delightful house in Cuernavaca and I stayed with him there several times. The garden consisted of three connected courtyards or *patios* with a fountain, numerous subtropical plants and great masses of bougainvillea sprawling over the walls and roofs. The Minister had persuaded his

American colleague, Mr. Dwight Morrow, the father-in-law of Colonel Lindbergh, to acquire the old buildings next door and they were converted into another fascinating residence, with a swimming pool and a small square tower, called a *mirador*, which commanded a splendid view of "Popo" and "Ixta".

It was delightful to be a guest of the Morrows and their daughters, and the bathing parties in their pool, with drinks in the warm sunshine afterwards, are among my most pleasant memories. On the day after my walk from the City I made a painting of the distant mountains from the mirador of the house. (Plate XXII.)

In those days Cuernavaca was a happy, dreamy place where one could relax among wonderful flowers in the sunshine and recover from the sometimes trying effects of the higher altitude of Mexico City. But friends who have been there recently tell me that it has been developed as a tourist centre and has consequently lost a great deal of its charm. I often stayed at the rather dilapidated but peaceful Borda Gardens Inn, which was once the temporary home of the ill-fated Emperor Maximilian and the Empress Carlota.

Later on, with one of the Ixtaccihuatl party and two other friends, I arranged to climb Popocatepetl, which approaches 18,000 feet. The journey to the mountain and the ascent to the snow-line were much the same as in the case of the other mountain, but this time we had to bivouac without any shelter. The climb to the summit was a long and fairly slow progress up a steep slope of snow that had become almost as hard as ice. As I was the only member of the party who had an ice-axe I led the way and cut steps where necessary. During the last 2,000 feet, as we had come straight from our desks without special training, we had to stop panting at frequent intervals. One of the party declared that he could never get to the top, but did get there; another swore that he would get there at all costs, but unluckily was overcome by mountain sickness and had to go down again without reaching it.

It was an exciting moment when I arrived at the brink of the crater of this immense volcano and looked down into its gloomy depths. The sun had only just lifted above the horizon and far away in the west, beyond the floating gardens of Xochimilco

XIX. In the Lynn Canal near Skagway, Alaska

XX. Bivouac on Ixtaccihuatl (16,200 feet), Mexico

V. COVERLEY-PRICE

XXI. The summit of Popocatepetl (17,794 feet) seen from the summit of Ixtaccihuatl, Mexico

XXII. Ixtaccihuatl and Popocatepetl seen from Cuernavaca, Mexico and the jagged shape of the Sierra de Ajusco, a low bank of grey cloud extended across the horizon. While the three of us stood on the sharp rim of the crater the sun shone upon us and began to tinge the distant cloud. We then noticed a dark cone standing against the cloud bank and we wondered what mountain it could be, for we knew of no other large volcanic cone in that direction. As the light strengthened the cone became more sharply defined and suddenly we realized that we were looking at the shadow of the upper part of the mountain on which we were standing. The shadow shrank rapidly and soon it had disappeared. The ice near the top of Ixtaccihuatl flashed and sparkled as the sun rose higher. Here and there in the superb panorama of the Valley of Mexico the light picked out buildings in the City and in some of the scattered towns and villages.

We walked for some distance round the rim of the crater, which is about half a mile in diameter and probably six hundred feet in depth to the lava floor. There was a strong smell of sulphur in the air and the interior of the crater was partially obscured by smoke issuing from cracks in the floor and from fumaroles in the walls. It is said that some of the Spanish invaders who accompanied Cortes collected sulphur from this crater for making gunpowder and, during the centuries since then, untold quantities of sulphur have been taken from it. Periodically the volcano increases in activity and there has been at least one considerable eruption since I was there.

As soon as we had got down from the icy upper part of the cone and were on hard snow we adopted the accepted method of descent and sat down to toboggan. It was a damping, but extremely swift, procedure and it did not take long to cover the 3,000 feet or so to the snow-line.

A volcanic cone, having a certain symmetry, has a peculiar fascination among mountains. One of the most striking active volcanoes in Mexico is Colima in the mountainous region near the Pacific coast. It stands among forests and vegetation grows almost to the top, except where the most recent eruption destroyed it. In the east there is another fine volcano, named Malinche, which can be seen from Popocatepetl. The name Malinche was given by the Aztecs to Doña Marina, who was the interpreter and, history records, the mistress of Cortes.

The mountains of Mexico are infinitely varied, from the arid ranges of Lower California and the northern states to the tropical areas of the south, where the so-called organ-pipe cactus and many other varieties grow in profusion to the size of large trees. In recent years these mountain regions have been made more accessible by new highways, but in 1931, when I drove The Greyhound round North America, some areas could be crossed only with mules or on horseback. The section of the pan-American highway from Laredo on the Rio Grande to Mexico City, which climbs among mountains for most of the 800-odd miles, was still for the greater part only a plan on paper.

I have told in the last chapter how I drove to Canada and then crossed the continent from Vancouver to New York before turning southwards for Texas and the Rio Grande. When I reached Laredo on the Mexican border I was beginning to feel tired of the long hours at the wheel, but there was still the best part of 1,000 miles to go.

The Greyhound's last lap, from the border back to the Mexican capital, was by far the most difficult part of the whole journey. The City stands a mile and a half higher than Laredo, but the total distance to be climbed through that region of almost continuous mountains was much greater than that.

As far as Monterey, which is surrounded by hills and dominated by the distinctive Saddle Mountain, the road was fairly good. On the night when I got there I had supper in the patio of a small hotel, among palm trees and masses of bougainvillea beneath a sky dotted with brilliant stars. Next day I managed to reach Ciudad Victoria, 180 miles farther south, but the loosely gravelled surface of the road was often in shocking condition. From there I had a choice of two routes, but I was told that, except for a few miles, both were mere mule tracks winding through the mountains. The rainy season had begun and the more easterly route was already an impassable quagmire. The other, heading south-west through San Luis Potosí and Queretaro, was only used in the dry season and was probably just as bad.

It was unfair to expect The Greyhound to emulate the gymnastic feats of mules, but I was determined to complete the journey if possible. I could obtain no map of the route. At four o'clock in the morning, hoping to cover the two hundred miles to San Luis Potosí in daylight, I drove out of Victoria and followed the stony track into the mountains. During the next twelve hours The Greyhound crawled up abominably steep gradients with numerous hairpin bends like the zig-zags of an alpine path, forded five small rivers in the bottom of ravines anything from fifteen to thirty feet deep, jolted and staggered among boulders and scrub and twisted among cacti for miles, where the sharp wooden spines scattered on the ground threatened to puncture all four tyres at any moment. Often I got out to remove large boulders or to prepare the way for a dash through an area of greasy mud. Several times I had to lighten the car, by carrying my luggage to the top of a fearfully steep incline, and to build stone ramps to help The Greyhound to surmount great steps of solid rock.

By the afternoon I was tired and hungry, having eaten nothing since before dawn. I pulled up on the brink of a ravine, for at least the tenth time, and got out to examine the ground. As usual the way down was all rocks and boulders and abominably steep. Oddly enough, there was little water in the bottom, but heavy clouds were piling up over the mountains and I knew only too well that, if I delayed, I might have to drive through another wild torrent.

I pushed my way through the cactus that choked the bottom of the ravine and reached the forty-foot cliff on the other side. I was just going to examine the track, a sort of glacis of boulders and shale, that zig-zagged up to the top when something glinting caught my eye. It was a splinter of glass and nearby was a dented fragment of a car's mudguard. Here, evidently, was the place I had been warned about, where a car had gone over the edge, killing the three people in it. There had been two cars, trying to make their way to San Luis Potosí, but they had both stalled, slipped back in the shale and turned over.

It was a grim moment. I was in the midst of a wild mountain region without a sign of human habitation. I had seen no one for hours. But I remember hearing a boom of thunder in the distance and the impression of my utter loneliness suddenly came into focus. I could no longer suppress the feeling that this last lap of the journey was a foolhardy effort; but I had to go on.

I got back into the car and started the engine. The sun broke
through for a moment and, as if to encourage me, the greyhound emblem on the bonnet glittered like silver. Very slowly
we bumped and slithered down into the ravine and somehow
reached the bottom intact. But there I felt like a man who has
walked into a minefield. It was out of the question to turn back,
but just as risky to go on. Once more I got out to inspect the
track; a precaution I had taken dozens of times. I scrambled
round two of the hairpin bends and found the place where the
car must have gone over. I could do little to make it safer, but
I pushed some boulders out of the way, rearranged some slabs
to widen one of the bends and then lugged a great chunk of
rock to the brink of the fatal precipice. I thought it might help,
if The Greyhound slipped back.

By now the clouds were thick again and there was a rumble
of thunder. The Greyhound took the first bend in a jerky rush
and, though a shower of stones clattered down behind, managed
to keep going until we had passed the scene of the accident.
But then the engine stalled and the car slid backwards in the
loose shale.

Luckily my special rock pulled us up. After a pause I tried
again, several times, but the tyres only ground into the shale
until I thought they would burst. I unloaded all my luggage
and equipment, carried it higher up the slope and dumped it
as an objective for the next effort. Then I arranged a few more
slabs of rock in front of and behind the wheels. This time I
made it. An avalanche of stone shot over the precipice behind,
but The Greyhound staggered on upwards until we were out
of the ravine.

After that we crawled on for miles, trying to keep on the
track that seemed to wander aimlessly into the distance. Every
moment I expected a puncture, or that something vital underneath would be smashed by a boulder. At last we came to a
wide valley leading to a little place called Tula, tucked away
just beyond the steel-blue hills. But it took ages to get there,
because the whole valley floor was a maze of ravines, cracks and
hollows and I had to pick a route by trial and error. Then,
without warning, a thunderstorm burst overhead. Barely two
hundred yards to my left a tree was struck by lightning, with an

explosion like a bomb. For several more miles I had to cope with oceans of greasy mud and dozens of young mountain torrents that had not been there a short time before.

After more than fourteen hours at the wheel, in which I had covered only seventy miles, it was a great relief to arrive somewhere. Tula's church stood on high ground in the midst of a cluster of adobe buildings. There was a deep ravine, with a bridge, between this nucleus and the rest of the town, which was hedged about with organ-pipe cactus and trees. While I was filling up with petrol three people offered me a room for the night and I chose that of an old lady whose house was just across the street. It had a large porte-cochère—a good shelter for The Greyhound—leading into a small patio and it reminded me strongly of some of the middle-class French homes that I had seen in Touraine. There were even a few pieces of old French furniture in my room.

Without delay the old lady prepared me a Mexican meal and, while I ate it, she came and sat beside me in the patio beneath an enormous mass of purple bougainvillea that sprawled from the tiled roof. She really was a charming person. While she fanned away the flies, she told me about the days of the Revolution and asked for details of my journey and about Mexico City, where she had never been.

After supper I went back to the little shop where I had bought petrol and asked if they could find someone who could guide me next morning to San Luis Potosí. Several candidates presented themselves, but the first had been drinking *pulque* all the afternoon and was not fit even to cross the street. Another who had been stranded in Tula on account of the rains, offered to go about half way, as far as his home village, on condition that I stuffed his wife and child in among the baggage.

The one that I chose had actually driven a car over the route, in the dry season, but after we had crawled a few miles he was by no means sure that we were going in the right direction. So much of the track was under water that we constantly lost all sign of it and it seemed a miracle when we picked it up again. The whole of this mountainous region was sparsely inhabited and even at the big ranches that we passed we saw only a few white-clad Indians.

My guide told me that some of these Indians were inclined to be hostile to strangers and at one ranch they not only refused to give us water for the radiator, but they threw stones after us as we drove away. At another place, however, we were given a most friendly reception. Inside a cactus enclosure we found a hut built of bamboos, mud and banana leaves where an Indian and his wife and another young woman were about to have a meal. They insisted that we should join them, so we sat on the ground by the charcoal fire, while pigs and chickens scavenged around us and under the donkeys tethered outside and lizards darted boldly into the circle for scraps of food. Meanwhile a wizened old woman, her dusky face full of wrinkles, knelt beside us in the mud while she flattened out the dough to make *tortillas* and laid them on a hot sheet of iron over the fire. The slap, slap, slap of her hands was a typical sound, heard all over Mexico.

About six weeks earlier, a few miles from here, a post office car had been attacked by bandits, who had piled a mound of rocks at a point where a ravine filled with cactus had to be crossed. When we reached the spot my guide, who knew the postman, told me how shots had suddenly been fired in the darkness. With great presence of mind—and phenomenal good luck—the postman had launched his car at the obstacle and somehow crashed over it. The radiator was badly damaged and there were bullet holes in the car, but he had got away in the darkness.

After many prolonged encounters with mud, rocks and ravines we at last reached San Luis Potosí, both feeling thoroughly exhausted. It had been a new experience to me to mend punctures with the wheels half buried in mud, but much worse was to come. Potosí stands at 6,000 feet and I still had a long way to climb.

Very early in the morning, almost before it was light, I set out again on the lonely trail towards the south. Somehow I managed to cover the fifty miles to San Luis de la Paz, though it took the best part of ten hours. But now it was a race against time. It was Saturday and I was due back in Mexico City, still more than two hundred miles away, on Sunday night. If I could reach Queretaro by nightfall I ought just to be able to do it, for the last part of the journey would be on a real road.

After an hour's hunt I found a cheerful young Mexican named Diego, who said that he knew the route and could drive if I wanted a change. I began to feel better, now that I had a companion again; but very soon we got into difficulties in the mud. Then, abruptly, the track disappeared in open plough-land. We crawled on, trying to pick it up again, until The Greyhound suddenly sank in a sort of bog. I got out and at once went up to my knees in black mud. The mud was well over the axles and even over the running-board on one side. This looked like the end.

Then I saw a peasant and his dog in the distance and I floundered across to ask him if there was any chance of getting help. Within half an hour he had fetched three other peasants and a yoke of the heftiest oxen I had ever seen. We began by removing all the baggage and tools to a patch of firmer ground and then we stuffed a lot of brushwood and stones down under the wheels. It was no use trying to dig away the soupy mud, but we levered up the car with a stout pole and then hitched the oxen to the steel cable that I had bought for just such an eventuality.

The oxen sank in up to their bellies, but they got The Grey-hound moving and in another minute or two it was more or less clear of the morass. But the little dog, bounding round with excitement, all but disappeared in the slush and had to be hauled out by the scruff of the neck.

The peasants were astounded that I had got so far and they said that it would be quite impossible to go another yard. The ground was sodden for miles around and already we could hear the thunder of another storm. It was now nearly dark, so I was forced to admit that this was my field of Waterloo.

I shall never forget the retreat to San Luis de la Paz. The black shadows cast by the headlights and by occasional flashes of lightning made the rocky ravines look even deeper than they were. In an attempt to avoid a landslide that had given us a great deal of trouble on the way out we drove up on to a boulder-strewn hillside. But then, without warning, The Grey-hound slipped sideways and stuck once again in deep black mud. My companion, Diego, was all for spending the night in the car, but I insisted that we should not give in until we knew for certain that we could not get out.

Five times we dug away masses of mud, forced chunks of stone in under the wheels and tried to extricate the car. At the sixth attempt, just as the rain began, we succeeded. It was a nightmarish drive, through torrential rain and forked lightning, back to San Luis de la Paz, but we got there at eleven o'clock that night.

In the morning I went to the railway station, an hour before the train was due, to arrange for The Greyhound to be sent to Mexico City, but not a single official was to be found and I began to think that perhaps nothing functioned on Sunday. However, the ticket office opened at last, as the train came in sight, and I just had time to scribble instructions on an envelope and to push it, with some money, into the hand of the solitary official.

As I sat sleepily in the carriage, watching the blue mountains and the sodden plains rolling past, I promised myself that if I ever saw The Greyhound again, I would have the silver emblem on the bonnet mounted on a wooden pedestal, as a souvenir of the car's gallant endurance. The car did arrive, a few days later, and it still wore its honourable coat of mud. But the tools—and the silver emblem—were missing.

A few months later, when I was due to be transferred to another post, I received a letter from the Secretary of the Royal Geographical Society reminding me that I had asked to be informed if there ever came a chance for me to join an expedition to South America. Professor J. W. Gregory, the Secretary told me, was planning an expedition to the Andes of Peru and, as I could speak Spanish, it was suggested that I might like to accompany him as interpreter. This was the opportunity for which I had been waiting, to paint among mountains in a little-known part of the world, and I at once got into touch with Professor Gregory. At the same time I asked the Foreign Office if I might be placed for about six months *en disponibilité*; that is to say, on unpaid leave. The Foreign Office granted my application and the Professor agreed to my joining him, and it was arranged that we should meet in Lima early in February, 1932.

Professor Gregory was well over sixty, but he was a man of indomitable will and enthusiasm and a most distinguished geologist. He had explored in many parts of the world and it was he who elucidated the main features of the structure of the eastern half of the continent of Africa during a journey that he described in his book *The Great Rift Valley*, published in 1896. For four years he was Professor of Geology at Melbourne and he occupied the Chair of Geology at Glasgow for twenty-five years. From 1928 until 1930 he was President of the Geological Society of London. He was endowed with great powers of physical endurance and an amazing memory; he regarded the world as a whole and applied intense industry to the solution of its geological problems; yet he was remarkably modest and unassuming.

It was sad to be leaving Mexico, for I had enjoyed my time there enormously, but I could look forward to a most interesting adventure in the immediate future. My luggage was packed, most of it to be shipped to my next post, and in the evening I took a last peep at the garden of my bungalow. The hundreds of heavenly blue flowers of Morning Glory that had been open all day on the whitewashed wall were now closed. I went by the night train to Veracruz and sailed for Havana on the following morning. My last sight of Mexico was the snowy head of the Pico de Orizaba fading in the mist.

I spent three days at Havana, waiting for a ship to Kingston, Jamaica, and there I changed into a third ship for the voyage through the Panama Canal and down the Pacific coast to Callao, the port of Lima. The whole journey took seventeen days. Professor Gregory arrived a fortnight later, accompanied by Miss McKinnon Wood, who had an expert's interest in collecting fossils. It was arranged that Mr. Tarnawiecki, a mining engineer of Polish origin who had worked in Peru for nearly thirty years, should accompany the expedition. His local knowledge, combined with considerable geological experience, proved invaluable.

Professor Gregory was chiefly concerned to solve certain problems of structural geology, for he had wondered, ever since his investigation of the Earth movements that had caused the formation of the Great Rift Valley, what disturbances had taken place in the Andes. First he wished to examine the coastal deserts of Peru, particularly in the southern section where there is a broken chain of mountains between them and the Pacific Ocean. Then he proposed that we should travel right across the Andes through a region geologically almost unknown; a journey of some four hundred miles extending from sea level to altitudes above 16,000 feet. Finally he planned to examine the eastern side of the Andes, following the Vilcanota river to its junction with the Yanatili. There, where this great tributary of the Amazon becomes the Urubamba, we hoped to find Indians with dugout canoes who would take us on for hundreds of miles down the river, northwards and roughly parallel with the main chain of the Andes.

This programme promised plenty of opportunity to paint unknown mountain scenery and I provided myself with a good stock of equipment, in special waterproof bags. From Lima we travelled southwards by car for several hundred miles and from three different headquarters in turn we traversed the desert in many directions, collecting geological specimens and examining the rocks of the coastal cordillera. This region is one of the most arid in the world. Lesser rains fall there about once in seven years and heavier rains at intervals of about thirty-four years.

Although I could not have been more amateurish as a geologist, my experience as a climber enabled me to clamber about among the bare, rocky foothills collecting specimens from different rock strata and making records with the aid of a compass and an aneroid barometer. Often, while the others were busy with geology, I went off alone to make drawings of the various peculiar formations that we saw. In this waterless region, most of it devoid of any sign of vegetation, we sometimes drove for miles over hard, flat *pampas* until brought to an abrupt stop in a patch of soft sand. Often we made our bivouac in the open desert and occasionally near the shore, where condors ranged up and down the coast and circled, with motionless wings, high above the cliffs.

The condor, one of the largest birds of prey, has a wing-span of nine to ten feet and it has been described as the "Monarch of the Andes"; but I seldom saw one far inland. Near the coast condors were plentiful and once, when I was returning down a long talus of scree after climbing in the rocky foothills, two of them pursued me for more than half an hour, circling so close above my head that I could see their gloating eyes and hear the wind in their pinion feathers. Doubtless they were hoping that I would fall and provide a meal, for they swept away as soon as I had reached safer ground.

It has been said that faith can remove mountains, but the one that we moved in the coastal deserts required the use of scientific instruments. This was Monte Criterion, which had been marked on the Admiralty chart—apparently on the basis of observations taken from the sea by officers of H.M.S. *Beagle* during that ship's famous voyage with Charles Darwin on board—as a mountain rising to 5,800 feet. We made quite a long search to find it, for it was not precisely where expected, and we climbed to the eight-toothed ridge along its top. Our aneroids, checked by boiling-point determinations at sea level, showed its altitude to be only 3,250 feet.

Our final headquarters in the coastal region was a little town called Nazca, where we were obliged to stay for three weeks while a prolonged hunt was being made for a sufficient number of mules to carry us and our equipment on the next stage of our journey into the Andes. During the delay we continued to explore in the desert and I made numerous sketches. Owing to the primitive conditions we had a foretaste of hardships to come, but I managed to continue the luxury of a daily hot bath, using a saucepan of water which I poured into a small enamelled basin the size of a Christmas pudding bowl.

CHAPTER VIII

ADVENTURES AS AN EXPLORER AND ARTIST
IN THE ANDES

THE French have a saying, attributed to Madame du Deffand, famous for her literary salon in the eighteenth century: *"Il n'y a que le premier pas qui coûte."* This saying can be applied aptly to many undertakings and particularly to exploration. Plans and preparations are necessary, but until the first step is taken they are valueless, for they can lead nowhere.

Our first step on the long trek across the central Andes of Peru, a multiple chain of mountains several hundred miles in width, was the most difficult to take. When we had finished our work in the coastal desert, checked our equipment and packed our food supplies we were all eager to turn eastwards through the foothills on the next stage of our journey. But still we had no mules.

On our arrival in Peru, about six weeks earlier, we had believed that it would be possible to hire or buy in the coastal region a sufficient number of mules to carry our baggage over the Andes. But we soon discovered that motor transport had almost entirely replaced mule transport near the coast, although the improvement of roads had not kept pace with this sign of progress. With the greatest difficulty Tarnawiecki, who had travelled widely in other parts of Peru, managed to hire two mules for a limited period. With these and a young muleteer he set off into the mountains to try to find the essential means of transport in some village where mules were still used to carry sugar, coca leaves and other products to Cuzco. The day when we expected him to return passed, as did several more days, and we grew anxious about him.

At last he arrived, with nineteen mules and two muleteers who looked like a couple of brigands in a pantomime. He had found them at a village four days' journey inland. Apaico, the

156

head muleteer, was as obstinate as his animals and Tarna-wiecki told us that he had practically had to threaten to shoot him if he would not bring his mules down to the coast.

The delay had been tiresome, particularly for the leader of the expedition, Professor Gregory, who, as a consecrated geologist, was straining at the leash to get at the Andean rocks. I, as a mere auxiliary with little knowledge of geology, had been doing my best to collect specimens and to master the use of various instruments that were supposed to supply us with information on which to base our maps and diagrams. But my chief functions, more or less self-imposed, were to act as interpreter wherever Spanish was spoken and to produce a pictorial record of the expedition. I was not of much use as a linguist in the high Andes, where Quetchua was spoken, and I was probably far below par as an amateur photographer. But I sketched avidly, as if my life depended on it, and I brought back from Peru more than a hundred and fifty finished paintings. How lucky I was to be able to bring them back will appear later on.

When we speak of the Alps we are generally referring to the clusters of snowy peaks in Switzerland, spread over an area about two hundred miles long and a hundred miles wide where, for the past century, Englishmen have indulged in two of their most risky forms of sport. When we speak of the Himalaya we are thinking of that much longer rampart, between India and Tibet, which contains Everest and many more of the world's highest peaks, of which the greatest have now been conquered by climbers of various nationalities. But when we refer to the Andes, which we seldom do, it is probable that we hardly know what we are talking about. To most people the Andes mean the backbone of South America and that is about all.

The whole chain of the Andes is something like five thousand miles long, perhaps three times the length of the Himalaya. In central Peru, where I went to explore, it is about four hundred miles wide, but farther south it is even wider. It contains a good number of high peaks to tempt the mountaineer—the highest is Aconcagua, nearly 23,000 feet—and many of them remain unclimbed. Description of the Andes is a matter for geologists and I will only say here that the structure is complex, varying considerably from north to south along the chain. In the region behind Lima, for example, where I went by railway—the highest standard gauge railway in the world, reaching 16,000 feet—there are jagged peaks without vegetation and often covered with snow. In the little-known section farther south that we visited the ranges, raised by folding and volcanic eruption, have been planed down to a more general level, raised and disturbed again and subsequently carved by rivers into deep canyons. Between these tremendous excavations there are lofty plateaux, at ten or twelve thousand feet, known locally as *puña*.

I was, of course, intensely interested in the geological work of our expedition, which aimed at making the first geological traverse of that region. But I looked at the mountains primarily as an artist and a mountaineer and I described in my diary what I saw, not as a geologist, but as a layman.

The western foothills of the Andes extend into the coastal desert like elongated tapering fingers. They consist of crumbling rock entirely devoid of vegetation, for, as I mentioned in the last chapter, this desert is one of the driest regions in the world. When rain falls farther inland, on the coastal cordillera, the water rushes down in deep gorges, carrying quantities of débris, but most of it soaks away into the dry ground and little actually reaches the sea. Some, however, is used for irrigating a few crops, including cotton, in the valleys cut through the desert and these are the only green strips to be seen. Some of the sketches that I made among the foothills show large expanses of white sand, looking almost like snow, high up among these coastal ranges where it had been carried by the wind.

If you were to pass along the coast in a ship you might see nothing of the gigantic chain of the Andes, for there is often dense fog, caused by warm air meeting the cold Humboldt Current. But if visibility was good enough to enable you to see a good many miles inland you might distinguish a long and almost level mountain barrier. This would be one of the series of gigantic steps, each many miles in depth, that lead upwards to the much higher continental divide. Beyond them lie high plateaux and more rugged ranges, separated from one another by deep valleys that run roughly north and south. It was over these plateaux and ranges, as over a long succession of waves, that we had to make our way.

We began our crossing, which was to take many weeks, by climbing through one of the gorges carved down the face of the first great step. Here we saw evidence of the terrific force of the water that descends periodically after rain higher up. The dry bed of the gorge was choked with débris, making progress difficult, and there were many boulders as large as houses that had been carried along in suspension by the thick water. Some of these had collided with great force and had split in half.

On the first night we were obliged to pitch our little tents on a ledge still far from water, with the result that the mules wandered in search of it. I went to bed with fever, an unpromising prelude to what lay ahead, but I dosed myself with quinine and felt better in the morning. Our plan was to get moving at dawn, but it took ages to round up the mules and nearly as long again to load them. For several days, until they got used to their loads, they generally bucked them off as soon as the last strap had been fastened. We were inclined to blame the muleteers for this, until one or two of us had been bucked off our riding mules and appreciated the violence of the eruption.

On the second day we marched considerably farther than we had intended, keeping on until we found a little pasture and some rather brackish water for the mules. Once we had surmounted the first two great steps or so we seldom had real difficulty in finding water, but several of the mules often strayed for miles during the night, generally going back along our route for some succulent morsel that they had noticed earlier in the day. One would have thought that they had no surplus energy for such nocturnal excursions, but they were certainly tough and needed to be. I was not always as annoyed as my companions at the inevitable delays in starting, for they gave me a chance to sketch the mountain scenery that varied widely from day to day.

The mule that I rode had its own ideas about procedure and there was little that I could do to change them. At first it liked to keep position directly behind one of the baggage mules and, if possible, between two others who formed a sort of bodyguard. But this arrangement did not suit me, for it generally meant lagging far behind the rest of the party, getting too much of the odour of mule and having my legs banged by the loads of the escort. By exerting every kind of legitimate influence I eventually convinced my mount that it would be better for everybody if it would proceed ahead of the main body. This enabled me to spot a good view before the others arrived, to make a sketch while they were catching up and to overtake them again before they were out of sight. It also meant that I could often choose the camping ground for the night.

Camping did not always involve the erection of tents, though we put them up whenever we could on the high *puña* because of the cold and rain. (Plate XXIII.) On a good many occasions, particularly down in the warmer valleys, we merely bivouacked in the open, rolling ourselves in our sleeping-bags with bits of mosquito netting over our faces. But sometimes the steepness of the ground forced us to do without tents, in spite of the cold, and we had to wedge ourselves up with rocks, saddles and bits of baggage, hoping that they would not roll downhill during the night.

As the days turned into weeks and we penetrated ever deeper into the majestic wilderness of the Peruvian Andes I evolved a camping routine that made my tent seem like a snug little home. It was only six feet long and three feet wide, with sides a foot high (when not sagging too much) and a sloping roof that rose to three feet. I could erect it in three minutes. I had a curtain of mosquito netting sewn inside the entrance and I always arranged my more valuable items of baggage inside the tent in the same way, with the sleeping-bag down the middle. I had, until it disintegrated, a tiny oil lamp that produced a flame about a quarter the size of that of a candle and I used this when candles were scarce, as they usually were. By its light I could just see to read for a few minutes and to write my diary for the day. In the morning I could pack up my tent and bedding in less than five minutes, but occasionally we all had to wait for perhaps an hour until the hailstones that had frozen on to the canvas during the night had thawed sufficiently to be brushed off. Inside my tent I was shut off from the great wild world outside and I could think about home and friends, who

XXIII. Camp at 12,000 feet on the edge of the *puña* in the Andes of central Peru

XXIV. Sketching in the Peruvian Andes: mule train crossing the
track of a landslide

had no notion that I was then lying on lumpy ground 15,000 feet up in the Andes. In later years I sometimes used the tent again in Roumania and Canada and it was strange that then, as soon as I crawled inside, I had visions of the *puña*, of range after range of lofty mountains, or of sub-tropical valleys filled with vegetation and butterflies.

I had had special waterproof pouches made to contain my sketching materials, paper and finished drawings and I generally put these in my saddle-bags. But their preservation caused me many anxious moments, when we had to wade through deep torrents among boulders and there was great risk of the mules, or ourselves, slipping. Moist atmosphere and constant changes of temperature, as we climbed to great altitudes or descended 6,000 feet or more into the warm valleys, were liable to affect my drawings and even the paints themselves. But water-colours were undoubtedly the best medium to use and I had learnt from experience in other hot and cold countries that tubes of paint are more serviceable than pans. I could squeeze out just enough paint, always fresh and clean.

I carried an enamel metal palette instead of the porcelain one that I prefer, for there was great risk of breaking this essential article, and I found that an old rubber hot water bottle was better than any of the usual too small metal flasks sold by artists' colourmen. In order to save weight, I took neither easel nor stool; in fact, it is easier to sketch in water-colours with the board on one's lap and there is usually at least a rock to sit on. Occasionally, when there was not much time to spare, I persuaded my mule to stand still—an art that he would have liked to pursue by the hour—and I made a hurried sketch from the saddle. Art connoisseurs ought to have a special category for mule-back paintings and I should like to introduce them to what, I fondly hope but doubt, is my own invention: the hot-water-colour. I produced this sometimes in Canada, when the temperature was far below zero. When I used cold water it froze instantly on the brush, so I painted with a thermos flask of hot water.

We crossed the continental divide at 16,100 feet and knew that from there on every stream and river was contributing to the Amazon. At these high altitudes the mules needed longer periods of rest and I made full use of the days in camp, making short excursions to obtain more sketches. Besides the herds of llamas that we sometimes saw, there were *huanacos*, a smaller version of the same kind of animal, and the graceful little *vicuñas*, still smaller and fleeter of foot. But there was practically nothing to be found in the way of game, except a few tough duck or geese, and there were no trees. The total absence of trees on the high plateaux made it impossible to have a camp fire, just when it would have been most welcome.

There are a number of villages and small towns scattered about among the Andean ranges and, if they lay anywhere near our route, we usually visited them. But they could produce little food and we generally had to rely on what we carried with us. Some of the villages that we saw, consisting of adobe and stone houses with red-tiled roofs, were quite picturesque from a distance, but they were not always very salubrious. The inhabitants, usually wearing the *poncho*—a llama wool rug with a hole in the middle through which to pass the head—might sometimes appear indifferent at our approach, or even a little surly. But we carried with us some letters of introduction from the Prefects of the districts along our line of march and these usually assured us a friendly reception. If there seemed likely to be any doubt we took no pains to conceal the arms that we carried and these served as a warning to anyone who might cast covetous eyes on our mules or equipment.

A few times, when overtaken by a storm, we were obliged to accept hospitality in a village, whose governor provided us with one or two empty huts for the night. But a night in one of these dark, dirty and rather tumbledown buildings usually provided me, at least, with an over-generous assortment of bites and I always preferred to camp outside any village rather than in it.

When, after travelling nearly a hundred miles, we reached a town called Cabana, Apaico, the head muleteer, reminded us that this was where his contract terminated. For nearly four days we lived in a totally unfurnished mud hovel while Tarnawiecki, our resourceful companion who had made the original contract with so much difficulty, endeavoured to negotiate its renewal for a further period or distance. Neither Apaico nor his two *compañeros*, one of whom he had picked up on the way, had ever been beyond this point and it appeared that they were terrified of bandits, who were alleged to be lurking all along the route to distant Cuzco.

Tarnawiecki promised higher pay, better food (if ever we could get it) and the bait of the unknown Inca capital as inducements, but still Apaico refused to go on. He asserted that his mules would all be stolen, that they would go lame, that they would die of the effects of altitude or that there was no pasture of any kind beyond Cabana. Tarnawiecki produced villagers to deny this last assertion and he indicated our revolvers and guns as bandit-deterrents. But Apaico would not move.

Then, after consultation, we suggested that Apaico should be allowed to replace some of the things that we had used up with a load of coca leaves, a form of currency that would be welcome in Cuzco or in the mountain villages. He could sell this at a considerable profit, for the Indians of the *sierra* constantly chew coca leaves, mixed with a little lime, and this seems to give them phenomenal powers of endurance.

This turned the scale in our favour and it was agreed that the caravan should go on to Cuzco. But we were not out of the wood yet, for Apaico had to collect his coca leaves and to replace one of his original *compañeros*, who had now thrown in his hand. There were several young men in Cabana who seemed inclined to join us, but, just when we were ready to start, the one selected was dragged from our clutches by his awe-stricken mother, who was apparently convinced that the bandits would devour her precious son. None of the other candidates knew much about mules, but Apaico picked another who looked teachable and away we went once more, climbing slowly for thousands of feet until we were again on the high *puña*.

Wading across rivers had become normal routine, but we were all a little dismayed when we came to a wide rushing torrent that was too deep to wade. There was, however, a suspension bridge, a very insecure-looking arrangement of ageing ropes more than 150 feet long and barely six inches wide, with an excessively flimsy hand-rope on each side. We managed in turn to balance across this without falling in the water and, after prolonged persuasion, the mules swam through the river, guided by ropes that prevented their being washed away. But nearly everything got wet, except food in tins and my painting materials, which I had bound up tight in a waterproof poncho in addition to the usual waterproof bags.

In some villages, when there was occasion to stop for an hour or so, we made use of the pause to complete some aspect of our work and this provided the inhabitants with unprecedented entertainment. They gathered round us open-mouthed, like children watching a conjurer, while one member of the expedition boiled a thermometer, another split chunks of rock with a hammer, a third mended some broken instrument and a fourth endeavoured to sketch them as they stood there.

Soon after we had left Cabana behind the muleteers began to show signs of uneasiness, reminding us that we were approaching the bandit-infested area. They begged us always to have our weapons ready and they relayed to us every portentous story that they picked up in the villages. One night, when we were bivouacking on a spit of land between two rivers about a mile beyond a tiny village, Apaico came to me and, almost with tears in his eyes, besought me to fire three or four shots from my revolver to let the villagers know that we had guns. I told him that, as we were so far away and as the rivers were making such a din, any potential bandits would never hear the shots and it would be a waste of ammunition. But, in order to reassure him, I put a stone on a boulder twenty paces away and hit it with a single shot. A dozen years earlier I had represented Cambridge University in a number of rifle and revolver matches and had often competed in shooting competitions at Bisley, but I surprised myself with this feat.

There were two or three short lulls in the bandit scare, but after each lull Apaico or one of his companions renewed their warnings with greater urgency. Yet however far we advanced the bandits were always supposed to be lurking just ahead of us. They might have been running away, with us in pursuit. But one day it really seemed that we were getting hot.

From the cold *puña* at 14,000 feet we began the long descent to the warm valley of the Pampachiri river and towards dusk, when we were about half way down, we stopped for the night in a dirty mud hut, clinging to the mountain-side, that was a part of the village of Chilcayo. Far away on the opposite side of the deep valley, at about the same level or perhaps a little higher, we could see another small village, named Chiara, perched on a spur. It looked almost inaccessible, but we had been told that our route lay through it and on upwards for thousands of feet until we reached the skyline again.

That night the people of Chilcayo said nothing about bandits, but in the morning, when we wanted to continue the descent, they told us that it would be impossible. There had been a landslide below their village—a very common occurrence all over the Andes—and a large part of the track to the river had been carried away. We were not going to let this deter us, so we set about finding a few men to help us to repair the track. (Plate XXIV.)

It then transpired that this particular landslide was not altogether a natural phenomenon, for the villagers had encouraged it to obstruct the trail in order to prevent the men of Chiara, who were described as desperate bandits, from coming over and stealing their cattle. However, we offered sufficient inducement to get the trail patched up enough to take the mules down to the river, but the work delayed us half the day and the mules practically stood on their noses during a large part of the perilous descent.

That night we bivouacked beside the river, amidst a profusion of cacti and wild flowers so thick that it was hard to find room to lie down. We had to cut tracks with machetes so that the mules could wander along the river-bed to feed.

The crossing of the Pampachiri was one of our most difficult passages, for the river was fully 150 yards wide and the current was very swift. The muleteers insisted that we should remain on our mules while they themselves waded hanging on to the stirrups, one on each side, to prevent the animals from falling and being carried away. For a large part of the crossing the water reached the saddle and I found it a most uncomfortable sensation, sitting on the mule's back in midstream with my feet round its neck and the water rushing past. This procedure had to be repeated until the whole caravan had passed over, so it was a prolonged operation. Only one baggage mule fell in the middle of the river and was swept about a hundred yards downstream on to some rocks, where the men retrieved it, apparently unhurt. As it happened to be loaded with my kitbag I was not too pleased; but eventually that kitbag was to suffer a worse fate.

Immediately after this successful performance, not without some misgivings, we began the arduous climb to Chiara and beyond. There was a sound of falling rocks behind us: presumably the inhabitants of Chilcayo were once more tinkering with the landslide. All the rest of the day we struggled upwards on an exceedingly rough and narrow mountain trail and it seemed sometimes that the mules must fall down a precipice. In the evening we reached the crest of the spur on which Chiara was perched and we made our camp in a very confined space about a quarter of a mile below the village. The mules were tethered, with a supply of fodder, close to the tents and the muleteers said that they would take it in turns to watch all night in case the bandits attacked. Before going to bed we fired one or two warning shots.

In the middle of the night there was a sudden scuffle and my tent and the one next to it collapsed. I crawled out of the jumble with my revolver in hand, expecting to find bandits in among us. It was just light enough to see that one of the mules had tripped over the guy ropes of the tents and was now rolling on the ground in a hopeless tangle.

It took ages to release the animal and we did not bother to put the tents up again. The rest of the night was cold and disturbed, with all three muleteers talking to keep their courage up.

In the morning, having scraped together some sort of breakfast and mended the damaged tents, we climbed on up to Chiara, where our reception was no less friendly than in any other village. In fact we parked the mules in the picturesque main square with its imposing entrance archway built of mud and stone and we managed to buy a little food. I sat in the sunshine and made a sketch of the village while most of the inhabitants looked on. (Plate XXV.)

In the part of the Andes that we were now traversing the scenery was very beautiful. Wild nature reigned supreme.

There were no roads, factories or works of masonry to mar the mountain-sides or to impede the rivers in their long journey to the Amazon plains. Except on the highest peaks and the steepest precipices, there was a coat of green everywhere. This grassland, sometimes spangled with wild flowers, existed even above the height of Mont Blanc and it made the mountains seem less formidable than those in the bare rocky regions without vegetation.

The anti-climax of Chiara made any further references to bandits fall rather flat, but the nervousness of the muleteers, which must have been genuine, did not noticeably decrease. One or other of them continued to keep guard at night, even in the most desolate places, and there seemed to be a risk that they might not keep fit enough to go on. But in spite of the usual delays due to the wandering of the mules, which had to be left free to graze, we made fairly good progress of anything between ten and twenty miles a day and reached the valley of Andahuaylas.

I had gone on ahead with some of the baggage mules while my companions spent an hour collecting fossils at a place where they were fairly abundant. I chose a spot for our camp, a little way from a village, and began unloading the mules and erecting the tents. Suddenly I heard a shout and looked up to see four horsemen bearing down upon me, all of them carrying rifles.

"This is it," I thought. "Here am I, alone with only two unarmed muleteers and most of our equipment and the bandits have caught us napping."

There was obviously nothing that I could do except wait and see what might happen. I walked slowly towards the cavalcade, who pulled up with a flourish in the midst of the scattered baggage. To my surprise, the leader of the party swept off his sombrero and said "Good evening".

I returned the greeting and waited while he dismounted and came up to me with a paper in his hand. This, he said, was a telegram that he had received from the Prefect's office at Abancay, the capital of the Department of Apurimac, informing him, the Sub-Prefect of Andahuaylas, a small town only a few miles away, that a party of four suspicious characters, one looking like a Bolivian, carrying arms and boxes of ammunition

and revolvers, had entered the district near Huancaray and
should be arrested at once and their arms taken from them.
Would I, he asked politely, please show him the contents of the
wooden boxes that now lay on the ground around him?

My relief was so intense that I had difficulty in suppressing
a desire to laugh, but I certainly smiled as I unclipped the lids
of the boxes and revealed tins of soup, packets of tea, sugar and
biscuits, several carefully wrapped scientific instruments and a
large number of small fragments of rock with labels adhering to
them.

The other official and the two soldiers who accompanied the
Sub-Prefect came closer to peer at this unusual armoury. Then
they all burst out laughing.

The tension was released and I joined in the laughter. I
asked the Sub-Prefect to let me read the telegram myself and,
before he could change his mind, I copied it hurriedly into my
diary. By this time Professor Gregory and Miss McKinnon
Wood had arrived on the scene, with a bag of fossils that they
had collected, and I explained to him what had happened. He
thoroughly enjoyed the joke and was concerned to know which
of us was supposed to be the Bolivian. As he and I were the
only two with beards, he felt that it must be one of us, though
we did not know if a beard was a Bolivian characteristic. But I
was wearing a sombrero and a cartridge belt with a large
revolver in its holster and I secretly believed that these might
be the insignia of a Bolivian.

We showed the Sub-Prefect our credentials, including the
permits to carry arms issued by the Peruvian Government, and
he said somewhat regretfully that, in the circumstances, he supposed he could not have the pleasure of making an arrest.
Subsequently he was able to fill in the details of the story.
Apparently the governor of a tiny village a long way back on
our route had taken fright when he saw us and, having no other
means of communication, had sent a special messenger sixty
miles through the mountains to the nearest telegraph station at
Puquio. The Sub-Prefect there, alarmed by the report of
heavily-armed invaders, had telegraphed the news to the
Prefect of Ayacucho, who had relayed the message to the
Secretary of the Prefect of Abancay. This official, determined

to nip insurrection in the bud, had at once sent instructions for our arrest to Andahuaylas.

When we looked at one another at this stage of our journey we had to admit that the sight was enough to frighten anyone. But the last thing we had expected, in the midst of the alleged bandit country, was to be mistaken for bandits ourselves.

No artist ever had a grander selection of landscape subjects than I had during those months of travel across the Andes; landscapes, unseen by anyone but a few Indians, succeeded one another in seemingly endless procession. Now and then, when my companions were busy collecting geological specimens or when we were resting in camp, I snatched a few impressions that I hoped would describe, better than words, the magnificent scenery through which we were passing. Sometimes, on the *puña*, it was hard to believe that we were standing at 12,000 feet in the midst of one of the greatest mountain regions in the world, for the gently undulating grassland stretched for miles around us, rimmed by low hills that might have been English downs. But at other times, when we reached the brink of an escarpment, there opened before us a panorama so magnificent that we were compelled to pause in wonder.

I remember an occasion, a day or two before we reached Cuzco, when we bivouacked uncomfortably on a cold and exceedingly steep slope, for we had been overtaken by darkness before we could find any suitable camping ground. For an hour or more we had probed our way downwards on a rough winding track, where the feet of the mules continually sent loose stones bounding off into the deep, black valley below and we slithered and stumbled in spite of our cautious groping. At last, as it seemed too dangerous to go on, we lay down beside the track, wedging ourselves among the rocks.

At dawn we were rewarded with a stupendous panorama. (Plate XXVI.) Far below, still shrouded in clouds, lay the valley that we had to cross that day. Beyond, in clear-cut silhouette against one another and against the early sky, range after range of mountains thrust their highest peaks up to the general level of the ancient plateau. We knew that, one after another, these ranges had to be surmounted and the deep intervening valleys crossed; a succession of gruelling climbs to the chill air of the *puña* and of awesome descents to the far-off turbulent rivers in their warm valleys. Often again we should have to make our way along the brink of precipices, through sunny valleys where the lofty organ-pipe cactus pointed to the sky and numberless butterflies fluttered over the wild flowers of every colour, and up and up by inadequate zig-zag trails where the mules would stop frequently, panting with the exertion of the long climb. And behind them would always sound the cries of "*Mula! mula!*" and the eloquent curses of the muleteers.

The adventure, though sometimes exhausting for the body, was never tiring for the mind. It was wonderful to be alive in such surroundings, to see this great wild country as God made it, untouched by the hand of man. Every fresh prospect enticed us to go on, though often we were content with the present and disposed to linger. In a few months' time we must return to civilization, but we felt sometimes that the life we were leading in the Andes was more real, more worth while.

For the purposes of our geological exploration there was no real need to go to Cuzco, which lay to the east of our line of traverse. But we had three good reasons for going there. In the first place, we wanted to see this ancient capital of the Incas of Peru and to examine the amazing stone structures that they had erected. Already, at widely separated points, we had seen examples of their architecture, but it would have been disappointing to miss others that lay within reach of our route. Then the contract with Apaico terminated at Cuzco, for only by agreeing to go there, the market centre for the region, could we induce him to take us so far on our way. Finally, there was the railway from Cuzco to the coast, the only means by which we could send on their way to England the large number of geological specimens that we had so far collected and any equipment that we no longer needed.

Almost the first thing I did on arrival in Cuzco was to have the best bath of my life. We were busy there for several days, sorting and packing our baggage, negotiating with a local muleteer to take us on beyond Cuzco and down the valley of the Vilcanota river for another hundred miles or so, and seeing as much as we could of the old city. I packed all the paintings and drawings that I had so far made, seventy-three in number, and sent them off to the coast with our other things.

We expected, soon after leaving Cuzco, to be going gradually down into the warmer country and we therefore decided to dispense with our tents and sleeping-bags. A good deal of our warmer clothing could also be discarded. Most of the remainder, in my case at least, was distributed all over the city. Some went to a laundry, a luxury it had not enjoyed for weeks, although I had frequently done my best to wash it—and myself —in ice-cold mountain torrents. A few things went to a tailor for repairs, while some boots and shoes, worn right through, were divided between two different cobblers in order that they might be mended quickly.

After living for so long in the open air it seemed an unwelcome restriction to have to stay at the hotel, except for the bathroom. But I spent little time indoors and wandered all through the ancient streets in search of subjects for my paintbrush. In the market, a colourful agglomeration of peasants and their produce, I made many rapid sketches of figures and costumes, noting particularly the different designs of the ponchos and the various ways of wearing them and the patterned wide felt hats with scarlet linings.

The plan for the next stage of our journey ended with a question mark. Would there, or would there not, be any canoes to take us down the Urubamba river? We still had many miles to go through mountainous country, but after entering the valley of the Vilcanota, which rises in the mountains south-east of Cuzco, we should begin the long, gradual descent to the eastern foothills of the Andes. Beyond them, still several hundred miles away by the route that we hoped to follow, lay the vast basin of the Amazon, a region of swamps and jungle where travel is seldom possible except on the rivers.

On the eastern side of the Andes the mountains and foothills are generally covered, up to an altitude of five or six thousand feet, with a dense cloak of forest. The climate is always warm and sometimes very hot and there are monkeys, snakes and parrots, besides many other animals and birds. This extensive region, in striking contrast with the higher mountain mass called the *sierra*, is known as the *montaña*. It is not an easy region to penetrate, for there are turbulent rivers flowing through deep gorges and the luxuriant vegetation itself is an impediment.

The Vilcanota flows for a great distance through a narrow gorge between high perpendicular walls of rock and it is so full of rapids that it is quite unnavigable, even in a canoe. (*Frontispiece*.) Many of the rivers of South America are so long that a single name does not suffice for them and this one, probably the longest tributary of the Amazon, is no exception. Down in the *montaña* there is a point at which it changes its name to Urubamba. Several hundred miles lower down, after it has been joined by many smaller rivers, it meets the Tambo river, which has had two other names higher up: first Apurimac and then Ene. At the junction the Urubamba becomes the Ucayali and carries this name for perhaps a thousand miles, until it meets the Amazon. This confluence is in Peru, not far from Iquitos, but the Brazilians apparently consider that the Amazon is a Brazilian river, so they call that part of it between the Ucayali and their frontier with Peru the Solimoës. Whatever the name may be, most of the water comes from the Andes— much of it from sources barely a hundred miles from the Pacific coast—and all of it flows eventually into the Atlantic.

Our plan was to follow the course of the Vilcanota, as nearly as we could, until it became the Urubamba and somewhere in that region, where it was more or less navigable for canoes, there was a dot on the map named "Rosalina". Here we hoped to find two dugout canoes, with crews of jungle Indians, waiting for us.

Our hope was based on a very slender premise. Professor Gregory had heard somewhere that two Peruvians were living in a village of the Machegenga tribe of Indians at a point on the Urubamba called Maranquiato, something like a hundred and fifty miles by river below Rosalina. He had been told that they were traders, cutting mahogany logs and sending them down the river—a feat which, it later became obvious, was hardly possible. It was said, however, that these two men could arrange for the Machegenga Indians to take two dugouts up the river to Rosalina. We could then travel down the Urubamba until it became the Ucayali and thereafter make other arrangements.

There was, our leader understood, just one snag. Beyond Maranquiato, where the Indians lived, there was a gorge—the gateway where the river finally broke through the foothills. This gorge was full of very dangerous rapids. Barely a dozen Europeans had ever attempted to pass through it and every one of them had met with disaster. Two or three of them, strapped to rafts, had emerged torn and battered below the gorge, having lost all their belongings. Most of the others had lost their lives.

Before leaving England Professor Gregory had written a letter to these two Peruvian traders, asking them to help us in the way suggested, and he expected to hear in Cuzco that the necessary arrangements had been made. I could not imagine how the letter was to reach them and probably they never received it. We had to leave Cuzco without knowing whether we could ever get beyond Rosalina.

In 1911 the American explorer, Hiram Bingham, discovered in the forest high above the Vilcanota gorge the ruins of a most remarkable citadel and temples dating from the period of the Incas. The place is called Machu Picchu and is accessible by train from Cuzco. We climbed out of the gorge to visit it and we bivouacked for a night in the midst of the ruins. The site suggests that this must have been an impregnable fortress and it is believed that it was the last refuge of the Virgins of the Sun, who fled from the sacred city of Cuzco at the time of Pizzarro's invasion.

The main ruins, perched hundreds of feet above the river with precipices all round, contain every kind of stone wall known to the Incas, including finely-cut ashlars keyed together without cement and cyclopean blocks estimated to weigh twelve tons or more. The surrounding mountains, though partially covered with forest, are vertiginously steep and beyond them can be seen several snow-clad peaks. The view looking down into the gorge from the ruins is almost terrifying. I made several sketches among the ruins and they now bring back to me clear impressions of the scene. But they remind me also that I suffered all night from mosquito bites and that my breakfast consisted of one banana.

Landslides scarred the mountains all around us and we had to cross a good many of their tracks with the mules. Each time it looked as if we were in for a hazardous undertaking, but the mules were as sure-footed as cats and invariably passed over without serious mishap. In the Vilcanota-Urubamba gorge we came upon the mother and father of all landslides where, some months earlier, the mountain-side had slipped over a distance of more than half a mile. The sloping débris of rock, now beginning to consolidate itself, had to be crossed if our expedition was not to end there and so we urged one of our two muleteers to lead the way. Luckily, having reduced our equipment, we had fewer mules than we had used in the high Andes, but it now looked as if their numbers might be suddenly reduced even further.

The muleteer hesitated, so Tarnawiecki boldly went ahead, leading one of the mules. We decided to proceed in succession at fairly long intervals, in case the scree should be set in motion again, and I waited until Tarnawiecki had gone about a hundred yards before following him with another mule. Picking our way with caution, we made a zig-zag track across the landslide, which seemed interminable; but at last we reached the far side in safety. Then three of us had to go all the way back to fetch the last four mules and the second muleteer who was waiting with them. I think I felt rather more nervous on my third crossing, again towing a loaded mule, particularly when the loose stones rattled down the slope at intervals, but nothing untoward happened and we went on our way down the valley.

Farther down the river, in more open country, there were two large *haciendas* and we stopped for a night at each. Besides the main buildings, with open verandas where we slept, there were a few native huts for the farm hands, who were cultivating maize, sugar, cocoa and a little coffee. Here we picked up some conflicting reports about the condition of the river below Rosalina and it seemed more doubtful than ever that we should be able to obtain canoes.

From this point onwards the trail became very rough and indistinct and often we were far from the main river. But I personally found it absorbingly interesting to be walking—and sometimes climbing and scrambling—through the tropical forest that covered the mountains completely, except where landslides had carried the vegetation away. Lianas formed a tangled network among the tall trees, whose leaves were often far larger than those in a more temperate climate. Many of the cacti were nearly a hundred feet in height and there were many varieties of palm that I had never seen before. Butterflies fluttered about us and any patch of moisture on the ground generally attracted dozens of them, including lovely specimens of the big blue morpho butterfly. Now and then a snake slithered across our path and I saw one spectacular reptile, about eight feet long and striped with brilliant yellow and jet black.

For several days we made our way through this tropical wonderland, bivouacking at night within reach of a mountain torrent. The air hummed with mosquitoes, which clustered on my hands whenever I tried to sketch, but even they could not destroy my enjoyment of the scenery. One day we had a splendid view of Salcantay, a magnificent snow-peak of 21,000 feet that had never been climbed. In recent years a number of expeditions have attempted to scale it, but it was not finally conquered until August, 1952, when a Franco-American party were successful.

Occasionally the nights were cool and we were glad of the single blanket that each of us had, but the climate became steadily hotter as we descended. Having no tents we had little protection against the heavy rain that fell at intervals, except a couple of light tarpaulins which could be slung over a framework of poles cut from the trees. Nearly every evening flocks of parrots and toucans set up a great clamour among the treetops, until they flew noisily to their roosting places.

On the 3rd May we reached the bank of the river at the point called Rosalina. All our baggage was unloaded, the muleteers were paid and the mules set off at once on the long trail back to Cuzco. We were now deep in the forest region, without means of transport in any direction.

It gave me a curious sensation to be stranded so far from civilization. If canoes could not be found, we should probably have to abandon everything that we could not carry and walk back at least as far as the *haciendas* through which we had passed. The only alternative would be to make a raft of balsa wood, if there were any of these trees in the neighbourhood, or to cut down a mahogany tree, if we could find one, and hack the trunk into the form of a canoe with our machetes. I doubt if we could have done this and I am quite sure that, without skilled Indian paddlers, we could not have gone far through the rapids without disaster.

In the days of the rubber boom towards the end of the nineteenth century Rosalina had been a village with a coffee plantation and clearings for a few crops. Trails led from it into the surrounding jungle where bold speculators, aided by a few Indians, tapped any rubber trees that they could find. These trails became overgrown and most of them disappeared long ago, but we had been told that one leading to Maranquiato, the home of the two Peruvians who we had hoped would supply canoes, could still be traced. Tarnawiecki, with his wide experience of travel in Peru, offered to try to make his way along this trail, if he could find two or three Indians to go with him. This was an heroic proposition.

Below Rosalina the river makes a great bend to the west and then turns northwards again to Maranquiato, a distance of about 150 miles. The trail led through the mountains inside this great loop, shortening the distance to about sixty miles. But that was a long way to walk through jungle on a long-disused track encumbered with fallen trees, rotting vegetation and frequent landslides.

Although there were said to be three or four Peruvians living somewhere along the river near Rosalina and perhaps a few scattered Indians of the Machegenga tribe, it appeared exceedingly unlikely that anyone would come to help us. But while we were debating what to do, two Indians, wearing rough cotton robes stained with the red juice of *achiote*, suddenly appeared on the opposite bank about fifty yards away and we saw that they had a small dugout canoe. Shortly afterwards there was a sound on the trail by which we had arrived and a young Dominican missionary, accompanied by two more Indians, came through the trees and greeted us in Spanish.

He told me that he had heard about us on the way down to the river and that he was returning to the mission, a few hours on foot down the left bank, where he had been working for a year among the Indians. The men on the opposite bank were

XXV. Chiara, a village perched high up on a spur in the Andes of central Peru

V. COVERLEY-PRICE.

waiting to take him across. He advised us to make our camp
on the other side, where he would show us the remains of an old
wooden building, sufficient to give shelter from rain.

During what remained of daylight the priest, ourselves and
our baggage were ferried across the river in the short canoe.
Only two people besides the two Indians with paddles, or an
equivalent weight of baggage, could be taken at each crossing
and the swift current carried the canoe so far downstream that a
lot of time was used bringing it up again.

The priest led us through the trees for about a quarter of a
mile until we came upon the strangest temporary home I have
ever lived in. Long ago, probably at the end of the last century,
it had been a two-storied wooden house thatched with reeds.
All that now remained were the corner posts and a few others,
supporting less than half of the upper floor and about the same
area of decayed thatch. There were no walls at all and therefore no doors or windows. The ground floor was literally the
ground: dry mud bearing, we noticed, the pad-marks of a
jaguar. An old wooden ladder, with most of the rungs broken or
missing, was leaning against the rotting boards of the upper floor.

We dumped our scanty bedding, collected some twigs and
made a fire and presently sat down to tea, with biscuits and jam
out of a tin. Before it was dark I returned to the river to wash.
There followed a few moments of panic, when I thought I had
lost the way back, but I saw the glimmer of a candle flame and
all was well. Before going to bed we all gathered round a small
acetylene bicycle lamp and a guttering candle to write our
diaries up to date. Mosquitoes and moths gathered round
them too.

During the night, which was pitch dark, I woke up hearing a
sound on the wooden boards overhead. Someone, or some
animal, was moving stealthily about up there. I heard Tarnawiecki stir beside me and I whispered "What's that?"

"Don't move," he said quietly. "I think I know what it is."

I wondered if it might be a large snake. But at that moment
Tarnawiecki, standing up, struck something hard against the
floor above. There was a sudden scuffle and a fairly large
creature landed on the ground a few feet away and streaked off
among the surrounding trees.

12

We were all awake now and someone struck a match.

"I thought so," said Tarnawiecki. "That was the jaguar." And he pointed at the fresh tracks in the mud.

In the morning we could see how the jaguar had got up there from the overhanging branch of a tree, which we promptly removed. Probably we had annexed his usual sleeping place, but anyway he never came back.

We were not sorry to have a restful day; restful, that is, for our bodies. But our minds were much exercised by the problem of our further progress. It had been agreed that Tarnawiecki should go to Maranquiato by the old trail, which he thought he ought to be able to cover in about four days, and the first necessity was to find some Indians to go with him, to carry his baggage and, supposing that they knew something about the trail, to act as guides.

In the jungle news travels in some mysterious way unknown to civilization and before midday we were visited by two of our nearest neighbours, Peruvians living several miles away. One of them had a rough kind of farm on a distant hill, where he employed a number of Indians. He promised to produce three of them in a day or two to accompany Tarnawiecki; their leader would be an Indian who had once been over the trail. We were to pay a moderate sum and to give the men machetes, as the trail was thickly overgrown in many places.

So far, so good. But an unexpected blow was to follow.

When we were sorting out the baggage, to prepare a bundle of provisions for Tarnawiecki to take with him, we discovered that a box containing tinned foods, candles, matches and other necessities that we had bought in Cuzco was missing. There were several other almost identical boxes and all should have been counted at every stopping place, but somehow this one had escaped attention. I remembered last seeing it when the mules were being loaded at a village several days' journey away. It was on the ground in front of a shed made entirely of old packing cases marked "DINAMITA". The loss of this box would not have seemed serious if we were going straight on with our journey, but with the prospect of considerable delay its recovery became a matter of possibly vital importance.

The Peruvian farmer said that he could sell us a few eggs,

some yucca and, if we were there for any length of time, an occasional chicken, but he had nothing that would keep well on a long journey. He promised, however, that when he next sent someone back into the *montaña* to fetch supplies, probably in a few days, he would tell the man to trace our Cuzco box and to bring it back with him.

When Tarnawiecki had gone, the rest of us settled down to wait. We hoped that he would come back in less than ten days, with two large canoes.

Chapter IX

TRAVEL WITH A SKETCH-BOOK IN THE
AMAZONIAN JUNGLE:
DISASTER AND SURVIVAL

THERE was little that we could do in our jungle home, but we soon fell into a routine that somehow filled the days. We got up at dawn, about half-past five. At first the scientists spent long hours writing up their notes, labelling geological specimens and walking along the one or two jungle trails near the river to examine the rocks. I finished some of my sketches and made new ones of the river, the densely forested foothills and the jungle trees. I walked as far as it was possible to walk along the trails and occasionally visited the farmer or our other distant neighbour, a man named Torres, to buy some yucca and bananas or a handful of rice and a few eggs. Our meals were much alike: yucca and bananas, coffee made with beans roasted on the lid of a tin and then crushed, and sometimes a supplement from our reduced store, such as biscuits, jam, a little spaghetti or a few small dried potatoes.

About a quarter of a mile from our encampment I found a creek flowing into the Urubamba, with a bank of coarse sand and a shallow rocky pool. This became my bathroom where I bathed in the early morning and again before dusk. I made a seat with some boulders and a towel and clothes rail with sticks, more or less out of the way of ants and spiders. The evening bath ceremony, before the sun dipped behind the hills at about five, became one of my daily pleasures. I would sit in the sun, watch the water tearing past and listen to the evening chatter of birds and the screaming flights of parrots going to roost. Then I would crawl along the bank beneath the overhanging trees and stroll back to our very inadequate house. One evening, as I was stooping near the water, a tarantula spider barred my path. I studied it for a moment, then threw a handful of sand and scared it away, hoping that it would not spring on me from a different direction.

The insects in the jungle were the worst thing we had to contend with. Some time ago I read a book, declared to be the authentic story of an explorer on one of the rivers that we were to pass later on, which hardly mentioned the all-pervading insects. Instead, the writer constantly fought with anacondas, battled with jaguars, alligators which he called crocodiles, tarantulas and other creatures and had numerous bloody encounters with savage Indians. Always he came off best. We, in contrast, were sometimes defeated by ants, that came in thousands and stole our sugar. Mosquitoes stung us mercilessly and sandflies got through everything. The only light we had after sunset came from a candle or a small acetylene lamp and sometimes these were extinguished by the sheer volume of the moths that flew into them. A bite from a certain large black ant over an inch long could paralyse a limb for several hours and this was proved by one member of our party. Some minute ants that made a meal off me left scars that did not disappear until nearly a year later. Occasionally there were snakes, but they made off in a hurry. But butterflies, including the lovely iridescent blue morpho, fluttered around us in hundreds and sometimes interfered with my sketching.

Every evening, for the first ten days or so, we discussed the possible fate of "the Cuzco box"—that precious box of tinned and dried food and candles that had been mislaid. Then we began to speculate about the possible date of Tarnawiecki's return, with or without canoes and Indians to paddle them. We never heard a thing about the box, but news from Tarnawiecki came at last on our twenty-fourth day at Rosalina.

That morning we heard two or three loud bangs in the distance and guessed that one of the settlers, perhaps someone at the farm, was killing fish with dynamite cartridges. Fishing with a line was quite impossible, as the current of the river was far too swift, but the Indians sometimes crushed a poisonous plant and put it in the water in a section of the river that they had netted. Presently an Indian came running from the river and he told us that our neighbour Torres had had an accident.

Two of us hurried to the plantation down the river, where we found Torres lying on the ground and groaning, while two Indians and a half-caste stood by helpless. It appeared that a dynamite cartridge had exploded in his hand, blowing off his fingers and a part of the palm and pitting his face with fragments. We did our best for him with our first-aid kit, stanching the bleeding and binding up the stump, but it looked as if one of his eyes had also been damaged. As soon as possible a messenger was sent from the farm to fetch the nearest available doctor with all speed, but we knew that it might take at least five or six days before the doctor could arrive. We left Torres with the rest of our lint and aspirin and could only hope that the wretched man would recover. The accident had been due to his own fault, for he had tried to light the fuse of the detonator with a cigarette, had not been sure that it had caught and had held on to it too long.

When we were nearly back in camp we overtook a dozen black-haired young Indians, wearing cotton robes of a delightful brick-red colour, who were walking close to the river. These were the Indians of the Machegenga tribe who had been sent by Tarnawiecki to fetch us in their two long dugout canoes. Most of them carried bows and arrows and each had a small pouch slung round his neck so that it rested between his shoulders.

It was an exciting moment when we realized that we could at last embark on the next stage of our journey and we began at once to pack up the camp. The rotting remains of the old building had been a curious residence, giving little shelter from the hot sun and still less from the tropical rain that sometimes descended in torrents and dripped through the decayed fragments of thatch. But for more than three weeks this had been our home, where we had worked and had our meals and slept. Every evening, as darkness descended rapidly on the jungle, Professor Gregory struggled to get the acetylene lamp burning, not always with success, and latterly we had not even a stub of candle by which to write our diaries. Usually we went to bed—consisting in my case of a single small brown blanket that had torn in half—soon after finishing supper, but I remember moonlight nights when we sat talking among the black shadows and listening to the mysterious sounds of the forest and the distant, ceaseless roar of the rapids of the Urubamba river.

One of the Indians could speak a little Spanish and I learnt from him that Tarnawiecki had decided to wait for us at Maranquiato, the village from which they had come. It had taken him six days to get there, for the old trail was in terribly bad condition and he had fallen down a landslide and sprained an ankle. The two Peruvians who lived with the Indians had been away cutting timber and several more days had passed before Tarnawiecki could get in touch with them and arrange for the canoes to be sent to us. Then the Indians, using paddles and poles, had had a prolonged struggle against the rapids to bring the canoes the whole way round the great bend of the river, a distance of at least 150 miles. When possible they had kept close to the bank, where the current was less swift, but they had had to drag the canoes long distances over boulders and sandbanks. The canoes, hollowed out from solid mahogany tree-trunks, were forty-one feet in length, about two feet wide and little more than a foot deep. The sides were about an inch thick and had to stand up to extremely severe battering among the rocks and rapids.

As soon as we were launched we were swept along at a great speed, rolling and plunging through the waves and darting from one side of the river to the other to keep in the main stream of the current and to avoid boulders, whirlpools and half-submerged tree-trunks. It was a thrilling experience and the Indians were adept at handling the canoes. They were all cheerful young men and they laughed merrily together, even when their voices could not be heard above the roar of the water.

Ahead of us there lay more than two hundred and fifty miles of almost continuous rapids before we could reach the broader stretches of the river beyond the last foothills of the Andes. Somewhere beyond Maranquiato, we already knew, was that terrible gorge where disaster had overtaken every European who had attempted to pass through it. But now we were told that there were other sections where the rapids were so bad that no canoe could shoot through safely and soon, hurtling along like a bobsleigh without brakes, we came to one of them. Adroitly the Indians forced the canoes aside out of the main current and beached them on a bank of coarse sand and boulders. We all got out and a portage of several hundred yards was made past the foaming cascades formed, like many of the worst rapids, where a tributary entered the main stream carrying boulders, sand and tree-trunks right across to the opposite bank.

During the next four days our progress was an almost unbroken succession of rapids and portages. Many times the canoes were swamped by waves in midstream and we had to beach them to bale out the water. Several times they became jammed fast between huge submerged boulders, so that we had to spring into the river and fight with them in the tearing current until we could get them free. Often, in spite of the skill of our crews, they struck a rock or a waterlogged tree trunk violently and all but capsized. We sat all day in water and everything was perpetually drenched. But it was intensely exhilarating and I seldom felt in real danger.

Before dusk each day we landed on a bank of sand or boulders and bivouacked between the dense jungle and the foaming, roaring river. When rain threatened, the Indians, using the machetes that we gave them, cut down the palm-like reeds of *caña brava* and in a few minutes erected lean-to shelters that gave some protection. Often we saw on the sand the tracks of a jaguar, a tapir or a deer and once, when a fine large tapir appeared near the bank, the Indians went in pursuit with their bows and arrows. I fired at another with my revolver, but the range was too great and our meals remained meatless.

So far my sketches and painting materials had survived, bound up tightly in their special waterproof covers. I made many drawings of the Indians, of our bivouacs and of the river between its walls of thickly entangled trees, but I wondered always whether I would get them safely through the rest of the journey.

On the fifth day after leaving Rosalina we landed near the little cluster of huts that was Maranquiato and were delighted to find that Tarnawiecki had recovered from his ordeal. He was a man after my own heart: tough, modest, friendly and

ingenious and it was entirely due to him that we had managed
to reach this distant point in the jungle.

At Maranquiato we met the two Peruvians, named Pereira
and Landa, who lived there in a large house well constructed of
wooden poles, reeds and palms and who did all that they
possibly could to help us on our way. Later on we met two or
three other men living as isolated settlers in the jungle. There
was a rumour that at least one of them was a murderer who had
escaped across the Andes where the police were unlikely to
follow. Possibly such outcasts or fugitives—if such they were—
may have been liable to arrest if they returned to civilization, but
they were helpful to us and it takes all kinds to make a world.

After little more than twenty-four hours we were on our
way again, accompanied by Landa who came in charge of the
Indians, whose language he could speak. That evening we
made our bivouac on a long island of boulders between two
branches of the river. Rain was threatening and low clouds
hung among the trees on the hills. A few hundred yards downstream, where the water boiled in a turmoil of white foam, was
the entrance to the ill-omened gorge, known to the Indians as
the *Pongo de Mainique*—the Gateway of the Parrots. Here the
river narrowed between densely wooded hills of rock and the
force of the current increased. As daylight faded, rain began
to fall, but I made a sketch of our bivouac, with the shelters
of fronds and the entrance to the gorge looking dark and
ominous under its roof of cloud. (Plate XXVII.)

When I look at my diary, a treasured souvenir with words
and sketches much blurred by water, I am vividly reminded
of that sinister evening of the 1st June. I remember the
depressing sensation of the first desultory raindrops, then the
fine drizzle that made all the vegetation glisten rather coldly.
Even now I can almost hear the parrots, as they came out
brusquely from the green monotony of the trees and streamed
across the river like a squadron of jet-fighters. By now I was
quite accustomed to jungle life; but I must admit that, when I
lay down to sleep that night, I had a vague feeling of appre-
hension.

On the 2nd June we woke up as usual, before sunrise. For
a few moments I kept my ear close to the ground, listening to

the sound made by the sand and pebbles as the current dragged them along the bed of the river. It made me realize more than ever how strong was the current. Just in case I fell in the river, I thought it wise to wear as little as possible. I put on nothing but a khaki shirt with a special large pocket to carry my diary and notecase, worn-out cotton trousers and the remnants of a pair of gym-shoes.

After breakfast of fish, yucca, bananas and coffee, we loaded our equipment into the canoes and pushed off. We were soon among the rapids, travelling very fast, and in no time we were soaked by spray. Sometimes the leading Indian in each canoe stood up, watching the converging lines of foam ahead and signalling instructions to the crew who were fully extended in their efforts to guide the canoe among the rocks and waves. Some parts of the river were deceptively smooth, but we avoided them; there lurked a whirlpool or a contrary current that would have caused us to swing sideways and capsize. We made generally for the very middle of the foaming Vs where the pressure of the water was equal on either side, though there were large waves where the currents met and often they broke over the canoe.

Everything was happening at great speed. As we entered the mouth of the gorge the steep sides—a jumble of rocks and trees —seemed to be rushing past like the landscape seen from an express train. For the leading Indians, tense with concentration, the vital seconds must have seemed as they do to a bomb-aimer during the run in to the target. "A little more to port. . . . A little more. . . . Not so much! Hold it!" And we flashed through between two vast boulders, bouncing on the glassy domes of a minor cataract.

Sometimes we were swept from side to side in confused water; sometimes we were heading directly for a boulder where the water rose in a seething mass of foam, like a saucepan of milk that is about to boil over. Somehow, with supreme efforts, we were deflected; but already, as we plunged past the rock through the spray, we were involved in another instant problem. Occasionally the current took complete charge and we raced on half sideways, like a stick in a millstream, while the crew battled to bring the prow straight again.

From fifty yards the gorge narrowed to perhaps thirty and the deeper water rolled in great waves among the foam that betrayed submerged rocks. Then, on our right, we came to some enormous limestone boulders, where half the cliff above had fallen into the gorge. Here we landed, not without difficulty for the canoes were half full of water and they banged hard against the rocks. After so much excitement it was a relief to step on shore and we spent nearly three hours here, peacefully collecting fossils that we chipped from the rocks with our geological hammers, while the water roared past a few feet below us.

The Indians, eager to press on early in the day, expressed their anxiety to Landa, who asked me to explain to Professor Gregory that every hour of delay meant greater danger. Already a wind was blowing upstream through the gorge, increasing steadily in strength. By midday its pressure would have built up the waves still higher and the canoes would be swamped as soon as they entered the current. There was no possible space even for a bivouac among those tumbled boulders and it would be much wiser, Landa insisted, to complete the passage of the gorge, only about another mile and a half, and to bivouac on a sandbank near the exit.

But our leader maintained that this fossiliferous limestone must be thoroughly examined; it was one of the significant geological formations that he had come to study. Three hours was not a long time to wait, but he promised that we should proceed at noon.

Meanwhile the Indians carried all our baggage, including some fairly heavy parcels of geological specimens, over the boulders for two or three hundred yards until they came to a place where the walls of the gorge became almost vertical and it was impossible to go any farther. Then they went back for the canoes and lowered them downstream with long ropes.

While we watched this operation—knowing that, if we wanted to go on, as, of course, we did, we must soon get back into the canoes—we could not help feeling anxious. In a few seconds both canoes were completely swamped and sank, though they were empty. No sooner had one of them been laboriously hauled half out of the river, to tip out the water and re-launch it, than it sank again. (Plate XXVIII.) The force of the water from the wider part of the river above the gorge was prodigious. Just below the place where we intended to re-embark the gorge narrowed to about fifteen yards—less than a cricket pitch. In this bottleneck it was as if the Cup Final crowds of the last ten years were all trying to rush through the Marble Arch together. But this was no smooth jet of water; there were conflicting currents and breaking waves all over the place. Here and there dim green humps of glassy water showed where rocks were lurking underneath. The only quiet patches were still lower down, where we could see the oily swirls of shifting whirlpools.

It was soon after midday when the first canoe was safely loaded with a good deal of the baggage in the comparative shelter of a vast jutting rock. It bobbed about like a demented cork. Landa and I stood with the Indians in the rough water, on the slimy boulders, and tried to hold it steady while Tarna-wiecki and the crew got in. Then it shot away down the gorge, bouncing through the waves. On the top of some of the baggage in the middle, covered with a waterproof groundsheet, I had at the last moment placed the pouches with my painting materials, including all the sketches I had made since leaving Cuzco.

Professor Gregory and Miss McKinnon Wood put the fossils that they had collected into one of the wooden boxes. I fastened elastic bands round my diary, in which I had made several rapid sketches of the gorge and of the first canoe being loaded at the embarkation place, and I stowed it in the large breast pocket of my shirt, fastening the button. Now it was our turn.

While the crew hung on to the canoe, we climbed in among the baggage, which included some heavy boxes of supplies and geological specimens, the shotgun and all my kit. Waves broke against the rocks and in a moment the canoe was half full of water. When the Indians got in, it sank.

We clambered out. Bit by bit we removed the baggage. With a great struggle we wrenched the canoe half out of the river's grip and tipped out most of the water. Then we started all over again.

This time we did it more quickly. It was just a matter of a

race against the waves. We had already shipped several waves when the last Indian climbed in. We swung out from the bank —and then the current grabbed us.

Like an express train, it seemed, we tore along through a swirl of white foam, heaving and bouncing wildly. The Indians lunged with their paddles in a futile attempt to bring the prow of the canoe downstream. They might have saved their energy. Wave after wave broke over us and in a few seconds the canoe had become a submarine, balanced on an even keel by a miracle. This could not last long.

For a short time we continued to swing down the raging river, as helpless as a match-stick in mid-ocean. As the precipitous walls of the gorge streamed by I caught sight, out of the corner of my eye, of numerous cascades, each like an intricate tracery of white lace suspended from the jungle above. Water dripped from overhanging trees, festooned with tangled lianas. I could not take it all in then, but I found it photographed on my mind afterwards.

Suddenly I realized that we were facing upstream, caught by a contrary current on the edge of a whirlpool. A moment later the canoe capsized.

Miss McKinnon Wood and I struck out for the right bank, some forty feet away. Others, perhaps wiser in that whirlpool-infested channel, clung to the upturned canoe that still floated beneath the surface. As I swam the grey wall of the gorge seemed to flow past me like the bank in a railway cutting. With difficulty we hauled ourselves out on to one of the limestone buttresses that rose sheer from the water for fifty feet. From our slippery perch we saw other members of our party clinging to the canoe, that had drifted into a small bay. Our leader, clutching my kit-bag that had enough air inside to keep it afloat, was being carried, uncannily, upstream by a wayward current near the opposite wall. Then he began to turn down the river and, as he disappeared from view beyond the buttresses, we had no doubt that he would soon be able to clamber out.

The nature of the gorge made it impossible for us to join the others, though we made many efforts to do so. Twenty minutes later we saw the first canoe returning, painfully slowly, upstream. With poles and paddles the crew gradually edged their way back against the powerful current, as close to the bank as possible. They shouted, above the roar of the river, that they could see no trace of Professor Gregory, or of the athletic young Indian who had been seated behind me.

We owed our lives to that other canoe. Without them we could never have got away. Tarnawiecki told me that the first hint of disaster was a kit-bag that floated past them through the rapids as they were emptying their canoe on a sandbank. No one saw precisely what had happened to our missing companions.

We were taken from the rocks and as cautiously as possible floated down to the narrow sandbank nearer the exit from the gorge. One of the Indians brought me the green ground-sheet, which he had found jammed against the rocks a little lower down. My pouches were still inside it. Tarnawiecki told me that, when his canoe became nearly submerged, it had been decided to drive it on to the first possible ledge or sandbank, but the ground-sheet had floated off like a large green bubble.

I laid out all my sketches in the afternoon sunshine, for most of them were very damp. My clothes dried slowly on me: all my kit had been lost. Before we lay down on the sand that evening we discussed what we should do. It was decided that Landa and I should go on down the river as fast as possible to the nearest telegraph station at Masisea on the Ucayali, a distance of several hundred miles, to telegraph the news of the disaster to England. The others would remain to search for the bodies of Professor Gregory and the missing Indian; then they would follow down the river. Meanwhile one of the Indians was to try to make his way upstream through the jungle in order to obtain food supplies from his village at Maranquiato.

When the next day dawned the little remaining food was shared out, Landa and I and six Indians got into our canoe and we pushed out into the stream. We streaked through the rapids, dodging rocks and whirlpools, and in a short time emerged into the sunshine at the lower end of the gorge. The exit, where the river finally broke through the last foothills, lay between two high cliffs of rock which rose abruptly from the water as if they were intended to carry a bridge across the chasm. Below this point there were occasional low hills, smothered with trees, and for a long time outlying ridges were visible beyond the left bank, but these gradually receded into the distance. After a few days all trace of the Andes had vanished and we were travelling through the vast region of the Amazon basin. Nothing but jungle and swamps, steaming under the hot sun, extended for hundreds of miles in every direction.

If Landa and I had not lost our equipment and if there had been no need to hurry, this part of the journey would have seemed like a prolonged picnic in wonderful surroundings. But we had undertaken not to delay until we arrived at Masisea and shortage of food made it urgent that we should as soon as possible reach some place where we could restock.

We travelled throughout the hours of daylight; my diary reminds me that we were generally up at half-past four in the morning and we made only the briefest of stops when it was necessary to bale out the canoe or when there seemed to be a chance for the Indians to kill some sort of game. During the first three or four days we passed through many stretches of rapids, some of which were so extensive and dangerous that we made short portages when we could. Generally there was heavy dew at night and, although the Indians made rough shelters with reeds and palm-fronds, everything was perpetually soaked. Nearly every dawn the river was shrouded in thick mist, which billowed up from the surface like clouds of steam as the sun rose. Several times, when there were difficult rapids ahead, we were compelled to wait until visibility improved. For hours on end we were exposed to the full strength of the tropical sun and even the Indians became almost exhausted by the great heat, which was reflected, like the dazzling glare, from the surface of the water. My dark glasses, like all the rest of my equipment, had been lost in the Pongo de Mainique and I found the glare extremely trying.

Every evening, shortly before sunset, we looked out for a sandbank for our bivouac, where we made a fire and lay down in our damp clothes. Here we found the tracks of various animals, including jaguars, tapirs, deer and capybaras, and two or three times we dug up nests of turtle's eggs that had been buried in the sand. These eggs, like small pingpong balls with soft shells, made a welcome but rather unsatisfying addition to our scanty diet. When boiled the yolks became firm, but the white remained liquid.

If I had had a rifle, or even my revolver, I might have been able to shoot something for the pot, although the tapirs and capybaras that we saw during the day generally made off in haste. But we now had no weapons except the bows and arrows of the Indians and, despite all travellers' tales about the deadly skill of natives with such weapons, it seemed that arrows could not be very effective in thick jungle. Occasionally, when capybaras were seen near the bank or swimming in the river, the Indians went in pursuit, but only once did they get one of these large rodents, which looked like giant guinea-pigs. They smoked it all night over a camp fire and we ate chunks of it next day. This was the only meat we had: by now our remaining roots of yucca had decayed and we had nothing but a few biscuits and unripe bananas and a little coffee.

One night, when I was lying on the sand close to the rushing river, a capybara ran out of the jungle, plunged into the water and swam away. Immediately afterwards I saw, by the dim light of the stars, a fairly large animal crossing the sandbank a dozen yards away. It went to the water's edge and then came stealthily in my direction. Soon I realized that it was a jaguar, about whose habits I knew nothing. I kept perfectly still. It came nearer and nearer and passed between me and the river, within three feet of my head. As it drew out of sight my eyes strained round in their sockets, but I dared not move. For a long time I listened, but could hear nothing except the sound of the river and the drag of the stones along the bottom, and at last I fell asleep.

In the morning Landa and the Indians, who had been sleeping round the remains of the fire, were astounded to see the jaguar's tracks, with one clear paw-mark right in the ashes of the fire. After passing me it had obviously stepped over one of the Indians, then withdrawn and followed an erratic course back into the jungle.

When at last we were free of the rapids we came to stretches of the river where it broadened out into vast steamy lakes hundreds of yards in width and the current became sluggish.

XXVII. Bivouac above the *Pongo de Mainique*, the fateful gorge of the Urubamba river, Peru

XXVIII.
Machegenga
Indians
preparing to
load the canoes
immediately
before
launching into
the rapids in
which Professor
Gregory lost
his life

XXIX. Nuuanu Pali, Oahu, Hawaiian Islands

XXX. Lake Kawaguchi, near Funatsu, Fuji Lakes, Japan

Hitherto we had covered probably fifty miles a day, but now our progress was slower. Now and then large pink river dolphins disported themselves about the canoe, threatening to upset it, and several times we found a number of alligators on the sandbanks where we proposed to land. Birds of many kinds became plentiful, particularly parrots, toucans and cranes. One afternoon I saw overhanging the water what appeared to be a huge bush covered with large white blossoms, like a rhododendron bush in full flower. The Indians paddled towards it and suddenly all the flowers took to the air—a cloud of lovely white egrets.

Early one morning my attention was drawn to movement near the top of a giant tree that towered above the dense wall of green on the left bank. Landa made the Indians stop paddling and we drifted along, watching a family of monkeys— the parents and two babies—swinging among the branches high above our heads. Later on we saw many more monkeys.

A week after leaving the scene of the accident we reached the mouth of the river Tambo, a large tributary which joins the Urubamba from the left bank, and from this point onwards the great river is called the Ucayali. We knew that, in a clearing amongst the dense vegetation not far from the mouth of the Tambo, there was a small Polish settlement named Atalaya that had been started barely five years earlier. While we were negotiating the conflicting currents at the confluence of the two rivers a tropical storm suddenly burst overhead.

I have been in many such storms, but I think this was the heaviest downpour I have ever known. In a few seconds all visibility was blotted out by the rain, which came down with such force that it seemed to rebound from the surface of the river to a height of at least two feet. We were several hundred yards from either bank and the Indians paddled like demons for the nearest, although we could not see it. Rapidly the canoe sank deeper into the water and soon it was completely full of water, only just floating level with the surface. It seemed certain that we should again capsize. I sat perfectly still, but prepared to swim at any moment. The crew, now extremely cautious, continued to paddle and somehow contrived to keep the canoe on an even keel. Then, after an age of anxiety, a grey mass loomed ahead and in a few more seconds the canoe was driven in among reeds and overhanging branches, to which we clung desperately.

We remained there for at least a quarter of an hour, while the rain thrashed the river into turmoil and stung our shoulders with its fierce needles. Not one of us dared to move.

Almost as suddenly as it had started, the storm ceased, the clouds passed on and the sun came through. It was quite impossible to empty the canoe in that position, so we pulled on the branches until we had got it well embedded in the jungle, then we climbed on to the bank—an indescribable tangle of mud, branches and reeds—and dragged the heavy canoe slowly in after us.

Fortunately we had landed on the bank on which Atalaya stood. Leaving the Indians to deal with the canoe, Landa and I plunged through the jungle towards the cluster of wood and palm huts about half a mile away. It was gloomy among the trees, but suddenly it grew even darker and in a few moments another downpour descended, accompanied by gusts of wind like puffs from a mighty bellows. One of these brought a large branch crashing to the ground directly in our path. As it fell it carried with it a tangle of lianas and snapped off or bent to the ground several palms.

A small store and a few other houses scattered among the trees constituted the whole of Atalaya and we went first to the store to get some food. The owner, Don Rodolpho, was out, so we called on two officials of the *Guardia Civil* and made a formal report of the accident to them. We then sat on the balcony of the store until Don Rodolpho returned after dark, when he provided us with a meal of fish, rice, beans, roasted bananas and coffee and allowed us to sleep on the balcony that night.

During supper he gave me the welcome news that the launch that came up the Ucayali once a month from Iquitos, to collect the odd bags of coffee, rice, peanuts and other crops that the few scattered settlers managed to produce, was expected at any moment. Luckily I had saved a good deal of my money in the pocket of my shirt and I decided to go on in the launch. I bought a few more gifts for the Indians, to supplement the

machetes and other things we had already given to them, and
Landa told me that he would go slowly back up the river with
them, a journey that would take several weeks. By the time
they reached the Pongo de Mainique the river should be very
much lower. But he would await the launch, to buy supplies
to take with him.

Next evening, after dark, a whistle was heard in the distance
down the river and immediately intense excitement broke out
in the village. The launch had reached the mouth of the Tambo
and should arrive in the morning. Meanwhile everyone was
busy, making up parcels of things to send to the market in
Iquitos, at least a thousand miles away.

When the launch pulled into the bank, towards midday, the
excitement knew no bounds, for its arrival, with luxuries from
the outer world, was always uncertain. For several hundred
miles below the Tambo there were dangerous currents and
navigation was only possible in daylight, owing to the numerous
shoals and waterlogged tree trunks. Only last month the sister-
launch had been wrecked, with the loss of seven lives.

When the first rush was over I went on board and chose a
place on the upper deck to sleep. Never have I travelled with
less luggage, for I had nothing but my sketching materials and
half a torn blanket. Unloading and loading continued in
desultory fashion for the rest of the day and most of the night.
Landa and I and two or three other men had meals with the
commander, Don Gregorio, at a table of boards on the upper
deck. Two fried eggs and a roasted banana for breakfast seemed
like a feast. Don Gregorio said he was anxious to get away early
next morning, as the river was rising and so muddy that the
shoals were often invisible.

The launch, which had crossed the Atlantic from Europe
about thirty years ago, was like a small tug and capable of
carrying thirty-five tons of cargo. The fuel consisted of metre-
lengths of wood, hundreds of which had to be loaded two or
three times a day from stacks made ready on the banks by
settlers. Other stops were made to collect a few bags of coffee
or rice or two or three scraggy bulls or cows that had to be
coaxed on board over a precarious plank, not always successfully.

But during the first few days the most frequent stops were due to grounding on shoals or collision with submerged tree-trunks and sometimes thick mist obliged us to wait. Often an hour or more was wasted, manœuvring with anchors and ropes to release the launch from whatever it had struck, but on several occasions the rudder, the screw or the bottom plates were damaged. Repairs that could be made from inside were carried out in almost complete darkness in the hold, amidst bags of coffee and rice, cows, pigs and hens. Underwater repairs were made by the engineer, who dived repeatedly through the muddy water—as thick as pea soup—and worked by touch for half a minute at a time until the damage was somehow patched up. Once everyone on board had to help to shift most of the cargo forward until the stern rose sufficiently to allow the engineer to straighten the rudder: then we shifted everything back again.

On another occasion, when a large branch had jammed itself between the screw and the rudder, it looked as if we were stuck for ever. Having nothing else to do, I volunteered to go over-board with the engineer, armed with a saw, and after more than half an hour of frantic struggle, mostly below the surface, we managed to free the obstruction. Afterwards we were both given a shower-bath with a bucket on the upper deck, but we were so hot that we remained damp for hours.

Yet another time a waterlogged tree jammed the rudder just as we were heading for a stopping-place and we rammed the mud-bank with a violent jolt that threw all the unfortunate cattle into a heap. By this time there were two women with babies on board and the pandemonium that broke out beggars description. Babies, hens, pigs and cows joined in a screaming, wailing din such as I have heard only during the broadcasting of modern dance music. Had our vessel been the *Queen Mary* we should have been towed off by a flotilla of tugs. Being what it was, it had to be satisfied with the power of its wood-fuelled engine, aided by myself and the few other men on board who pushed mightily with the trunks of two small trees that we had cut down at the edge of the jungle.

We reached Masisea, another settlement in the forest, after midday on the 14th June, eleven days after I had left my companions in the fatal Pongo de Mainique. There was a telegraph office from which I sent a message to the British Legation at Lima, asking them to forward the news of the accident to London. Some letters had been forwarded here to await my arrival and one of them, from the Foreign Office, told me that I had been appointed to the British Legation in Bucharest and was to proceed there as soon as possible.

The commander, Don Gregorio, lent me a hammock made of string and I slept in this, slung between stanchions on the upper deck which was crowded with cargo and several other men in their own hammocks. On the night before we reached Masisea I was woken up suddenly by what sounded like a revolver shot close to my head. I heard groans and the sound of footsteps on the deck. By the time I had disentangled myself from the hammock, two or three men had appeared with a lantern and an agonized voice called out that someone had been shot. By the light of the lantern we found blood on the deck. We followed the trail to a young Peruvian, who had a long gash across his scalp. Further investigation revealed that this had been caused, not by a bullet, but by the sharp edge of an Indian club, made from the stem of a palm-frond, with which the man's cousin had struck him while he slept. The assailant was discovered crouching in the stern and he confessed that this was his way of settling a quarrel that had been going on for days. We put him in the hold among the coffee bags, pigs, cattle and cockroaches, with a guard to ensure that he did not emerge until he could be handed over to the police. The wounded man was passed to me to bandage and happily he soon recovered.

For another six days we went on down the Ucayali, now a very broad river and navigable by night as well as day. Occasionally we collided with waterlogged tree-trunks, but there were no longer any shoals. The stops, to take on fuel and cargo, were as frequent as ever. I noted them in my diary and on the last day counted a total of more than seventy.

I spent much of my time watching the bird life of the river, the dolphins playing in our wake and the numerous alligators sunning themselves on sandbanks. Now and then, when a village or a saw-mill broke the green monotony of the jungle,

I made a sketch. As we approached the confluence of the
Ucayali and the Marañon, where the main stream becomes
the Amazon, we overtook several rafts of mahogany logs with
logs of light balsa wood attached to give them buoyancy.
Here the flood water had spread far into the jungle and great
masses of weed floated on the surface. I saw a good deal of
the river by moonlight, because the noises at every halt—
caused by the rudder chains, the ship's bell and steam whistle,
shouting voices, the dumping of hundreds of logs in the hold,
pigs squealing, cocks crowing, babies yelling and so on—made
sleep impossible for a large part of each night.

Arrival at New York in a transatlantic liner is a sedate affair
in comparison with our arrival at Iquitos. We had spent part
of the night, under an enormous yellow moon, anchored off the
island and at 4 a.m. the commander woke up everyone in a
great flurry, having mistaken the time for five o'clock. In spite
of sleepy protests, the upper deck was cleared of hammocks and
terrible bellowings from below told us that the cattle were
being prepared for landing.

I was not sorry to have reached the end of this section of my
long journey, interesting though it had been. Ten days cooped
up in such a tiny vessel, with barely a square yard of the little
deck space free from encumbrances, had been a trying ordeal.
I had nothing to pack; I was still wearing the old shirt, the
worn-out cotton trousers and the disintegrated gym-shoes in
which I had swum through the rapids of the Pongo. While the
launch steamed slowly towards the quay, with much tooting
of the whistle and a cacophony of noises from below, I leant
on the rail and made a rough sketch of the Iquitos skyline in
the early morning light. It was a peaceful scene, with reflections of the church, the low white buildings and the launches
and river steamers rippling gently in the lake-like expanse of
the river. Iquitos is 2,000 miles from the delta of the Amazon,
yet at this point the river is already two miles wide.

We pulled up with a tremendous clatter close to the *São
Salvador*, a Brazilian river steamer that was due to sail in four
days' time for Manáos, 1,200 miles down the Amazon. Meanwhile it was going to a sawmill nearly two days away to load
a cargo of mahogany.

I shook hands with Don Gregorio and thanked him for the loan of the hammock, which had alleviated much of the discomfort of the voyage. Then I went ashore, showed my passport at the Capitania del Puerto and booked a room at a small hotel. Feeling like a tramp and certainly looking like a "Distressed British Subject", I called on the British Consul to ask for advice about where to buy some clothes. Had I been dressed in full diplomatic uniform, Mr. Massey could not have received me more kindly. He invited me to stay at his house until I sailed in the *São Salvador* and he asked one of his staff to show me the shops where I could have clothes made quickly: there was no ready-made clothing that would fit me. I told him that one of my first calls would be the photographer, to have my luxuriant beard photographed; then the barber, to have it removed. I asked him to compare me carefully with the photograph in my passport so that, when I returned clean-shaven, he would know that I was the same man. He lent me a tropical suit of his own and I went off to shop.

That evening we met for supper at his home, where I had been revelling in the luxury of a shower-bath. He was astounded at the change in my appearance and laughed heartily over the transformation from a filthy tramp into a diplomat. Over iced cocktails, the first I had tasted for months, I told him briefly about the expedition and we continued to talk until late.

In less than four days Portuguese tailors, Peruvian carpenters and others had made me two suits, four shirts, underclothes, pyjamas, two pairs of walking shoes and a splendid box of solid mahogany in which to pack them. The clothes fitted well and I doubt whether I could have had such an emergency wardrobe made to measure anywhere in London in so short a time.

The voyage to Manáos took six days, during which there was nothing whatever to do except eating and sleeping, both of which were good for me. But I have never had the ability to do either for long periods on end and I studied the river for hours, anticipating that I might never pass that way again. It is impossible to describe the width of the Amazon, for it divides into several channels that form immensely long islands and at this time of the year it was in flood. Where there are low hills and where the general level of the ground is above flood level the river has definite banks, sometimes several miles apart, but in the lower reaches the water extends far into the jungle and in many areas, for a period, only the tops of the taller trees are visible. Although the jungle walls, sometimes near and sometimes far away, might seem monotonous to an unobservant person, I found it fascinating to watch the numerous species of birds, the monkeys and alligators, the innumerable varieties of tree and palm and of course the traffic on the river. Whenever we came to a stopping-place I snatched the opportunity to sketch and I made many notes from the deck as we went along.

On arrival at Manáos I found that I should have to wait there for six days until one of the Booth Line steamers was due to sail for Liverpool. The Acting British Vice-Consul, Mr. J. P. Turner, most kindly had me to stay with him and he took me every evening to bathe at the delightful British Club at the edge of the forest. Having booked my passage to England, I was invited to join the twenty or so cruise passengers on their sight-seeing trips and this gave me the opportunity to see some of the enormous Victoria Regia water-lilies that were abundant in one of the creeks. One day several of us went for a tour in a small motor-boat in the flooded forest, where we sailed in and out among the tree-tops. We narrowly escaped disaster when someone disturbed a hornets' nest suspended from a branch and we got jammed among a lot of palm fronds in our haste to get away.

Some day, perhaps, if Europe continues to saw at its own throat and to promote the survival of the unfittest, the centre of world interest may shift to South America. Life there can be extremely attractive and there must be many people who would rather deal direct with nature than collect higher pay for less work in a factory in the Old World. Then Manáos and other places in the heart of the South American continent will come into their own. In the days of the rubber boom someone spent a million dollars on the opera house at Manáos, but I found it closed. Grandiose ideas can only be fruitful when the life of the local inhabitants is vigorous and fitted to support them. It seemed to me then that Manáos, having once been a boom town, was trying vainly to flourish on export trade with countries that were suffering from poor economic conditions. There was a factory where rosewood was being treated to make perfume and another where Brazil nuts were being cracked, shelled and packed in tins and cedar-wood boxes for export to countries where they would be coated with sugar and used to break people's teeth. In another factory, a magnificent tiled edifice that was far too elaborate for its purpose, I saw rubber latex being prepared for export—on a much reduced scale. Elsewhere efforts were being made to promote the sale of coffee, of an insecticide called *varvasco* that was said to be effective in preventing the adhesion of barnacles to ships' bottoms, of *uacima*, a substitute for jute in making sacking, and of *balata*, a latex similar to rubber that could be made into good machine belting. I could not help feeling that these efforts were a mere scratching of the surface. The Amazonian jungle is rich in timber, much of it almost as hard and as heavy as iron, in plants of medicinal value and in many other valuable products and it might be wiser to make full use of them, precisely where they are, before attempting to find a better world on the moon or on one of the planets.

Soon after I went on board the steamer for the voyage of about 860 miles to Pará one of the passengers, a Roumanian lady who had not realized that I was a new arrival, asked me what I thought of the trip "a thousand miles up the Amazon". When I told her that I had not come up the Amazon she seemed incredulous and asked how on earth I had got to Manáos. I said that I had come from the Pacific coast and that I had already travelled between two and three thousand miles by river. She appeared unconvinced, but our conversation flourished rather more when I told her that I was on my way to Roumania and that I had already visited Bucharest, some years ago.

Four days later we were in Pará. The night before we sailed for England I remained for a long time on deck. It was impossible to sleep on account of the noise of the winches, hour after hour, as they raised from lighters and poured into the holds six hundred tons of Brazil nuts.

As the ship gathered way, heading out into the Atlantic through the muddy water that poured from the Amazon, my thoughts were thousands of miles away, in the high Andes and with the laughing Indians in the foaming rapids of the Uru-bamba. Often since then I have longed to live that life again.

It was only when I was back in London that I heard what had become of my companions left behind in the Gateway of the Parrots. Fortunately they seemed to have fared rather better than Landa and I, who had known real hunger for a few days. The Indian despatched upstream when we left had by chance seen some of his tribe on the farther side of the rock-slide in the upper part of the gorge and had shouted the news of the expedition's plight to them. They were able to tell Pereira, the Peruvian who had remained at Maranquiato village, and he lost no time in making a rough raft and loading it with foodstuffs. This was launched into the rapids and it arrived, after a very severe battering, in the shallows below the gorge, where it was recovered by Tarnawiecki and his men on the following day. Pereira then collected all the local Mache-gengas and they managed to repair an old trail past the Pongo sufficiently to be able to reach Tarnawiecki's camp. On the third day after the accident the body of Professor Gregory was found on a beach below the camp and he was buried under a cairn on the left bank of the river, among the mountains that he had explored.

The rest of the expedition then continued down the river to the mouth of the Tambo, taking nearly two and a half times as long as Landa and I had taken over our hurried journey. From there, with a fresh crew of Piros Indians, they went on to Masisea and were able to fly in a Naval Air Line plane to San Ramón in the Andes. Thence they went by car and rail to Lima.

Some of Professor Gregory's notes and many of the geological specimens were lost in the river and several of the scientific instruments were lost or damaged, but most of the rest of the equipment, except my own kit, was luckily in the canoe that got through safely. The scientific material saved, together with that sent home from Cuzco, was later examined by specialists in England, but no complete account of the results of the expedition could be written without Professor Gregory's guiding hand.

Soon after my return to Europe I was asked to address the Royal Geographical Society on the subject of the expedition, an honour that should have fallen to Professor Gregory. My future wife was in the audience. At the request of the President of the Society, Admiral Sir William Goodenough, the lantern slides that I showed were all made from my own paintings and more than a hundred and fifty of the pictures were exhibited in the Society's House for several months.

CHAPTER X

PAINTING MOUNTAINS ALL ROUND
THE WORLD

IN recent years there seem to have been more books than
usual about mountains, a large proportion of them dealing
with the Himalaya. This was natural while Everest and other
Himalayan giants remained unclimbed, but now that it has
been shown how the obstacle of great altitude can be overcome
with the aid of special equipment the Himalaya have come
down a little. Extreme altitude was a peculiar barrier; a factor
that had to be added to the problem of the climb itself. Now
it is becoming possible to compare pitches on Himalayan peaks
with those on well-known mountains in other parts of the world.
There is reason to hope that the Himalaya will gradually
become more accessible and that more people will be able to
enjoy their beauty.

In a letter that I received at the New Year, 1956, a fellow
member of the Alpine Club suggested that interest in the
Himalaya had passed its peak. All except seven of the really
big mountains, he said, had been conquered and numerous
detailed histories had been written about the conquests. It is
probably true that the interest of the general public, stimulated
by press reports of sensational first ascents, has waned; but
climbing as a sport is not dying out and I think it likely that
increasing numbers of climbers will turn their attention to the
Himalaya. But whether the Himalaya have "had it"—in so
far as public esteem is concerned—or are only beginning to
become popular, no one need despise the lesser mountains of
the world that were first climbed many years ago.

Almost any mountain, even a little one, can loom large
when there is nothing near to surpass it and it can give us a
personal experience that we might never have elsewhere. I
have enjoyed days on mountains in many parts of the world

and some of my happiest memories are connected with quite minor peaks. Several of them are so well known that it may seem jejune to mention them.

The volcano is a type of mountain in a class by itself. I have walked up to the craters of a good many volcanoes, both active and extinct and, with a few exceptions, I would not rate them very high as climbs. But they are often found in the midst of spectacular scenery and it is usually well worth while plodding up the long steep slopes of old lava to look down into the crater and to see the view from the top. Yet for me, as an artist, their greatest fascination lies in their distinctive, graceful shapes and in the luxuriant vegetation that grows in the rich soil about them. The typical conical form is by no means universal and there are many ancient volcanoes that have been weathered down to the shape of jagged mountains and are now clothed with trees and scrub from base to summit.

I remember walking, in the heart of the Andes, down a steep escarpment and across an undulating plateau many miles wide to what appeared to be a low range of hills, but I did not realize, until Professor Gregory drew my attention to the geological formation, that this was a gigantic volcanic vent. Then, while I made a sketch looking back along our route, I appreciated that we had walked across a kind of monster soup-plate, with an irregular shallow rim, lying at an altitude above 12,000 feet. Not every volcanic vent forms a cone when erupting; sometimes the lava oozes from crevices and spreads over the surrounding country, like water coming through cracks in ice on a pond. Several times in the Andes we saw water-carved ravines that had exposed a number of thick super-imposed layers of lava and there is at least one place where no less than nine such layers can be seen.

One of the most famous and lovely groups of volcanoes is in the Hawaiian islands, which I visited in 1937. The archipelago was discovered in 1778 by Captain Cook, the most distinguished of the pioneers in Australasia, during his last great voyage and he named it the Sandwich Islands after John Montagu, fourth Earl of Sandwich, who was First Lord of the Admiralty at the time. On his second visit he was killed by natives in a skirmish on the shore of Hawaii, the largest of the islands. They might once have been a British colony, for Captain Vancouver took possession of them in the name of King George III, but the British Government never ratified his action. For more than a century they remained a kingdom under native rulers, until a republic was proclaimed in 1894. Four years later they were annexed by the United States Government and American influence is now abundantly obvious.

The highest volcano in the group, Mauna Kea, now extinct, is nearly 14,000 feet, but Mauna Loa, which is nearly as high, and Kilauea, are still active. It gave me more pleasure to gaze on the mountains from a distance than to climb their long slopes, but there are not many other places where it is possible to stand on a high mountain that commands such magnificent views over land and sea. The vegetation, too, is outstandingly lovely and colourful. The native flower, cultivated in profusion, is the hibiscus, but there are numerous other tropical trees and plants, including the poinciana regia and the "golden shower", which I found almost too startling to paint.

Most of the ships that visit the Hawaiian islands call at Honolulu on the island of Oahu and I suppose that many of the passengers, when they have the time, drive up the motor road to Nuuanu Pali to see the view looking towards Diamond Head. (Plate XXIX.) There is a gap here in the mountain side which must be one of the windiest spots on earth and it was extremely difficult to find any shelter from which to make a sketch. When I tried to stand at the roadside, where a low wall protected my legs, I felt as if the whole top half of my body would be blown away by the continual blast, almost like that from a jet engine.

Before leaving Oahu I was taken to Pearl Harbour, the largest United States Naval Base. No one could then have foreseen its fateful destiny. But the mountains and flowers and the heavenly green-blue ocean held most of my attention and I could hardly bear the idea of going away without having bathed at the famous Waikiki beach. I was horrified to find the beach barricaded by a solid wall of hotels and houses: there appeared to be no public bathing place at all. I was told that, if I wanted to get to the beach, I must rent a room for five dollars. Waikiki is a wonderful place for surf-riding, but I felt that a short swim would not be worth five dollars to me and I walked away disappointed. Then I noticed a small hotel, a few hundred yards along the shore, with some little bathing cabins and I persuaded the man in charge to let me use one of these for twenty-five cents. Waikiki is worth at least that.

When I left Canada I had accumulated several months of leave and I decided to use them to complete a voyage round the world. From Honolulu, therefore, I sailed for Yokohama with the intention of spending about two months in Japan. Then I proposed to go to Peking, the wondrous oriental city that I wanted to see above all others, and to return to Europe by way of Indo-China, Malaya, Burma and India. Unfortunately the Japanese, who were at that time carrying on their undeclared war against China, interfered with this delectable plan and, owing to the fighting that was going on, I had to cut out Peking altogether.

I happened to be travelling in the same ship as Sir Robert Craigie, the newly appointed British Ambassador to Japan, and on the day after we left Honolulu we heard that the British Ambassador to China had been wounded by a bullet from a Japanese aircraft while motoring on the road from Nanking to Shanghai. For a time it seemed possible that our Government might break off diplomatic relations with Japan and that Sir Robert might have to turn back without landing; but, as events turned out, he was to have a busy time in Tokyo. When he hinted that a temporary addition to his staff might be welcome, I saw at least some of my leave beginning to dissolve. But I did not altogether shun the idea of working for a short time at the Embassy in Tokyo and I said that of course I would be willing to help if needed.

The China incident is now old history and, as it has nothing to do with my theme, I shall not discuss it here. The Japan I like to remember is far away from Tokyo and nearly all the sketches that I made there, at the risk of being taken for a spy, are views of mountains and lakes and ancient temples.

My first sight of Japan, in the early morning, was a line of jagged, misty hills where I could just distinguish cultivated terraces and a few scattered villages. I shall never forget that, as I drove in an Embassy car from Yokohama to Tokyo, through a continuous and much-beflagged built-up area swarming with Japanese precariously riding bicycles, my nostrils were assailed by a succession of indescribable smells such as I had never known before. I was accustomed to oriental—and African—odours, but this concatenation was phenomenal.

I suppose that most Englishmen, if asked to provide a symbol for Japan, would suggest the form of Mount Fuji, the sacred mountain that has been depicted by every Japanese artist and probably by every Japanese child in its first efforts to draw. The cone is over 12,000 feet high and it certainly has a graceful shape, but I do not myself consider it more beautiful than Popocatepetl in Mexico or Demavend in Persia. The ascent is a rather long walk uphill and in my opinion the most pleasing impression of the mountain can be obtained from a distance.

But Fuji, like so many of the Japanese mountains, is often obscured by cloud and mist. When I first saw Japanese prints of landscape subjects many years ago I used to wonder why the artists seemed so addicted to views of mountains and trees half hidden by mist. However, it seemed an economical way of painting and, as the pictures had a fascinating simplicity, I liked them. I had not been long in Japan before I realized that the country really was like that. I was astonished to find how true to nature were many of the prints that I had seen. When I went to Lake Chuzenji, the Fuji Lakes, Miyanoshita and other mountain and lake districts and sat down to paint my impressions I found at once that my sketches had something that was characteristically Japanese. (Plate XXX.) I made no attempt to affect any Japanese style of painting, but there were the mountains and the pine trees, half-seen through the mist, and the soft reflections with, perhaps, an isolated fisherman's boat floating apparently in the air.

After working for a month at the Embassy I was released to continue my leave, but I never recovered that lost month. For another month I toured about the country, experiencing several minor earthquakes, that are as commonplace there as they are in Mexico, and the stormy weather that came during a typhoon that struck Hongkong. Reluctantly I accepted the advice not to attempt to go to Peking and I sailed in a French ship from Kobe for Hongkong.

XXXI. "Blizzard at Camp III on the North Col of Everest, 1924." A reconstruction (published in *The Sphere*) based on descriptions by the climbers and personal experience of blizzards

A. V. COVERLEY-PRICE

XXXII. Mount Kilimanjaro (19,321 feet), Tanganyika Territory, seen at dawn from an aircraft at 12,000 feet

Three days later we anchored off the China coast, about a dozen miles from Shanghai, and I found myself on the edge of the war zone. Several Japanese destroyers appeared and at intervals during the next twenty-four hours I saw considerable numbers of Japanese aircraft flying inland. Now and then there were sounds of gunfire and of bursting bombs. Despite all this, a fresh consignment of passengers, largely Chinese, arrived on board and a French gunboat came down the river to take off some European passengers who were returning, rather bravely it seemed, to Shanghai. Two of the new arrivals on board told me grim tales of the bombing of the Cathay Hotel and of other incidents in which they had been involved.

The sea had not yet subsided after the typhoon and we rolled heavily while steaming southwards through the Strait of Formosa. As we approached Hongkong the whole sky was ablaze with a lurid sunset which made the scene that met our eyes almost theatrically unreal. At the entrance to the channel leading to Kowloon, where the ship was to dock, bare rocky slopes, golden in the sunset glow, rose steeply from the water. At the base of these slopes, high and dry above sea level, there lay at intervals several large vessels of up to 20,000 tons. They had been thrown up there like flotsam by the fury of the recent typhoon, when the wind had reached the unprecedented velocity of 165 miles an hour. In the midst of the harbour other vessels lay on the bottom, with only the tops of their masts and funnels showing, and the stern of one large ship, which had been hurled on to a quay, overhung the road while its prow was buried deep in the water. It seemed unbelievable that such large ships should have been thrown completely clear of the sea.

There was a full moon that night in a clear sky and, as I crossed to the island in a ferry, the reflected lights of Victoria and The Peak danced merrily on the dark water, in fantastic contrast with the scene of devastation now concealed by the night. On my first morning there I walked to the top of The Peak before breakfast and looked out over the marvellous panorama of sea and islands, shimmering softly through a thin veil of mist.

I had no further opportunity for painting in mountainous country until I reached Malaya, but the journey there was one

14

of the most interesting sections of my whole tour. When I sailed
from Hongkong for Saigon the air was exceedingly hot and
moist and the commander of the ship showed me on his chart
the estimated course of another typhoon that he was trying to
evade. But we soon found ourselves on the fringe of the disturbance, in high winds and confused seas, and I was glad when
we reached the shelter of Cap St. Jacques and steamed slowly
up the river, amidst numerous junks and sampans, to Saigon.

Indo-China made a vivid impression upon me and I longed
to have much more time to study, in particular, the birds. The
country is a paradise for the bird-watcher and I have never
seen anywhere else so many different species that were new to
me. My chief goal in Indo-China was Angkor, but I wanted
first to spend a few days at Phnom-Penh, the capital of Cam-
bodia. I travelled northwards by bus through flat country
where extensive floods made the long journey unusually uncomfortable. But there were so many aquatic birds to watch that
I never had a dull moment.

Phnom-Penh is a fantastic place, with palaces and temples
that look like a Hollywood version of those in Bangkok. As far
as I could make out, some of them were coated with plaster into
which had been stuck millions of pieces of broken crockery and
glass, of every conceivable colour. As an artist, I was particularly interested in the School of Cambodian Arts and Crafts,
where the pupils were learning to work in silver and bronze in
accordance with traditional designs. I paid a visit to the royal
white elephant, a vast creature of a dirty pink colour, and saw a
most striking performance by Cambodian dancers, whose costumes and formal postures are similar to those of Siamese dancers.

Angkor exceeded all my expectations. It would be worth
while travelling three times round the world to see this colossal
architectural achievement, the ruins of a city that disappeared
in the jungle completely for four hundred years. I would
gladly have spent several weeks there, sketching among the
ruins and the gigantic trees that embrace them and examining
the miles of intricate and beautiful stone carving. But I could
spare only a few days. Then, almost overwhelmed by the
staggering impression of all that I had seen, I crossed the
frontier into Siam and stayed for about a week at the British

Legation in Bangkok with the Minister, Sir Josiah Crosby, whom I had last met in Panamá.

It happened that Sir Josiah, an oriental expert with an unfailing sense of humour, was engaged in some important negotiations and one evening he received a long telegram from the Foreign Office which, owing to some error in transmission, appeared to be impossible to decypher. His staff struggled with it for a long time far into the night until at last, in desperation, he asked me to take a hand. Not long before, in Tokyo, I had laboured night and day decyphering telegrams and I suppose I had acquired a knack of solving such problems. Anyhow, in half an hour I managed to unlock the secret and the Minister at once brought a couple of bottles of champagne into the Chancery to celebrate the victory.

During my leisurely journey down the Malay Peninsula to Singapore I was struck by the peculiar formation of some of the densely wooded hills and mountains. In the north in particular there were many pinnacles of perpendicular strata rising like islands from the plain, a geological oddity that I could not explain. The weather at this time was intensely hot and, although I wore dark glasses against the glare, I arrived in Penang with a touch of sunstroke. I had no idea what the remedy should be, but I swallowed several aspirin tablets and immersed my aching head in a cold bath. In a short time I felt much better.

After visiting Kuala Lumpur I arrived in Singapore under the impression, derived from enthusiastic press reports, that this was now an impregnable naval base. During my stay there the commander took me on a tour of the base and I was entertained on board H.M.S. *Terror*, a monitor with two 15-inch guns built in 1916 that now formed part of the defences. The Governor of Singapore, Sir Shenton Thomas, introduced me to the Director of Civil Aviation, who piloted me in his Moth aircraft for a survey of the island from the air. The large new civil airport, circular and slightly domed like a plate lying upside down, was a most impressive achievement, having been made on difficult ground; but I began to have doubts about the impregnability of the place when he pointed out to me the three 15-inch guns in their emplacements facing the sea and the very exposed collection of oil tanks and administrative buildings.

We could see far over Johore and a part of the Dutch island of Sumatra was visible to the south. The following day was Armistice Day and I had much food for thought.

On the way to Calcutta I stopped again at Penang and spent a few days in Rangoon, a city that appeared to my foreign eyes to have been the scene of a recent massacre. Everywhere the pavements and walls were spattered with ominous-looking red blotches resembling bloodstains. I soon discovered that it was a local custom to chew betel-nut and to spit out the red juice without much attention to where it went.

The India that I went to see was the India of the history books that I had read avidly at school and I planned to spend a few days in each of about a dozen chosen places that could be reached without great difficulty on the way across to Bombay. I particularly wanted to see some of the finest examples of Indian art of all kinds and I believe now that, by approaching India from the east instead of from the west, as most British visitors have done, I was better able to appreciate the fundamental simplicity of Indian spiritual art. Oriental, rather than European, conceptions of beauty were fresh in my mind.

But I was ready to sacrifice—and did in fact abandon—a part of the plan in order to have at least a glimpse of the Himalaya. There was not time enough for an expedition among the mountains, but I got to Darjeeling for a few thrilling days and very early one morning I waited on the top of Tiger Hill, itself more than 8,000 feet high, in the hope that the clouds would part and reveal the mighty range. Some Australians and an American who were with me abandoned the vigil at seven o'clock and went down to breakfast, but I hung on, pencil in hand and with a sketch-book open on my knees.

Half an hour later the clouds began to disperse and gradually a few blue windows appeared. I watched where I thought the first snow peak might appear, high above the dark ranges that filled the intervening miles. In one window, far above where I was gazing, a small patch of dazzling white near the darker edge of a great billowing cloud seemed to remain strangely motionless. I could not believe that, from that great distance, any mountain could appear so high above the horizon.

Now the clouds were drifting faster and in a few more

minutes the whole top of Kangchenjunga was framed in the
window against a background of blue that seemed more substantial than the mountain. Some parts of it were even higher
than the first tip that I had seen.

Breakfast was forgotten. I could not tear myself away.
Steadily the horizon cleared and in less than an hour the whole
panorama of the Himalaya lay before me. Never, in all my
mountain experience, had I seen such a magnificent sight. I
had an appointment with a friend at the Planters' Club to visit
his tea plantation and late in the morning, at the last possible
moment, I went back down the hill to Darjeeling. My first sight
of the Himalaya had been dramatic, unforgettable, and I imagine
that no other mountain scenery will ever displace that spectacle.

Once, in the early 1930s, I had a hope of going to the
Himalaya to climb, but other things occupied all my time.
But a few years ago I renewed my acquaintance with the
Himalaya in an unexpected way. The attempts on Everest
were being resumed and the editor of *The Sphere*, in which
articles about the expeditions were published, wished to have
some special drawings that would illustrate, even more clearly
than photographs, the problems involved and the splendour
of the highest mountain in the world. The art editor, who was
seeking an artist with a first-hand knowledge of mountains,
got into touch with the Royal Geographical Society. One of
the Society's officials, who remembered my drawings of Peru,
most kindly mentioned my name. The art editor asked to see
some of my work and, apparently satisfied, he commissioned
me to produce several special drawings that were to be ready
for the printer in a few days' time.

That problem weighed heavily on my mind. I loved painting
mountains from nature: I had climbed many and I knew the
nature of rock and ice, the infinite variety of snow conditions,
the appearance of climbable and of unclimbable pitches and
the qualities of the different substances that compose a mountain. I was familiar also with the equipment used by climbers
and the attitudes that they were obliged to adopt on different
sections of a climb. But now I had been asked to construct
mountain scenes with the aid of photographs, maps and descriptions and this was a branch of art that had few exponents.

I put all that I knew into those special drawings. There was no question of slavishly copying photographs. Some of these, taken at moments when the light was poor, were vague and insipid; others, taken in strong sunlight, showed areas of black that bore no relation to the lovely transparent tones in the enshadowed areas of snow. Important features sometimes appeared flat and insignificant, and like most photographs taken without adjustment of the subject or of the lighting, the pictures usually lacked artistic composition and could not convey the feeling of the "atmosphere" of a great mountain. In making my drawings I tried to express what I felt about the mountains, both as a climber and as an artist.

There were of course limitations. The drawings were to be reproduced by special printing processes and they would be considerably reduced in size. Such is the case of the illustrations in this book, which were made from original drawings, not from photographs. The rather intricate process of drawing in black and white that I used covered the widest possible range of the medium, but I had to allow for some inevitable loss of contrast in reproduction. My pictures had to be finished within a few days and I knew that each would require many hours of work. These drawings were intended, primarily, to be illustrations; they had to be clear and convincing and necessarily very different from the rapid sketches that I like to make in the field to record a passing impression. One night, in order to give a drawing the high degree of finish that it required, I got up at 3 a.m. and worked in my studio until seven.

One of the drawings, which I had to compose from imagination, was supposed to represent a scene that had been described by Eric Shipton, when the snow gave way on a steep slope. In making this—and other reconstructions—I took pains to make special studies of the actual type of equipment used. Then I showed all the drawings to Shipton and obtained his full approval before sending them to the editor. (Plate XXXI.)

After the publication of these drawings I was asked for more and since then nearly 150 of my pictures of mountain scenery, both in the Himalaya and in other parts of the world, have been published. All except some of the Himalayan subjects were painted on the spot or from my own sketches.

I think I was fortunate in going to India a little while before the last great war and before the end of the British "Raj". Towards the end of 1911 I saw the film of the Delhi Durbar, when King George V was crowned Emperor of India and the capital of India was transferred from Calcutta to Delhi. Ever since then I had hoped that I might some day see in reality something of the pomp and circumstance and gorgeous pageantry of the East. Shortly after my arrival in Calcutta my hope was, to some extent, realized when I watched from a balcony the procession accompanying the Governor of Bengal on his departure for Bombay at the end of his term of office. He rode in a carriage under a splendid gold and red umbrella, with a colourful escort of Bengal Lancers.

A few days later, after my return from Darjeeling, I saw the arrival of his successor. The only differences that I noted were in the person of the Governor and the direction of the procession; otherwise the ceremonial was identical on both occasions. It was a pallid version of a royal or vice-regal progress, but still splendid, though I could not help feeling that it was the kind of show that could have been put on daily— matinée and evening—if required.

In Delhi I had a privileged—and closer—glimpse of the splendour that surrounded the Sovereign's representative in India. The Viceroy's private secretary, Gilbert Laithwaite, most kindly invited me to stay with him and one evening I had the honour of dining at Viceroy House. State dinners, whether given by Emperors, Kings, Presidents or Governors, are fundamentally similar all the world over, but in India the setting and the pageantry had always been exceptionally sumptuous and I am never likely to forget that splendid function. After dinner I had a conversation with the Viceroy, the Marquis of Linlithgow, largely about Japan where he had once been on a short visit.

My route back to London took me from Bombay through the Persian Gulf to Basra; from Baghdad, where I arrived on Christmas Day, across the desert to Damascus and thence through the Taurus mountains to Istanbul.

On the morning after my arrival in Damascus two convicted murderers were hanged in a public square less than eighty yards from the hotel where I was staying. The execution took place at 3.30 a.m. and the bodies were removed at half-past seven. I knew nothing of this until I came down to breakfast at eight o'clock, but a soldier who accompanied me round the Citadel an hour later had been one of the guard at the execution and he insisted on describing what had taken place. Obviously he had been considerably shaken and I think it did him good to work off his emotion by talking.

When I crossed the mountains of the Lebanon by car, from Damascus to Beirut, the sun was shining and there was snow on the ground. These minor ranges, insignificant in comparison with the Himalaya, were looking so lovely that again I altered my plan in order to have time to sketch among them and to make some drawings of the beautiful ruins of Baalbek.

On the road to Aleppo I narrowly escaped being robbed by bandits, thanks to a puncture. I was annoyed at the time because there was no spare wheel and my driver seemed to be fumbling interminably in his efforts to repair the inner tube. But when we reached Aleppo I heard that, precisely at that time, a dozen cars had been held up on the road a few miles ahead of where we had stopped and the passengers had been robbed of all their valuables.

I have had quite a lot to do with the Middle East, a region that fascinates me, and, although I made my first visit in the belief that I should be unlikely to have another chance to go there, circumstances took me back several times until I had more or less covered the whole area. At one time I might have claimed to be an "expert" on the Middle East, though "expert" is a very relative term, and during the early part of the last war I was in the department of the Foreign Office that dealt with Middle Eastern affairs. After the war, when I had severed my connection with the Foreign Service, I felt that my Middle East experience must have come to its appointed end.

But in 1952 I was asked if I would like to go to Iraq, Syria and the Lebanon to write an article, with a series of special drawings, dealing with the work of the Iraq, Mosul and Basrah Petroleum Companies. This delightful commission took me by air to Tripoli in the Lebanon, whence I followed the oil pipelines all the way to Kirkuk, Mosul and the Persian Gulf. For hundreds of miles I drove through the open desert, but from the oil field at Ain Zalah in the north of Iraq I had my first magnificent view of the snow-covered mountains of Kurdistan.

During that memorable journey, which lasted for several weeks, I made pictures of almost every aspect of oil production, from the rigs where new wells were being bored to the tankers loading oil from pipelines laid under the sea. Far out in the desert I made sketches of men laying a new pipeline; I worked inside the gleaming power house at Kirkuk; I painted, not without difficulty, in the scorching heat of Basra and Fao. Among the hills near Mosul I encountered, for the first time, an enormous swarm of locusts. At Palmyra, where I spent the best part of two days sketching, I used a stone from the Temple of Baal for a seat; while painting on the island of Ruad, looking back towards the mountains of Lebanon, my seat was an ancient Phœnician wall. Near Tripoli, where I drew a general view of the oil installations and the tankers filling up a mile from the shore, I sat, for a change, on the floating roof of a modern oil storage tank containing 25,000 tons of oil. Needless to say, I did not smoke.

Along the coastal road beside the Mediterranean all the spring flowers were shaking their heads in the wind, but it was cold along the heights of the Lebanon and snow still sparkled against the blue sky. Though I kept fairly close to the 30-inch pipeline, the ghosts of history were never far away and frequently they enticed me to their ancient strongholds. One of these, high above the famous Homs gap through the hills, was the splendid Crusader castle known as the Krak des Chevaliers. While, from the deserted battlements, I looked out over the ancient hills and drew their gently undulating outlines, I could not help wondering whether any of the English crusaders, whose effigies I had often admired in our cathedrals and churches, had tethered their horses in the vast dungeon-like stables down below.

Flying back to England, I had a wild tossing in cumulus cloud high over the Alps, but landed safely at Zurich with one of the four engines out of action. In a few hours I could have been on another mountain, but I had to get home with my sketch-books and to prepare my article for publication. There were still several pages in the sketch-books that I had not filled and I wondered what subjects would find a place there. In due course they were filled—with mountains.

When looking through some of my old sketch-books I come across a mixed bag of subjects, many of which I may almost have forgotten. But the drawings, whether slight or highly finished, bring back memories more vividly than photographs generally do. They recall some of the sensations that I had when I was making them and sometimes they tell me a lot of other things as clearly as if I had written them in a diary.

Take, for example, one of the South African sketch-books, with water-colour drawings of Table Mountain, flat-topped mountains in the Great Karroo (Plate XVII), native huts on the edge of the Kalahari desert and the awe-inspiring gorge below the Victoria Falls. One picture, made among the great whale-back humps of granite in the Matoppos Hills, is a careful drawing of the tomb of Cecil Rhodes, with brilliantly coloured lichen on the rounded boulders. It was hot—intensely hot— and a large lizard such as I had never seen before, tinted with all the colours of the spectrum, came out from under a rock and raised its head to gaze at me. I began to draw it; there is its head in the corner of the sketch; but suddenly it whisked round and darted away into the deep shadows.

Next, in an American sketch-book, I find an impression of the lovely Blue Mountains of Virginia and I remember how I stood leaning against the back of my car to make that sketch. While drawing, not very far from Lexington, my thoughts strayed for perhaps the tenth time that day to the American Civil War and I remembered that General "Stonewall" Jackson had been Professor of Artillery at the Virginia Military Institute at Lexington. Often history and geography get all mixed up with my drawing and sometimes they provide a reason for the sketches.

Near the end of the same book there is a picture of Antigua, shattered by an earthquake in Guatemala, and on the next page a lovely volcano in the same country. They remind me of the colourful market scene outside the capital, that I had no time to finish. I travelled up there, through magnificent mountain scenery and tropical vegetation, with a party of British naval officers from H.M.S. *Durban* and I remember the generosity of the British colony who, to cool us all during the terribly hot journey from Puerto Barrios, provided a quantity of beer that would do honour to a public house. I remember, too, the wretched peasant woman who stepped on to the line in front of the train and died in a few minutes beside the track. On the last page of this sketch-book there is the bow of the cruiser in which I was travelling, closing the harbour of La Guaira. High up on the orange-red cliffs a puff of white smoke shows where a gun was firing a salute on our arrival. The captain of this beautifully designed cruiser eventually became an Admiral and Governor of the Bermudas. The ship, in her old age, rendered her final service when she was deliberately sunk off Arromanches to form part of a breakwater for the Normandy landings during the last war.

From La Guaira I drove up to Caracas, the capital of Venezuela, and it was there that I met an exceedingly efficient business man who had been a Royal Flying Corps pilot in the 1914 war. There were not then many roads in the mountainous country of Venezuela, but one day he took me for a drive of about two hundred miles to show me some of the finest scenery. He handled the car as if it were a light aeroplane performing aerobatics and several times I thought we were about to take to the air, over a precipice. A friend of his told me that, during his service in the Flying Corps, he had been a skilful pilot and a strict disciplinarian. Once he had had the misfortune to fly into a tall wireless mast and had remained suspended in his machine near the top, injured but not unconscious. A man on the station climbed the mast to find out if he was still alive; but, on peering into the cockpit of the wrecked machine, he was sternly reprimanded for not saluting an officer.

In an old sketch-book of the 1920s there are impressions of Vesuvius, Etna and Stromboli. The crater of Vesuvius, the first volcano I ever climbed, was usually approached by the mountain railway or on the back of a mule, but, in order to save money, I elected to go up on foot. In the vineyards of Boscotrecasa near the foot of the mountain I was surrounded by a crowd of young boys who pursued me for a long way, offering their services as guides. Eventually, by quickening my pace, I managed to shake them off and I plodded on up the long slope of pulverized lava under a hot Italian sun. I reached the top in an hour and a half and spent some time watching the eruption of hot lava and stones through the cloud of steam rising from the depths of the crater. I sat down on the rim of the crater to make a sketch and only then discovered that my notecase, containing lire to the value of about six pounds and my return ticket to Naples, was missing. It would have been much cheaper to have gone up by rail.

I have alluded, in Chapter III, to the tour that I made in East Africa during the last war, when I accompanied the late Lord Moyne and an economic expert for official talks with the principal British authorities throughout the region. We made the long journey from Cairo, a total distance of about seven thousand miles, in a twin-engined Lockheed aircraft and the first stage took us to Khartum. All the way I watched the green strip of the Nile and the burning desert, trying to identify places that I had visited during my camel journey twenty years earlier. When we stepped out of the plane at Khartum, to stay a few days in the Governor-General's white palace, we were dazed by the sudden impact of blinding glare and scorching heat.

In the intervals between our conversations I managed to make several sketches, although I had to work extremely fast in order to lay on washes before the colours dried. While I was painting in the palace gardens, the Governor-General, Sir Hubert Huddleston, came and joined me, telling me the names of trees and plants that were new to me. I think he was pleased to find someone who took an interest in them. One afternoon, sitting on the kerb of the pavement, I made a study of the famous statue of General Gordon on his camel, a sketch that was presented some years later to the Royal Corps of Engineers (in which Gordon served) and placed, I believe, in the office of the Engineer-in-Chief at the War Office.

Our next stop was at Asmara, the capital of Eritrea, a difficult place to approach or to leave by air as it lies at 8,000 feet among high mountains. When we left we climbed rapidly in order to get over them, but we ran into a severe storm that buffeted the aircraft alarmingly. Although we were within fifteen degrees of the equator, it became intensely cold and soon, in the midst of thick cloud, the engines began to falter. Peering through the windows, we could see ice forming on the wings—the quickest example of refrigeration I have ever known. The pilot turned and dived back for the aerodrome, where we landed less than twenty minutes after leaving. The British Military Administrator, with whom we stayed that night, must have been disconcerted to see us back again so soon after he had got rid of us.

Early the following morning we soared in sunshine over the fantastically shaped mountains of northern Ethiopia and looked down on the sites of battles which had led to the defeat of the Italian forces there in 1941. Some of the mountains, precipitous and crenellated like medieval castles, looked as if they had been erected by a giant Vauban.

At Addis Ababa, another high capital in the midst of the mountains, we stayed at the British Legation with Sir Robert Howe, who later became Governor-General of the Sudan, and we had the honour of being entertained at a banquet given by His Imperial Majesty Haile Selassie, an impressive figure of great dignity. I had a conversation with him in French, for about a quarter of an hour, during which we discovered many points of mutual interest.

I had feared that the whole of my time might be occupied with official business, but I enjoyed an afternoon's duck shooting on Akaki lake and one day the Minister's wife took two of us for a three hours' ride over the surrounding hills. My dashing little pony cantered passionately over the rough ground, where there seemed to be numerous holes concealed by tufted grass, and I felt that sooner or later we must come to grief. But the pony was as sure-footed as a mountain goat and never made a single *faux pas*. There was not much time for painting, but I snatched a few rapid impressions of that very attractive mountain region.

As we flew southwards to Nairobi, almost continuously over mountains, my thoughts were of the explorers and pioneers who had opened up all that wonderful territory and of the late Professor Gregory who had been the first to explain the formation of the Great Rift Valley. Far away in the west we could distinguish through the haze a faint shimmer from the surface of Lake Rudolph. We skirted the massive blue pyramid of Mount Kenya, protruding above the clouds to 17,000 feet, and a few hours later we were engaged in an official conference with the Governor of Kenya, with whom we stayed for the next three days. Changes and contrasts came so thick and fast that it was hard to keep things in perspective.

After a succession of conferences with Ministers and Generals, I told the Governor's A.D.C. that I would feel much better if I could see a giraffe for a change. The A.D.C., a wizard at organization, contrived to telescope one discussion into another and when, partly owing to the hot weather, the talkers had talked themselves into a stupor, he found time to drive me in his car into the game reserve. I said that of course I did not want to drag him out, but he replied that I should have to drag him back.

For two hours we drove into the blue distance. From the top of every rise there was a magnificent panorama of hills and valleys and rolling plains. Then we saw a zebra, grazing under the flat-topped trees that studded the plain. Soon a large herd, several hundred strong, came into view and we got out and walked to within a hundred yards of them. Farther on there were more herds; then a giraffe placidly nibbling the top of a tree. When I approached he looked as if he wanted to warn me not to come too near, but was too polite to say so. There were about forty more of these living skyscrapers a little farther on. For some minutes they stared at me with an indulgent expression, then turned slowly and cantered away with great Nijinsky strides.

From Nairobi we flew north-eastwards to Mogadishu, the capital of the former Italian colony of Somaliland. Very early in the morning, while the ground below was still in semi-darkness, we had splendid views of Mount Kenya and Mount Kilimanjaro towering above a sea of clouds. At 12,000 feet I took out my sketch-book and made drawings of the two mountains. Kilimanjaro was a hundred miles to the south, but its snow-capped head, rising above 19,000 feet, seemed to dominate the landscape. (Plate XXXII.)

Having talked ourselves hoarse in the terrific heat of Mogadishu, we flew on across the "Horn of Africa" to Aden, which lies partly inside the broken crater of an extinct volcano. We dined at Government House, but this time I was not involved in the lengthy conversations and I found time to see something of that fantastically hot place. The best moment came when the Air Officer Commanding, the Australian Air Vice-Marshal Macnamara, V.C., took me for a refreshing bathe in the sea, though we had to share it with innumerable jellyfish.

On the long hop back to Cairo we passed, I believe illegally, over a corner of the Yemen and gazed down on the beautiful panorama of green mountains and deep valleys. There was an astonishing number of cultivated terraces clinging to the steep slopes. We spent an hour or two on the island of Kamaran, which is normally a quarantine station in the Red Sea for Mecca pilgrims coming from the east. At the time of our visit it was serving as a place of detention for various delinquents, including wheat hoarders from Palestine, who certainly could not indulge in any further mischief on those twenty-two square miles of empty sun-baked sand.

Having re-fuelled at Port Sudan we followed the west shore of the Red Sea northwards. I have never seen any other landscape that looked so exactly like a map. It seemed unreal. The sea appeared intensely blue and incredibly calm, except close to the shore where a strip of translucent green was fringed with white lace. Directly below us were brown mountains of barren rock rising from pale ochre sand and far away across the sea we could sometimes distinguish faintly the mountains of Arabia. The colouring was precisely like that of the large maps that covered the walls of my office in Cairo and I almost expected to see an occasional black dot on the ground with a name neatly printed beside it.

We landed near Cairo that evening, as darkness was falling. It had been a most interesting journey, with mountains nearly all the way. Less than two years later, when I was temporarily in charge of the Egyptian Department at the Foreign Office, the news came that Lord Moyne had been assassinated in Cairo.

Inevitably, it seems, this story about painting among mountains has become, to some extent, an autobiography: an account, essentially discontinuous, of those parts of my life that I have most enjoyed. My life, since I left school, has been varied in many ways: service abroad in the Diplomatic Service covering more than twenty years was enough to ensure that. But, all the way through, painting has been my principal hobby, walking and climbing in mountain regions my favourite recreation. My love of the mountains has taken me to many places where, as an artist only, I might not have ventured, and my love of painting has helped me to understand mountains in ways that I might not have appreciated merely as a climber. I am never happier than when walking among mountains with a sketch-book. Sometimes I feel the urge to climb rather than to sketch; but, when the climb is over, I must paint the mountain, perhaps for the same reason that makes a young man keep a snapshot of his sweetheart in his pocket-book.

Painting among mountains is not always easy. It is almost impossible in intense cold or in a strong wind. In very hot weather, or when the eyes are dazzled by reflection from snow, it is often difficult to make even a quick sketch. But the artist who paints for pleasure need only work when he feels like it. It is useless for him to be disheartened when the results fall far short of the natural beauty that impelled him to take up his brush. A slight sketch or a highly finished picture: with neither can he capture the whole truth of the magic moment. It must suffice to put down enough to remind him of the scene that he has chosen and to recall his own feelings at the moment when it gripped him.

When I paint mountain pictures for reproduction I try to do a little more than this. The paintings must have certain qualities to suit the printing process that is to be used; the tones and the details will be unavoidably modified by the limitations of the process and by reduction in size. But it is also necessary to take into account the fact that the people who will look at the pictures are not standing beside me while I paint them. I must therefore describe each scene sufficiently to help others to understand the character of the component parts. But I can never hope to make them feel the cold tang in the air, to see the movement of the cloud shadows, or to hear the gentle rustle made by the wind combing the wild flowers.

My pictures in this book are only a few lifeless reflections of some of the wonderful mountain scenery that I have enjoyed; but I hope that they, and what I have said about mountains, will direct a few of my readers towards the "rocks and hills whose heads touch heaven".

INDEX

(*Note.*—Roman numerals indicate illustrations.)

15